C✦MPASS

10 PARENTING PRINCIPLES FOR GUIDING GIRLS INTO BECOMING ADULTS

DR. URSULA BELL

DALLAS, TX

Compass: *10 Parenting Principles for Guiding Girls into Becoming Adults*
Copyright © 2017-2022 * Dr. Ursula Bell. All Rights Reserved.

Scripture texts in this work are taken from the New American Bible, revised edition© 2010, 1991, 1986, 1970 Confraternity of Christian Doctrine, Washington, D.C. and are used by permission of the copyright owner. All Rights Reserved.

No part of this publication may be reproduced, stored in a retrieval system or transmitted in any way by any means, electronic, mechanical, photocopy, recording or otherwise without the prior permission of the author except as provided by USA copyright law. This book is designed to provide accurate and authoritative information with regard to the subject matter covered. This information is given with the understanding that neither the author nor Higgins Publishing is engaged in rendering legal, professional advice. Since the details of your situation are fact dependent, you should additionally seek the services of a competent professional.

The opinions expressed by the author are not necessarily those of Higgins Publishing.

Published by Higgins Publishing
www.higginspublishing.com

Higgins Publishing is committed to excellence in the publishing industry. The company reflects the philosophy established by the founder, based on Psalm 68:11, *"The Lord gave the word and great was the company of those who published it."*

Book design Copyright © 2017 – 2022 by Higgins Publishing. All Rights Reserved.

Compass: *10 Parenting Principles for Guiding Girls into Becoming Adults*
Dr. Ursula Bell

Library of Congress Control Number: 2022916667

Pages cm. 380 * Includes Glossary, References, and Index. (September 2022)

ISBN: 978-1-941580-32-5 (pb)
ISBN: 978-1-941580-24-0 (hb)
ISBN: 978-1-941580-25-7 (eb)

1. Parenting: Family & Relationships / Peer Pressure
2. Parenting: Family & Relationships / Bullying
3. Parenting: Family & Relationships / Life Stages / Teenagers

For information about special discounts for bulk purchases, subsidiary, foreign and translations rights & permission, contact@higginspublishing.com.
Published in the United States of America.

*To Karen Michelle Bell and Courtney Honor Bell,
I dedicate this book to you.*

Acknowledgments

My sincere gratitude to God for the strength and guidance He provided me to bring this book to fruition. God provided us the principles to use in raising our daughters which have proven to be effective and highly productive. I am very grateful for God's blessing in accomplishing this piece of work.

To Manny, the love of my life, my best friend and husband, I extend my deepest thank you for encouraging, advising and supporting me through my aspiration, and for journeying with me with utmost grace, patience, companionship, dedication, and love as I wrote this book. I could never have accomplished this work without your selfless cooperation.

To my mom and dad, and my lovely sister, I say thank you so much for your love, support, and prayers throughout my writing of this book.

To Pam Steinkirchner, current principal at St. Mark Catholic School, a special thanks for your leadership, artful administration and dedication to our daughters' holistic education. You are the quintessential administrator who teaches them to be better peers to each other and enhanced citizens in their communities. Your love, attention and kindness to our daughters will forever be deeply appreciated. Thanks for taking the time to read my manuscript, and encourage its publication.

To Patti Orchowski, Joyce Burke, Carole Mitchell, Diana Davenport, and Peggy Coleman, the terrific teachers who generously and lovingly impart their knowledge and make our daughters enjoy learning, I extend immense gratitude. Despite the ever-challenging curriculum, you make learning fun for our daughters thus helping them like going to school. Thank you so much for reading pieces of the book and for supporting the publication.

I am especially indebted to Sarah and Trish Hodson, Hugo, and all Karen's friends who sweetly accepted for their real names to be mentioned in the book. Thank you all for your cooperation.

I am grateful to Ursuline Academy of Dallas and Overbrook School of Tennessee for supporting me in sharing our daughter's experiences at their respective schools.

To all the organizations, individuals, and groups who are referenced in the book, I express immense gratitude to you for having readily available material that I could plug into for empirical backing of some of the discussions. The research, literature, and data provided on your sites and your life's work permitted me to better articulate my perspectives and share evidence for some of the discussions in the book.

Thanks to the amazing women in the media and women of prominence whose names are mentioned in the book. You are part of the model paragon for our evolving daughters.

Contents

Acknowledgments 5

Preface 11

SECTION 1 15

THE BACKDROP: A LESSON ....

    Lessons from Mother...

    The Open Secret 19

    A Third-Grade Boy of Sorrow 24

    This Little Lady's Secret 26

    The Ready Belt 28

    A Lone Voice in Our Midst 30

    Rampant and Enduring... 33

    Intentional or Unintentional 34

    The Family Court Judge... 36

    Potentially Transgenerational.. 37

    What the Deal Is 43

    All That Glitters Is Not Gold: The Hidden Truth 47

    Contempt Breeds Contempt 52

    Bridge to Self-Confidence 55

SECTION 2 61

EDUCATION...

    Shared Responsibilities 62

    Right Here at Home 64

    Ordinary Recipe, Extraordinary Results.......................... 68

Contents

    Transitioning to the Hill 74

    LEDD—My Blueprint 83

    Make the Mark—the Gift of Time 87

    Partnering for Success 91

    To Each Their Own 100

    Far from the Truth 106

    The Exceptional Nation 113

    The Choice 117

    Peer Pressure, Fitting-In, and Vulnerabilities 122

    Mel 124

    Ingrid 128

    Eve 132

    Transitioning to College: Mind the Gap! 137

SECTION 3 161

BULLYING, INTIMIDATION, AND PEER VICTIMIZATION ....

    A Nightmare 162

    A Surprising Early Beginning: Bullied at Four 163

    The Amazing Sixth Grade Mom: No Place for This in Our Family 171

    Middle School Longtime "Friends" 172

    Cyberbullying: Cowardice 177

    Mary-Lou 178

    Behind Professional Walls 180

    We Are Not Alone 191

    Where Are the Solution Starter Kits? 193

Dance, Study, and Fight Together for Solutions 197

Fighting It as a Village 200

Sowing Seeds 216

SECTION 4 225

FAITH JOURNEY ....

Faith ....

Graciously and Faithfully, Father 231

The Journey—with Twists and Turns 240

Love and a Grateful Heart on the Enduring Journey 257

SECTION 5 259

FRIENDSHIP ....

The Concept of Friendship ....

Reciprocity 263

Time Factors into its Growth 264

Qualitative versus Quantitative 265

The Best Friend 277

Notes Following This Discussion 284

SECTION 6 289

A FEW IMPORTANT TOPICS ....

Diversity and Inclusion ....

The Facts of the Matter 291

Note Worthy 293

Impactful Words and Actions 294

The Bottom Line 300

Killers on the Roads 306

Contents

    In the Know 307

    Knowing May Be Half the Battle 310

    B and G 312

    N and V 315

    CY 319

    Answering Our Daughter's Questions 323

    Little Things Make the Difference—Lady 329

    Keep the Peace—Family Matters 336

    Cradling Love and Trust 340

    Breaking Is Infeasible 341

    Staying Close 344

    Peaceful Gatekeepers 345

    Forgiveness 346

SECTION 7 351

MY OPEN LETTER TO OUR DAUGHTERS - PRINCIPLES ....

APPENDIX 357

    Karen Michelle Bell's Persuasive Speech: "Stop Bullying Now" ....

GLOSSARY 363

INDEX 365

REFERENCES 375

Preface

Most parents want to raise their kids right, motivate and empower them to be the best version of themselves in every situation that life throws at them. So often, parents begin guiding and teaching them through various undefined pathways from their infancy. However, during adolescence our children experience not only physical, but also rapid cognitive and psychosocial growth which makes it a prime time for parental guidance to be more intentional. Having raised two daughters using several intentional strategic principles to guide them into adulthood and experiencing the results thereof, I am well equipped to speak on these topics. Raising children right is not an easy task and the teenage years are often the most challenging for some families.

The world is full of challenges and adolescents encounter their share daily. While some of them experience serious difficulties external from their homes, at school while in class, on the playground during recess, at the lunch table, in the locker rooms, on the drill team, in the library etc…, others' experiences are within their internal family circles which compounds challenges of external nature.

Adolescence is the phase of life between childhood and adulthood, and the World Health Organization (WHO) defines adolescent as any individual between ages 10 to 19. The stages in adolescence are ages 10 to 13 known as early adolescence, 14 to 17, middle adolescence, and 18 to 21 is late adolescence. This is a unique stage in their development, and a period when our teenage daughters are in the process of transitioning from a child to an adult, and an important time to establish solid foundations of strategic principles for guiding them into adulthood.

Preface

Everyone has a story to share, and some stories are sad while others are happy stories. Yet other stories are a combination of sorrowful and joyful moments borrowed from experiences for motivational, inspirational, educational or transformational purposes. There are different types of stories told in *Compass*. Some of the stories include physical punishment as a means of correcting children, bullying, peer-pressure, faith, friendship, family, drugs, vaping and alcohol, diversity and inclusion, education and its significance to our daughters and our society, and others.

Every story is important because of its meaningfulness to the situation and in *Compass,* stories are shared as meaningful situational examples that provide the rationale for establishing strategic principles for resolving the challenges presented. Each story embeds the principles that are invaluable for parental use in guiding adolescent girls with the ultimate goal of seeing them as empowered, assertive, gracious and formidable adults of their time. Some of the stories were shared by brave teenage girls, mature friends, young adults, colleagues, while others were gleaned from national reports, our society, personal experiences etc…and they all culminated to inspire the creation of *Compass*.

Educating and guiding young girls is a significant task especially with parental goals of preventing them from falling prey to some of the worse societal ills, and increasing their potential to significantly impact tomorrow's world as leaders of their time.

A mother of two daughters and a doctor in healthcare administration with decades of experience in health sciences, I understand the potential consequences of raising girls in an age of moral decadence, frantic consumerism, individualism, and many other dangers to which our teens are exposed daily. And how essential it is for parents to raise them using all available tools for success! Utilizing the established and shared principles to raise our girls was pivotal because each principle was mutually beneficial to us, and served as a roadmap for guiding them into empowered adults.

Compass is a book that is carefully written with all women in mind. It provides powerful insights to several issues that should interest every parent and female, and presents 29 fundamental strategic parental principles for guiding teenage girls into empowered adults. The principles served as critical tools for guiding our daughters into the magnificent young adults they are, and would provide parents and their adolescents a solid foundation of knowledge and understanding of how to deal with multiple everyday challenges. The ultimate goal of using these principles is to raise and transition kids into strong adolescents, gracious teenagers, empowered adults, loving mothers, and effective leaders and contributors to their world. Depending on the principles used, the situation and rationale, they could be transformational, motivational, inspirational, empowering…and life-changing. Principles are personal beliefs and values set by parents to use in guiding their actions and interactions with their children, and desirably, will be followed by the family. Fundamentally, having parental principles for use in navigating issues and challenging situations with children, and for guiding them from adolescence to adulthood is central to their personal and professional successes.

SECTION 1

The Backdrop: A Lesson

Lessons from Mother

Born and bred by staunch Catholic parents in a very traditional Catholic house and community, I learned very early in life that my faith in God is what will lead me everywhere I intended going. My parents, devout Catholics, taught me that as humans, our relationship with each other should mirror the relationship that God wants us to have with one another, to the extent He asked us to "love thy neighbor as thyself." At a very tender age, my mother, Marty, told me that this meant we had to love or learn to love people and treat them just like we loved and treated ourselves. Because my mother surrounded me with loving-kindness and care, I understood very early and quickly what I had to live up to. As I remember growing up, I was not only provided an amazingly lovely childhood by my parents, I was also meticulously cared for by a mother who was there whenever I needed her. When I was ill, I saw her face first before any other loved one. She always had the kindest words for me and my siblings no matter the circumstances.

But I learned very many other things too. Most significantly for me, my mother never once in my entire childhood smacked or hit me. She was, and still is loving to me like an angel of God. To her, nothing I did was worth a smack. And I certainly did things that could have pushed her to the edge to give me a smack. She never did.

I have tried to imagine and remember, but I recall no yelling either from Mom, even when I pushed her buttons. Instead, we had serious discussions when things were not the way she expected or wanted them to be. When my older sister and I disagreed, she'd ask us why and encourage us to be good children of God, loving sisters who support each other instead of arguing over what she typically called "nonsense." She would hold long conversations with me to remind me that I was going to be "the nun of the family" and that I should pray to God for a better understanding between my sister and me without resorting to arguments. She would call me "Sister Cecilia" on occasions since my middle name is Cecilia. I still think it is unimaginable or surreal not to scold or yell at my kids.

Every Saturday evening, as the sun set and twilight graced our city, she would take us to "the mission" for confession and encourage us to confess our sins of the week and say our penance. Arguments between my siblings and I were rare. We were a very loving, close-knit family, and our parents did not have to work hard to keep us grounded. Mother often whispered to me on my way to school, "Remember at school today that you must be good. You do unto others out there as you would have them do unto you, and you also must love your neighbor as yourself, okay?"

These most precious memories of childhood regarding the love, care, and kindness bestowed to me by my parents created the backdrop of my relationship with my daughters, and my personality. Considering my mental and emotional stability, I conclude that parental behavior is pivotal to the psychological well-being of young girls. I am not a clinical psychologist, but I believe it is difficult although not impossible to argue that when girls grow up in a loving, caring, and nurturing environment, they hardly become someone less than what their communities anticipated.

Mother's loving and nurturing ways, her lessons of love, and her words of kindness are forever ingrained in me. I use some of her parental concepts and style to raise my own daughters. I believe that parenting is a very challenging task. Parents and families each have individual styles of parenting, and children are born with varied temperaments.

Even children born of the same parents have different temperaments, which makes it tedious to have a one-size-fits-all response to questions regarding raising children or parenting concepts. Notwithstanding, when the desire is to raise strong, well-rounded girls with great potential to succeed in the fierce world of this century, parental behavior must set the pace for success from the child's cradle. Parental behaviors can either lead their children to succeed or destroy them in certain ways. Yes, I believe that. Certain negative parental behaviors can either destroy their daughters completely, partially, or scar them in some way. Mother used to say to me, "You should be a girl who stands up right. I am not going to give you the opportunity to slouch in any way. When we talk with you, I like that you sit up right or stand up straight. Hold up your head always. This is how my own mother told me to stand. Look at me in my face because I have love in my eyes for you to see. I am telling you what I do not want to see you do. I will always tell you where you go wrong so that you can correct it, but while I correct you, you must look me in the eye, and sit or stand up straight. Okay? When you slouch, you are indicating that you are powerless. I would not like you to feel you are a powerless girl. My intent is to ensure you do not repeat what you did today. That is all. I tell you not with anger, scorn, or dislike, but with love and care. I am your mom. Do you understand, "Sister Cecilia?" With those words, no matter how guilty I was for doing something really "nonsensical" such as "forgetting" to attend after school tutoring lessons at my teacher's house, I'd raise my head, knock off my slouchy posture, and look her in the eyes.

Truly, she is an angel incarnate. She is a woman full of love, patience, forgiveness, and kindness. Even in correcting me, she empowered, and taught me something new each day. I would sit up right in front of her during our discussions and look straight in her eyes even as I said, "Sorry for what I did, Mom." She was always quick to respond, "I forgive you. You are a very good girl for acknowledging your mistake." Mom never intimidated any of her children.

I learned later as an adult studying health science that when girls feel intimidated, especially by a superior female figure in their lives, the superior person consciously or inadvertently makes them feel scared and consequently shuts down their assertiveness. I understood from the lessons learned from my mom that what then ensues is fear of the individual, or fright that could cause the girl to assume a physically uncomfortable posture such as slouching or tilting her head to one side of their body instead of sitting upright. This might ultimately result in a timid or shy and unassertive woman.

Not every mother in our community held conversations with their daughters when they went against their parents' rules. There were girls whose experiences were very different from mine. I had friends who, though they were from some of the most prestigious families in the city, were beaten by their parents while I visited them. I hardly knew what to think about that at the time, but I did not want to be beaten like that. What I gleaned ultimately is that persistent intimidating parental behaviors toward their daughters could have negative psychological impact on the child. I am not sure if Mom knew this or even thought about it at the time. I cannot imagine she did.

Mom is naturally a very sweet woman. I am grateful she never hit me because I suffered nightmares from witnessing other aggressive encounters that had nothing to do with my family and me. Parental attitude and response to their children's unacceptable behaviors or attitudes can make or break a child. Some parents yell, some smack, while others beat their children when they cross a line or do something wrong. Yet others hold serious discussions to admonish the child such as my mother did with me. This brings us to a discussion about smacking children. Knowingly, there are opponents and proponents of child smacking. I staunchly side with the opponents of smacking. My parents never smacked me, so I am not inclined to smack a child. Had my parents ever smacked me, I still would consider smacking out of place as a means of correcting a child. Besides, smacking your daughter really does not teach her what the right thing to do is. It certainly just hurts her physically, emotionally, and psychologically. Whether it is a baby, a toddler, or a teenager that you smack or beat, beating your daughter does not arm nor empower her to be self-confident. Conversely, it can have potentially negative psychological repercussions on her. I understand several mothers smack or hit their girls. My understanding emanates from the experiences explained in the following paragraphs.

The Open Secret

In the spring of 2002, Manny, my husband, and I were at London Heathrow. We had been traveling within Europe and were going to take a train back to our house in Reading. I was pregnant with our second daughter. We were in the accompany of our first daughter, Karen, who was almost four at the time. We were all descending an escalator when we heard a baby grumbling. It sounded like he or she had been refused a favorite toy, and she was expressing her discontent with the person who had refused her the toy. As we approached the grumbling sound, it was evident that the grumbling baby was a little girl in a blue pushchair.

She appeared to be approximately three years old. She was holding a small feeding bottle with what appeared to be Ribena in it. She was wearing a blue pair of sweatpants, a pink sweater, and a pair of solid blue sneakers. Her mother was carrying the baby's bag and a pink blanket. A man who I guess was the child's father was in their company. He was standing by some luggage. The child's mother pushed the pushchair back and forth to calm the baby, but the child continued grumbling. We were checking the boards for the arrival of our train when I heard the baby slightly cry out. Our daughter told me, "The baby is crying. The baby is tired and does not like the noise here. Mom, it's loud and noisy here."

I responded, "Yes, little one. Maybe baby is tired and sleepy or baby does not like the noise here. Baby's mother will take care of baby."

The woman asked her daughter to be quiet. "Stop the noise. I am tired. Stop crying."

The baby responded by continuing to cry even louder.

The woman yelled at her baby, "Stop the noise, stop it!" As she spoke, she slapped the baby once on her little face, then twice on her tiny thighs. Then she screamed at the baby to "stop now!"

I cringed at the behavior and the woman's words to her little baby girl. Kay held onto me tightly, saying, "Mom, baby, baby is crying. Look at baby, Mommy. That is sad. Baby's mother is smacking her, Mom!"

"Mo-o-ooomm!" Kay was pulling my right arm, insisting I should check the situation with the baby and its mother. I held her tightly. I dared not look at the woman's direction. I was furious but kept it internally. Then I said to Manny, "She asked the baby to stop the noise, but she inflicted pain on her tiny face and thighs. Consequently, the baby is screaming even louder." Manny responded, "Oh yeah, she did, didn't she? Some of these women are shameless. Just beating on a toddler like she doesn't care. That is shameful."

As the baby yelled even louder, the woman smacked her again on the thigh and said, "Now stop it, yeah. Stop."

It was horrible to watch the open abuse of a baby who was probably tired, needing comfort, food, or something soothing rather than pain. I grumbled and told my husband how despicable that mother's behavior was.

I said, "If she hits that baby again, I'll ask her to stop it now and tell her to check if the baby is wet or tired or sleepy, needing a cuddle." I insisted to Manny, "She needs to be grateful God has given her a baby girl she should cherish instead of beating. Many people around the world are praying and asking God to bless them with a child. She has one, but she does not appear to be grateful she does."

Manny looked at me sternly. "You don't speak to her. That is her child, and she can tell you off. She has the right to tell you to go to space if she wants to. Too many people beat their kids in this country and all over the world anyway. Authorities are not doing anything about it, so you will not. I understand it is frustrating to see that but stay out of it please."

It was a busy time of day in a highly busy environment. People who were around there just looked away as she intentionally inflicted pain on her baby more than twice.

Some people say a gentle smack on a child is fine. I say it is not. And this mother did not gently smack her child. No! She was beating, hitting her baby, and consciously inflicting pain on the toddler. I moaned to Manny, "She is probably tired from traveling. Her child appears to be tired too, but she is unable to assist her tired and angry baby. Pity!"

She was awarding that corporal punishment on the baby for moaning while she, the adult, was fatigued. The child cried out as loud as it could, but the sounds of the airport noises drowned her tiny voice as the mother punched her little face while the father watched on distantly, very nonchalantly. It was painful to witness. The woman did not apologize to her child. She did not pick up the baby to comfort her, nor did she ask her lovingly to stop. She looked away and pushed the baby's pushchair as she cried until she was evidently tired of screaming from the pain her mom imposed on her.

All the way home, Kay wanted to know if the baby girl was safe with her parents. She asked several times if the baby was fine, why her mom spanked her, and pleaded with me to never spank her because she believes it hurts. She worried, "Mommy, do you think the baby is still sad and crying? Mommy, will baby be fine? Mommy, you do not smack me, do you?"

I reassured her, "I wouldn't want anyone to smack me, so I wouldn't smack anyone, especially not you, darling. Remember to do unto anyone, even babies, as you want them to do unto you. Okay, darling? Mommy does not smack you. Don't worry."

She smiled and held my hand tightly, swinging it up and down. "Oh yes, Mommy! But did the baby's mom not know that? Mommy, she does not know that. Baby doesn't want a smack!"

I told her that baby's mother had to learn that because it appeared she did not know that yet. I continued to enlighten my daughter. "Baby's mother could have helped baby in several different ways instead of hitting her. She could have removed baby from the pushchair and cuddled her to make her sleep. Maybe baby was tired and needed her mom or dad's arms. Maybe baby was wet and needed a diaper change. I don't know. Maybe the noise was too much for baby, I don't know, darling. What we can be sure about is that baby's mom will learn that it is not nice to hit her baby. She may never hit baby again."

My little one pursued, "I hope she doesn't hit her baby again because it makes baby sad."

I agreed with her and told her we had to forget the incident. Even though she agreed when I asked that we forget the incident, that night during bedtime prayers, she said, "Mommy, Mommy, I have something I want to pray about. Let's pray for baby to be happy and for baby's mother to not hit her again. I know Jesus can help baby if we pray for her."

I assured her, "Jesus will help baby if we pray. You tell Jesus what you want Him to do for baby."

So she shut her eyes, put her hands together, made the sign of the cross, and said a prayer to Jesus for the baby. In her little voice, she asked, "Jesus, please keep baby safe. Tell baby's mom not to smack baby ever again. Angel of God, my guardian dear, to whom God's love protect baby. Ever this night be at baby's side, to light and guard, to rule and guide. I love you, Jesus. Amen."

She opened her eyes and smiled. "I am sure Jesus and the angels will keep baby safe. Huggy-huggy, Mommy!"

I quickly opened my arms. She hurried into them, and I hugged her, kept her in my arms for a little bit. She held me tightly. "Yes, Mommy, Jesus is protecting baby." We held our hug even tighter for a little while, kissed good night, and then I tucked her in for the night.

I was dumbfounded at Kay's reaction to the incident at Heathrow airport. It was evident that the incident had shaken my own daughter. I wondered how the woman's attitude was affecting her daughter and how shaken the child may be. I thought within me that if she continued hitting her daughter through life, she was slowly destroying her own beautiful product and setting her up to potentially be an aggressive woman herself who may end up spanking her own children. However, I reassured Kay, "You know, darling, the little girl's mom certainly loves her. She probably was very tired and could not understand that her baby was equally very tired. Jesus is taking care of them now. You know He loves babies, don't you? He says children are the apples of His eyes, so He is protecting baby and her family."

Prior to this incident and over the course of time, I witnessed several women in England publicly hit their little ones on countless occasions. Some of the women from whom I witnessed the child smacking or beating incidents appeared to be younger teen moms. However, the woman at the airport was not a teen. Per my estimation, she could not have been a teen. She looked more like a young adult. It appeared to me at that time that smacking their kids was common, so casually done in public that it had become an open secret, and each time it happened I neither heard nor saw witnesses speak up against it.

A Third-Grade Boy of Sorrow

One afternoon in the spring of 2012, Courtney (Missy/Mi), my second daughter, returned home from school and said she has something sad to tell us. She was in third grade at the time. Kay and Mi attended a Catholic school in the city where we lived. We had gone to the school on a few occasions to settle issues that had no bearing with their academics, so I wondered what she had to tell us that she defined as sad. I was impatient for her to tell us what the issue was, although I did not push to know. I knew she would eventually tell me when she was ready. Her older sister asked her what it was, but she said she would tell us after she completed her homework. When she finished doing her homework, she said she'd tell us after dinner. I was curious to hear what she had to tell us, but I had to be patient.

At the opportune time, my third grader explained to her sister and me that she had a good friend in her class who was sad. I asked her to tell us her friend's name, and she did.

She told us, "My friend told me today that his father and his mom are divorced, so they do not live in the same house. He said he lives with his mom and his stepfather. And he said when his mom is not at home, his stepfather beats him with a wooden spoon. He is sad, Mom, and that is so sad. He was in tears when he told me, and he is very sad."

I wondered aloud if the woman knew that her husband was abusing her child in her absence. My third grader responded, "I don't know, Mom, but sometimes he has redness on his cheeks and around his eyes. I do not know if that is from beating or from the playground. He says he is sad, but he cannot tell his mom."

I agreed and insisted, "That is very sad, sweetheart. I am sorry your friend is experiencing that. Let us hope he tells his mom and that the man does not hurt him further. Maybe if his dad visits, he'll tell him too, and he can warn the stepdad to stop hurting your friend or take him away from them."

My daughter, Mi cried, "He is so cute, Mom. He is a nice child. He does not deserve to be beaten with a wooden spoon. No one does, but he is a very nice kid, so I don't see why the stepdad beats him with a wooden spoon or why he beats him at all."

Her older sister affirmed, "No child deserves to be beaten. Adults should not beat children just because they are at a disadvantage from being smaller and weaker than the adult is. No one should beat a kid. His stepfather should be ashamed of himself for beating another person's kid. He is a child abuser. I hope he tells his mom about this."

The kid's painful confidence to Courtney about his stepfather beating him with a wooden spoon was another trigger for me. My third-grade daughter was nine years old when she shared her friend's troubling situation with me and her sister, meaning her friend was being beaten at approximately nine years old. How sad! Why do adults smack, hit, or beat children? Not that age matters, but what I am thinking right now is that at the age of nine, emotional scars sustained from parental abuse rarely fade. Moreover, by beating this kid, the stepfather is potentially destroying another person's child psychologically. Although my daughter's friend is a little boy, his experience might have been the same if the kid were a little girl.

This Little Lady's Secret

Courtney aka Missy, used to be a girl of few words. Before she turned eight, she would only talk when it was necessary for her to do so. Some of our friends called her "a little lady." She carries herself with utmost grace and self-respect and knows how to make her point appropriately when required. At home, we used to say she is eight going on fifty. Her behavior among her friends back in TN prompted some parents at her school to wonder how I got her to be so well mannered and behave as respectfully as she did.

When she was in first grade, we allowed her to go for playdates at her good friends' houses without me. Parental feedbacks post playdates and casual visits were always the same no matter whose house she visited. My friends would gush, "She behaves so maturely. I want to know how you did it. How did you do it? Do you have a special potion to share? Please share."

My response has forever been, "Hard work, patience, and prayers. It's the work of God, not mine." On a certain day, one of her good friend's mother was determined to know what I do to my child to make her behave differently from her peers. Her friend's mom was one of my good friends too. She found me one afternoon, and during our conversation, she stated clearly, "I spent much time with some first-grade girls yesterday, and it is amazing to see how Missy behaves among her peers. She is so poised. She behaves like a little lady. What did you do to make her so composed? Do you beat her to keep her quiet?"

She was laughing as she asked me the last question. Her last question befuddled me. I thought she was paying Missy compliments, but I understood she wanted some of my recipe for having "a little lady," as she had described Missy.

I smiled and responded, "Are you kidding me? Why would I beat her? Do you beat your girls? Missy is naturally like that. That is her personality, nothing I did right or wrong. It is the work of God. I am a staunch opponent of adults hitting children, and I have never hit or beaten either of my daughters. I have never, and will never hit Missy. My daughters are my greatest blessings, so I am immensely grateful for having them. I will never hit them. I hope you do not beat your children to keep them quiet or for whatever reason. I know that would not mean you are not grateful to have them. Do you hit them?"

She laughed. "Uhh...you know, people beat children when they do things they don't like or when they can't be still."

I used the opportunity to gauge her perspective on the issue. I quickly asked her, "Who do you call people? And who beats those people when they do something wrong or can't be still? Should adults beat their children because they are defenseless? So when a child does something they do not like, is that the right way to communicate with the child? You are an emergency room doctor. You tell me what you would do if I brought my child into your ER after beating her and she fainted from the beating. How would you consider me? Will you report me to Child Protective Services? Or ask your nurse to? Or will you overlook the root cause of the child's visit to your ER?"

She looked at me astonished, and then she burst out laughing: "Seriously? Wow...okay. I just asked because I don't understand how she can be that well behaved, and she is just seven years old, my kid's age."

I smiled. "You asked me a seriously good question, so I thought we could talk about it. I like the question. You know, I believe in open and honest communication with our girls, and that is how we operate at my house. Our rule is that no one hits the other. We respect each other's body and keep our hands to ourselves. When we disagree with each other, we dialogue. That is it. My two girls do not fight. In fact, they have never fought, and no one has ever laid hands on the other at my house. Do you consider this difficult to do?"

She replied, "Wow! Hmm…Okay. Well, many parents beat their children to keep them still. Hmm…I smack when it's necessary!" Then she quickly changed the topic of the conversation. I did not want to make her feel uncomfortable, so we continued to discuss an entirely different subject.

The Ready Belt

When she was in sixth grade, Kay had several friends sleep over at our house to celebrate her birthday. The girls always had plenty of fun when they got together for a sleepover. A lot of noise was coming from the second floor of the house where the girls were spending time and having fun. I went up to speak to my daughter because one of her friends came downstairs to ask me for assistance with the sleeping arrangement they had been trying to figure out. After our discussion, my daughter and her best friend visited me in the family room, and we chatted for a while. Both girls discussed the sleeping situation, which they did not like. They wanted to sleep next to each other because they were BFFs. They suggested the other girls would not mind, but I responded by reminding them the other friends just had a discussion as a group and agreed that the BFFs should not hang out all night with each other. I told my daughter that as the host, she should understand all her other friends wanted equal attention. Her friend understood, but my daughter resisted my arguments, closed her ears with both of her hands, and said, "I'm not listening, Mommy, no, no, no, nooo." She walked off as she hummed the word "nooo."

I told her, "You better behave appropriately and listen to me attentively. We will have to talk about your attitude tomorrow after your visitors leave. For now, you girls go and mingle with your other friends."

Her friend quickly exclaimed, "Oh, Karen, you are so lucky. If it were at my house, my dad would have pulled his belt and beaten me right away."

I followed up by asking her friend, "What did you just say?"

The kid repeated what she said, "If it were me, my dad would have beaten me right now. You dare not do that at my house or else he pulls his belt."

I turned to my daughter Kay, "Did you hear that?"

She responded, "Yes, Mom. I am sorry. I didn't mean to be rude." My daughter and I looked at each other, and we smiled. She returned to hug me and insisted she was sorry. I asked the girls to go have fun and be ready for bed at a reasonable time. Kay later told me that her friend had confided in her that her dad beat them with his belt.

As a person, have you ever wondered how you would feel if in sixth grade, your father beat you with his belt? Would that endear you to him? Will it scare you? How would you feel? Would you feel humiliated or special? Would you consider his actions the right way to teach you right from wrong and make you feel empowered to be yourself but remain respectful to him? If your response to these questions is no, and you believe you will feel humiliated and sad instead of happiness if that happened to you, then you should not beat your children. They have the same feelings as you do. Their emotions are like those of their adult parents. Instead of having a ready belt to hurt their little bodies when they are rude to us, a basic solution may be that we should firmly tell our children that as parents we will not tolerate or accept rudeness from them, and have them experience a significant consequence when they are seriously and knowingly rude. Such a consequence may be no sleepovers for a month, no birthday party this year (Oh this is a big one that can bring immediate change after many tears), no desert, no hug or kiss for a day, etcetera.

A Lone Voice in Our Midst

I have wondered why some parents think I beat my children. I have two daughters who I have never hit in their lifetime. I have scolded them but never beaten either of them. Two parents from two different schools asked me if I beat my children. At Court's eighth birthday party, a couple of women and I discussed child upbringing and exchanged ideas regarding sibling rivalry, competition for parental love, and family harmony.

We had what I considered great conversations that day. We shared our various perspectives and listened keenly to our varied parenting precepts. A very sweet woman in the group who became a good friend of mine had three very young daughters growing up together, so she explained some of the challenges in raising three young girls of ages between four and eight. She explained the fights and squabbles that happen among the kids and said occasional smacks help provide brief periods of calm between the girls and in their home. This was coming from a very sweet woman, very loving to her girls, very caring and kind to them. In fact, on the day of my daughter's birthday, she had to travel across the city to attend the party after she celebrated her daughter's birthday earlier in the day. Some of the women agreed that sometimes "tough love" does not hurt because child upbringing is highly challenging especially in contexts such as having several little ones to tend to at the same time.

I explained to the women that on my part, I have tried to raise my girls without inflicting corporal punishment on them and how it has been easy to do so. I shared my perspective, which includes the fact that if I were in their kids' shoes, I wouldn't like to be beaten, but it was also important to tell them that beating their child takes so much away from the child—and them. I insisted that as a family, we had agreed that no one had the right to hit the other. I shared how we'd taught our daughters that we must respect each other's body, that when we hit or beat it, we hurt it, and if we love deeply as we should in a family, we should not resort to hurting each other, and especially not in that manner. Our family believes that each person in the house should keep his or her hands to him or herself. They appeared astonished to hear that our two girls had never fought with each other. That made some of them exclaim, "Hmmm! Wow! Oh, no way! Really? Never? You mean Karen and Courtney have never fought physically? No way! How is that possible?"

It was an exciting discussion for me because I realized I had an opportunity to share with the women some of the negative effects of hitting our daughters. I affirmed, "They have never ever tried to physically fight with each other, although they argue now and again." I eagerly insisted, "When you beat a child, you tell him or her that it is okay to physically hurt or inflict pain on another person. They therefore learn to hit, believing it is fine to do it, after all, the people who are their examples, such as mom or dad, hit each other or hit the kids. When they see you hit their sisters, they each see it as 'it's fine to hit,' and that makes it easy for them to fight and hit each other as well." I paused. They were each silent, smiling and looking at me as if I was incomprehensible. That neither disturbed nor bothered me.

I pursued, "I understand it may be hard but Just try not to hit them when they are naughty. Instead, discuss with them to understand what the problems are. That is what I do, which is not always easy. When they argue over something and I realize that they cannot resolve it independently, we discuss the issues. When one or both of them misbehave, I invite them for a conversation about the misbehavior. We assess what prompted the poor behavior or naughtiness, why it is not considered good behavior, and we examine the possible alternatives to the behavior, and then we move forward after they understand the reason for the conversation and my expectations for the future. We share what we learn each time we determine that either of the girls has behaved in a not very decent manner either toward a friend or each other. When it is necessary, we let them experience the consequence of deviating from acceptable behavior or attitude by taking away a privilege—a dessert, a favorite toy, or a playdate. And even such discussions are very rare because the girls generally carry themselves with grace. Why would you hit them? You love them, and by hitting them, you are neither communicating nor affirming that love you have for them. I believe that when you hit them, you actually take away something good from them, and you hurt them. I firmly believe that hitting any kid is counterproductive."

That was enough to make some of them exclaim even further their astonishment at my parenting concepts. I realized mine was the lone voice in the room with such perspectives. I could hardly understand why. Nevertheless, the conversation made me understand that I was probably the sole opponent of smacking kids among the women present during the discussion. Whether my thought was right or wrong, it appeared a lone voice opposing corporal punishment or child smacking as a form of punishment was heard in the party of mothers present there. I did not know what to make of the idea of "yeah, they need tough love," but I thought of what I could say or do to explain to more women that beating their children is not a sign of love, even if or when "tough love is necessary."

There are many ways to express tough love for our daughters aside from spanking them. Every child looks forward to their birthday celebration once a year. If that celebration is taken away to help them understand that a parent is serious about acceptable and unacceptable behaviors, and as a means of correcting bad behaviors and naughtiness, what else can be a more serious manifestation of "tough love"?

Rampant and Enduring

Corporal punishment appears to be rampant not only in England, where I publicly witnessed it on countless occasions, but in this nation as well as in many other countries. After discussing the issue with several other parents, I conclude that it certainly is a rampant and enduring problem in modern societies. A well-respected chaplain with whom I worked did not hesitate to tell me that he believes that beating a child helps mold them better. He has four children, and he has beaten them mildly and minimally over the years "when they pushed the buttons too far," he insisted to me. When I asked him what he meant by "pushing buttons too far," he was silent.

He, however, affirmed, "I beat mine, though not often. It is hard to raise children without beating them. It is just difficult with children. Sometimes they don't listen."

Our conversation on this particular day was brief, but we established ourselves as a proponent and an opponent of corporal punishment for children. I let him know that I have never beaten and will never beat my daughters. I also advised him to quit hitting his children for whatever reasons because he is being unfair when he hits them. I shared with him the potential psychological effects of beating kids. He understood my point but maintained that beating kids was a good way of teaching. We respectfully disagreed with each other's perspective, and he verbalized admiration for parents who exercise patience with children instead of "whooping them when necessary."

Besides him, some parents have expressed to me that beating the child "teaches them a lesson." The nation watched the First Lady, Michelle Obama, respond to Barbara Walter's question that she once smacked one of her daughters, but she was very quick to reasonably emphasize that she would not repeat it and that her reaction to the child at the time was not the best. What she told Barbara Walters indicated that she regretted that one-time smack as she said: "There are better ways to correct a child." I strongly concur with the First Lady that there are myriad other ways to correct a child than lifting an angry hand on her.

Our young children are not stupid. They do not have to be hit, smacked, or beaten to "learn a lesson," or appreciate "tough love" as put by some proponents of corporal punishment. Very early in life, children develop cognitive skills such as understanding skills, thinking abilities, attention skills, and even memory skills that we should nurture through communication and dialogue when they are naughty or behave poorly.

Intentional or Unintentional

One summer evening, the light that usually shone like ten million bright stars at my house suddenly faded. Kay, our oldest daughter, who habitually recounted her school day once she got into the car, would not utter a word during our drive home. All attempts to make her tell me what the matter was had failed. That was odd, and it was a clear signal that something went terribly wrong at school that day. After she completed her homework and ate dinner, we sat down to talk. She had been intimidated at school by her teacher. She explained that she did not speak during our ride home because she was very hurt, humiliated, and was trying to make sense of what she endured in class that day.

Although many would agree that humiliating an adolescent girl in front of her peers can be any young girl's nightmare, one of her teachers had elected to be oblivious of that. Deciding that Kay was not her favorite student did not mean anything to the kid. After all, she believed she was a well-rounded student who had excelled in her Catholic preschool and elementary school, and was on a very good track in middle school. Kay was simply saddened that this teacher could not contain her dislike for her to the point she had to humiliate her again. She explained that she and one of her classmates were working as partners for a class project, and her friend said a joke while they worked and both girls giggled about it. The teacher, who was attentive in her small class size, walked up to both girls but addressed my daughter alone. While pulling Kay's hair which was packed in a ponytail, she asked her, "What's going on here?"

Kay explained that they were working, but the teacher rightly remarked, "No. You are talking. You are being disrespectful. Stop talking!"

This was the second time this same teacher had pulled her hair in class in the same manner. The first time it happened, she reported it to me. We discussed it briefly, and although she felt hurt and believed that her teacher treated her unfairly given the circumstances of the incident, I convinced her it was not the teacher's intent to belittle and humiliate her. The fact that her hair was pulled in class by the teacher hurt her more than anything else in the teacher's behavior. The teacher had laid hands twice on this adolescent girl, and she had no justifiable reason to do so repeatedly. We may never know if she intended to overtly humiliate Kay or not. Manny and I agreed that although she might not have thought of the effects of her action on the adolescent student, it was a very poor choice on the teacher's part to lay hands on her student no matter the circumstances. We thought Kay might have been working and talking with her peer. No matter what the student did, and although the teacher did not beat her with a rope, a belt, or a strap, she felt spited and humiliated by her teacher's injurious behavior. I discuss this here as an example of what young girls may feel when their beloved parents beat them, no matter what they did wrong. And it does not matter that the belittling action was carried out intentionally or not to hurt or humiliate them, it does just that to them.

The Family Court Judge

Perhaps the worse and most notorious situation of parental abuse of power and use of force on a child is the November 2011 CNN Newsroom report about a Texas family court judge who was videotaped beating his sixteen-year-old daughter with a leather strap. The video was made in 2004 but was exposed on YouTube in 2011. The video showed the family court judge, a highly educated individual who passes judgment on other families with issues, and counsels families on better behavior, beating his own sixteen-year-old daughter countless times with a leather strap. The video was agonizing to watch, and it was bewildering to hear the judge repeat several times over, "Bend over the bed, bend over the bed, bend over the bed" as he beat his almost-adult daughter on her thighs, her right buttock, her back, and wherever the strap could land on her body. The beastliness in the judge was evident when he continued his assault on the young woman even while she cried aloud like a baby in distress.

This incident rightfully generated a national debate regarding parental child abuse through beating. As a family court judge, this man could not have been more wrong or stupid to believe that this was the best way to discipline the young woman who is his daughter. When Kay saw the news and the video that went viral, she exclaimed, "I hope this horrible man who calls himself a judge is stripped of his title. What he did has nothing to do with discipline. He is an aggressive man and should be put on the stand so we can all see what defense he can put up for such a prominently violent act. He is nowhere ready to judge others when he is like a monster dad."

What remains astonishing to me in this situation were the messages on the Internet that supported the judge's action. My gut told me that the supportive messages were testimonies that this is a familiar paradigm for discipline in several families. However, the paradigm needs to stop because of the potential horrific repercussions on the young girls and women who suffer the beatings.

Potentially Transgenerational

My guess is that beating a child as a form of discipline has existed for centuries now. I did not hold this conversation with my parents. I never saw Mom beat anyone, but I know many children were being physically punished in other families in our community and beyond. Beating children as a means of "teaching them a lesson" can easily become transgenerational within certain family circles. Some parents resort to corporal punishment because their parents beat them. Their parents beat them because their own parents beat them, and their own parents had been beaten as well by their own parents. Therefore, the cycle of beating their offspring continues incessantly, and the destruction is probably felt by generation after generation of children from such families. Within such families, the belief is that this harshness should continue because…well, just because their mom or dad did it or because this is the family's known and acceptable way of making corrections. There has been a general understanding in the family for years past that this is the way to make corrections, and it is the naturally accepted parenting model… because this is it, and we move on without remorse after beating the heck out of our beloved daughter.

I have learned over time that critical thinkers and great leaders often assert that "because it was done like this before I got here does not mean it is the right thing to do. We've got to change some things around here." So too, I insist here that just because your mom or dad beat you, because their parents beat them when they were naughty, or because generation after generation of your family have endured physical punishment for things done incorrectly does not necessarily mean it is the right thing to do. At times, as adults, some individuals who grew up beaten in abusive homes or environments think of the hurt they felt, maybe the shame they endured because of the harm from physical pain, and understand their personal chagrin due to the beatings they were subjected to as children. In such situations, they may likely learn from their parents' or families' errors or the repercussions of such hurtful behavior and stop the cycle by never beating their own children. Notwithstanding, in other families, the feeling appears to be one of, "I was beaten by my father and my mother. I did not die. I survived it, and I learned. Here I am. Give me the belt. It does not kill. Bend over!"

Transgenerational beatings have to stop somewhere. One person in such families who felt hurt and humiliated by the torture inflicted on him or her needs to help arrest the cycle, the help can simply be done by encouraging those in the family that are still doing it, to end it. There is no beauty in it. Just because your father and mother beat you since their parents beat them does not mean you should or have to do the same your kids. Where is the rationale in inflicting pain in the same children you need to teach, love, protect from harm, and shield from danger? How does beating them teach them anything? How does the pain from that benefit them or teach them? Such a mentality or philosophy is evidently ingrained in the minds of some families, as seen on some of the Supernanny episodes and America's nanny shows, where some parents could be seen beating their children because they were beaten and it is acceptable practice in their families.

Jo Frost the star of Supernanny brought her savvy from the United Kingdom to help families with *patience, energy, and tolerance-demanding children* (PETD children) deal with the challenges of raising a PETD child. My premise for PETD children is to avoid the tag of "difficult" children. PETD emanates from my personal proposition that highly naughty children require their parents to exercise a high level of patience when teaching them wrong from right to get them to behave in the appropriate manner. Patience is an imperative ingredient in any parental recipe for dealing with a terrible two, a rambunctious toddler, an obstinate preschooler, a stubborn adolescent, or a wild young adult. Patience is when a parent maintains a calm-and-collected approach in correcting or dealing with their child.

Patience has proven to be an invaluable tool for success in my personal parental handbook for over almost two decades.

The parents of PETD children should be energetic rather than apathetic because the behaviors of such children require energy and time to educate for behavioral metamorphosis. The energy needed to help a PETD child must not be solely physical. If your PETD child is aged between infancy and middle adolescence, your energy reservoir better be replete with the appropriate psychological, emotional, as well as physical tinges of positive energy. As parents, we should bear in mind that every developmental stage for our daughters comes with its own challenges. At puberty, for some parents, the challenges might triple or even quadruple. An excellent level of psychological and emotionally appropriate energy could provide not only a great footstool on which to stand but also a reasonable guide on how to approach acute aches that sometimes result from psychosocial impacts of a changing mind, body, and soul of an otherwise sweet girl.

As a mom, I continuously ask God for the grace of positive energy to deal with my daughters' challenges or behavioral opportunities. My argument is that most of the adult attitudes in our families can be easily infectious. Hence, positive energy would most likely deliver positive changes to the situation at hand. If we try to be engaged, positive, and understanding in dealing with our daughters' issues, they will calm down once they notice our support for them, instead of piercing their already torn minds, thoughts, and actions. My belief is that humans naturally gravitate toward positive rather than negative energy. Remember, children are humans no matter how tiny or young they may be. A crying baby wants to be soothed rather than smacked so that its troubles or pain may inflame. A stubborn adolescent or a truant student may be using truancy as a medium to scream for attention and help. Dedicated positive attention and some good energy have a higher probability to help than the reverse.

I staunchly believe that parenting tolerance is a virtue. I can hardly imagine it not considered such when our children's attitudes or behaviors sometimes push us to a very high level of frustration, yet we should be understanding with resolve to help them. Using my personal parental playbook, my theory argues that while a patient parent maintains calm when dealing with a challenging situation with a child, tolerance is different. Parents who acknowledge and appreciate the different behavioral tendencies and potentials between them and their children are more likely to manifest tolerance. Behavioral differentials between a parent and his or her daughter, which are fundamental, may be due to age, maturity, or personality, but it does not matter in the PETD theory. What is critical to note here is that tolerant parents are less prone to smack or beat their offspring no matter what the children do. They tolerate the child's temporary inadequacies and react more understandingly to them but this does not mean that they tolerate the naughtiness. They are tolerant because they can deal with it without feeling uncontrollably frustrated at them which leads to the spanking.

Raising two girls is tough and challenging for me. They are not perfect girls, and they are very dissimilar one from the other. Though mostly very grounded, I have had to pray for tolerance with Kay and Courtney as I raise them with the determination to never slap, smack, or beat either of them no matter what.

I remember a frustrating incident in a retail store in Europe when Kay was just three years old. She was interested in strangers, and no matter how many times I reminded her of "stranger danger", she would speak to unknown individuals, smiling and saying hello to them whenever she pleased.

On this particular day, she quietly wandered out of sight as Manny and I looked at pieces of garments for her. One little second and my baby was gone. Her dad and I ran through the aisles of the store, calling out "K, KK, Kayyyy!" but there was no response. I asked Manny to continue walking through the aisles while I ran frantically to the entrance/exit to make sure no one exited with my kid. Then as I asked for the store manager, I heard her little voice coming from very close by. I followed the sound of her voice, walking toward the closest aisle. There she was, smiling and talking to a woman who was attentively listening to her. Once I saw her, I ran like a crazy individual and asked, "Why did you leave without telling us?"

She just smiled and said, "Mommy, look, this is a lady I met." I was honestly so mad at her, but at the same time I was grateful to find my kid after a minute or two of frenzy and near cardiac arrest. Elated, I just picked her up and hugged her. I was so shaken by this incident, we immediately exited the store. After we found her, I did not yell at her, but I explained to her the dangers of wandering off like that without telling her mommy or daddy.

From an opposite stance, one Saturday morning I witnessed a true beating of a little boy who was playing hide-and-seek with his sister in a grocery store and went missing from their dad's fatherly eyes for a minute or two When he finally saw them, he was furious at them, and right there in the store, beat the little boy for hiding away from his view.

A tolerant parent is one who is capable of enduring the negative aspects of his or her child's behavior or attitude without utilizing corporal punishment as a medium for correction while working with them to obtain enhanced behavior or even mannerism. Tolerance assists parents to objectively understand the challenges involved in raising a child, respect for the child's body, and not believe that beating resolves his or her child's behavioral idiosyncrasy. Tolerance is therefore the acceptance that *"hey, my kid is different than me, younger, and less mature than I of course, and I am cool with that. I understand, and I can deal with that respectfully."*

The lessons learned from watching some of the live Supernanny episodes demonstrated that some families are raised to believe that corporal punishment is an acceptable way to correct children of any age and that inflicting pain on defenseless children is fine. Several parents beat their children on the show even as the cameras rolled at their residences. They had no issues with it probably because they had been brought up to believe that there are no problems with beating a naughty, challenging, or disobedient child. Even the Texas family court judge, a well-respected man in his community, resorted to assault and abuse to correct his teenage daughter. You want to ask yourself after watching the judge's beatings, "How worse can it get?" "If this highly educated man can be this abusive, low, and violent to his own daughter, what can we expect of people who do not know what possible repercussions of beating a child are?"

Spanking children is clearly an insidious problem within certain family circles. It is domestic violence, and it is abuse and assault. If you belong to such a family or know someone who does, then remember PETD children need understanding and try to deal with them according to my PETD theory.

What the Deal Is

"What is the big deal about spanking my child?" Asked one good friend of mine. I share this in *Compass* as my own way of calling attention to the immense concern of beating children as a means of correcting them. This is my own way of sending a loud cry that can reach very many people about this issue because it is occurring within families of all social and economic backgrounds, and all racial and ethnic backgrounds. The deal is that victims of this type of abuse are often either afraid or ashamed to report or discuss it, and in some cases, it is the family's secret, so silence is maintained until it can no longer be kept a secret because someone has had more than enough of it, such as in the case of the Texas family court judge. Corporal punishment is not part of an appropriate parenting model or way to correct a child or "teach a lesson" to our young and vulnerable ones.

Besides, what the big deal is, is that there is no justifiable defense for smacking, beating, or hitting your child, and you can stop doing it. It is very inappropriate and carries potentially devastating effects for your daughter. If you intend raising your daughter to become a strong woman in the society, do not hit her because she is defenseless and presents traits of a PETD child. Understand that your daughters might translate the fact that you hit them as an indication that you condone with violence. When a child believes that her parents utilize violence or aggressive reactions as a means of remediating disputes and disagreements, she might resort to hitting her friends, her little nieces, her nephews, or her siblings when in disagreement with their opinion or behavior. Smacking or hitting might signify to them that it is acceptable to use violence as a medium for conflict resolution. As reasonable adults, we should understand that such a belief may encourage callousness later in life on the part of our children. Indeed, the belief that violence or beating is an okay behavior might escalate to absurd proportions, including but not limited to fighting, ruthlessness, aggressive desires, mean-spiritedness and bullying.

I have worked and spoken with several women who indicated that they know children who are hit by their parents before their first birthday and that some parents hit their children well into their teenage years. I have also spoken with young girls who have suffered humiliating parental physical abuse used as a form of correction. What we need to understand as responsible adults is that physical discipline is morally wrong and unacceptable. By hitting your daughter, you infringe on her rights to physical integrity, as well as her general emotional and psychological wellbeing. Does your child cry louder and harder each time you hit her? Why do you think that happens? Is she emotionally distressed, or is her loud cry secondary to the physical pain you just inflicted upon her? Do you like to see her in that mood—highly distressed? What about her psychological health? Do you care about it? Then know that each time you hit her, it is an assault and it affects her emotionally and psychologically in a negative way. I would argue that physically abusing a child, more likely than not, presents a reflection of the parent's emotional state than the child's behavior. Some parents beat their child because they are frustrated with a completely different situation—displacement. Try and learn not to displace your anger or frustration on your little one if this applies to you. Be fair and honest with yourself and your emotions, knowing that you can actually draw strength from her through discussions and open communication rather than through aggression and assault. Spanking your daughter may not help her in the long run because by beating her, you are suggesting to her that you have lost self-control and that force, violence, and repression are an alternate and acceptable means of control. Repression is not a fertile ground on which we can expect to plant and grow the seeds for a strong, assertive, self-confident lady.

Parents assume the critical role in assisting their children from their toddler age to appropriately adjusting their behaviors to ally with social rules and expectations. Understanding parents acknowledge the challenges in raising a child and leverage their children's capabilities of comprehension even as babies to assist them in attaining a high level of self-respect, parental respect, obedience, and regard for socially acceptable behaviors. They respect the children, even as toddlers, but they uphold age-appropriate limits on their need to test, try, and to explore their immediate surroundings. Typical examples of such testing behaviors may involve shoving, hitting, biting, cursing, and spitting but such parents assist by teaching them self-control by not hitting them. By hitting them or anyone else, you show them the very wrong example and suggest to them that you have lost self-control, and that force, repression, and violence are an alternate and acceptable means of control. I suggest that you use behavior guide and model to teach them how to cooperate with you in resolving problems rather than hitting them.

As modern parents, very many of us treat our children respectfully. Children should learn to respond respectfully to their parents because it is the right thing to do rather than because they fear physical punishment and reprisal. The fear of corporal punishment should not be the driver of our children's good behavior. Protecting your daughters from physical violence and emotional and psychological harm is every parent's unwritten responsibility. Why then do some parents elect to inflict corporal punishment? If you are reading *Compass* and you are a proponent of child spanking, ask yourself why you do it. Is it the right thing to do? Is it your inner emotion or displaced anger that overpowers your reason and prompts you to beat the child? Are you being fair to the kid by hitting her? Would you have liked to be beaten if you were in her shoes? Are there reasonable alternatives to beating her?

The other deal of the matter is that my interactions with some psychotherapists, and clinical psychologists with whom I worked in the past revealed there is a correlation between harsh discipline in childhood and aggressive behavior in later life. I learned from some doctors and researchers that a significant number of individuals have reported a relationship between corporal punishment in childhood and, later, mental illness such as depression and anxiety, mood and personality disorders, as well as the use of drug and alcohol. When raising young girls, supportive and caring environments are better than aggressive and suppressive environments. My suggestion to those who are pro-spanking is to value your daughters more to the extent that you do not see the need to hit them for whatever reason. You can help build their self-esteem and sense of confidence by being fair and understanding, tough, honest, and nurturing, and tolerant and insightful instead of beating and maltreating them because of their unwelcomed attitudes and shortcomings as immature little people.

Section 1: The Backdrop: A Lesson

All That Glitters Is Not Gold: The Hidden Truth

Kristina, a beautiful young woman, grew up an only girl in a family of three boys. We have known her family for several years. She affirmed to my family that she could never do anything right by her parents, who are both civilized and educated. She said her father called her names, and when she frowned, he hit her bottom with whatever he could lay hands on. He told her that her mother conceived her by accident after her parents decided they would not make any more children. Her father called her "the intruder!" He would return from work and ask, "Where is the intruder? Did she decide to go to hell?" She could neither express her feelings nor confide in her mother because it enraged her father to see them together. Some days she knew her mom had cried, but she did not ask because her mother would say nothing. On the contrary, she would blame her for her troubles with her husband.

Kris looked me with teary green eyes and then began sobbing. "Although my mom hit me only on occasion, she could not stop my father when he beat me."

Kris's parents sent her to very good schools and appropriately provided for her, but she insists they do not love her and she does not feel loved by them. "I was depressed most of the time. I was often embarrassed when I brought friends home, so I ceased taking friends to our house. I lost many good friends after middle school. In high school, I made difficult choices and joined the wrong group because I believed they loved me. The others were too good for me. I was too quiet and shy. Girls who lived in my neighborhood stuck together. I kept my distance because I did not want them to know my story. They might tell their parents or not even believe me. I hung out with students I had nothing in common with, and they were very nice to me, but I was often emotionally disconnected from them. I always felt sorry for myself. I felt ashamed and different from everyone else. I felt like I was never good enough, so I rarely spoke in class. I had a lot of anger in me.

I envied girls whose parents loved them. I sometimes cursed them out for no good reason. I would push a nice girl into her locker and call her names because I was jealous of her. At lunch, I poured my soda on a very nice girl who did nothing to deserve that. I was just being mean because of my personal issues and frustrations. Each time I did those things, the school administration reported it to my parents. That gave my dad a perfect reason to beat me up. But that was my own way out and I did not stop. I knew I was taking it out on other girls.

Now in college, I do not trust anyone, and I am often hostile to both boys and girls. The hurt in me may begin to subside now that I see a psychotherapist and a psychiatrist, and I take antidepressants. I do not care much for my parents, although I forgive them. My brothers and I have a good relationship. They helped me to not run away from home and shame my family."

Kristy paused and took a deep breath, cleared her throat, dried her tears, and took the hand I extended to her over the coffee table. Her eyes appeared forlorn on her young but somber face. Her gaze was empty.

I told her, "You are a brave young woman. I commend your strength, fortitude, and power of forbearance."

Her head tilted toward the right side of her body, and still holding my right hand, she proceeded in a subdued tone, "When I was four years old, I remember one evening after dinner, I sat on Mom's lap for comfort and played with her hair. I did nothing wrong when suddenly, Dad grabbed and pulled me away from mom and threw me on the mat and yelled at me, 'Get out of here! Get out of here now before I smash your face.' He left bruises on my back and thighs. But Dad is considered a good family man and a community leader. He beat me till I left home for college. Leaving home for college is the best thing that ever happened to me. I do not like to return home, but my brothers constantly persuade me to. It hurts…it hurts to talk about it. It hurts to go back. It hurts when I see them. It hurts when I don't see them. It just hurts, but I want to be away from them now that I can. I can fight for myself here, and I can fight hard for myself now. I have also confided in one of my professors. She is now my guardian angel. Although she says I must return home, where I came from, I was clear to her I will not. I am an all-American girl. I will fight it out here for myself. I am too hurt…"

I agreed with her that she is an all-American girl. "You are right, being all American is a magnificent thing. Once you have forgiven them, remain open-minded about what ensues between you all. They are your parents and must regret their actions. Pray to God for guidance in the decisions you make. You only have one set of parents. If you can wholeheartedly forgive them, you start at an excellent place there. It must be difficult to forget your pains. You are a very strong young woman. You are capable of rebuilding." Kristy cried, "I was, I am, and will always be an intruder in their eyes. Aside all the beatings, I was called the family intruder. I still have nightmares from all the spankings I received. Some nights I must drink myself to sleep because I feel like, like, like I am hurting from the pains of dad's spankings. I try to not keep alcohol in my room, but when I need it, it helps me go away from my pains for some time. My sleeping pills also help. I cannot do without those pills."

It was inconceivable to me that this family had such an antic in their immaculate and gorgeous home. I understood from our meetings that beating children was endemic in her father's family, but I was at loss for words to know that this respectable man was a monster in his daughter's eyes.

I looked out the window from the quiet end of the diner where Kris and I had sat down to chat. The sun was beginning to disappear underneath the blue skies. My response to the sound of tick-tock, tick-tock coming from across the hallway was to slowly raise my eyes to the wall. The time read 5:15 p.m. I was hesitant to tell Kris that I had to go do the after-school run. I had to get my daughter before 6:00 p.m. from after school, where I placed her so I could meet with Kris. She knew it was time. She held my hand tightly and muttered, "I do not need a drink after this conversation. I just had four hours of excellent therapy session."

I got up and smiled. "Neither do you need to beat yourself up any further. You are your own best advocate, your own best friend. Your most crucial relationship is with yourself. Love yourself. You are worth more than you might believe. Drinking yourself to sleep will never provide you a tangible resolution to the endured pain. Come with me, listen to your inner person, hold on to forgiveness, and try to renew yourself through pardon. You are capable of doing anything you want to do. You are a magnificent young lady."

My visit with Kris was initiated by her. After visiting my family on several occasions, she became very fond of my daughters. She once told me she admires the way my family relates to one another. She visited us frequently. We are good family friends. On the day of our rendezvous, she said she needed to speak to someone she knows will not judge her, someone who respects children. Our visit was a tipping point in my reserve regarding the open discussion of the issues surrounding children, especially girls who have been smacked, hit, beaten, you name it, by their own loved ones. Our meeting enabled me to concretize the assumption that the abuse of children by adults, or their parents, for that matter, could be foundational to destructive and violent behaviors later in adult life. Kris was crystal clear she had abused and bullied girls at her elementary, middle and high school from motiveless malice. In high school, she insisted she hung out with the wrong crowd and made senseless decisions because she suffered low self-esteem. She suffers from chronic depression, drinks alcohol to abate her emotional and psychological aches, has trust issues, and has been unable to build lasting relationships with most of the people she's known through the years—the list is endless.

Although people say children are the most resilient of humans and have a high potential to self-renew, recovering from the devastating effects of abuse such as suffered by Kris, the Texas judge's daughter, and a plethora of young girls in this nation can be very challenging. Smacking is neither a good nor legitimate way to discipline or teach your daughter the right kind of behavior required of her. The humiliation of corporal punishment and its accompanying anger and devastation neither incite a desire to please nor create the type of self-discipline that parents anticipate from their children. As they mature, girls who grew up in a home where their parents physically abused them may have a higher tendency than girls raised in a more loving home without physical torture to consider violence of any kind, especially spousal abuse, as an acceptable part of life. The probability for such girls or women to break up with an abusive spouse may be slim because as children, they experienced similar conditions and are more prone to believe that is acceptable. It will not be surprising that these may comprise some of the women who would end up beating their own children and hurting them just like they themselves were hurt.

Do not destroy your daughters and their respective lives through smacking or beatings—whatever you call the act of hitting your child on purpose as a means of teaching her that what she has done is wrong or unacceptable. Remember the high price such girls might pay throughout their existence: physical torture, humiliation, emotional scars, and damaged self-worth that usually lead to other psychological issues with potentially intractable psychiatric disorders. Avoid even what you may think is a gentle smack on the back of the hand or the buttock because it teaches aggression, and may beget just that. Beating your daughter, no matter at what age, is not worth anything, it would diminish the self-esteem of any teenager, and may insinuate that aggression is acceptable.

If you hit your daughters prior to reading *Compass*, remember that it is a human right to maintain physical integrity and to not be hit. Children are humans, and so their rights to be free from hitting must be respected. Their defenselessness and dependence on the adults in their lives for protection and love should be taken seriously, and not minimized when we are frustrated with them.

The principles of **dialogue, understanding, tolerance, open, and honest communication** should be prioritized for teaching, correcting and guiding girls and children in general, whether they belong to the PETD category or not. Further, the insistence on, and persistent use of **"consequences for unacceptable behaviors"**, is an invaluable principle for successfully guiding teenage girls into adulthood. Further in the book, I discuss tolerance and how to have meaningful dialogue, open, honest, and effective communication with girls. The goal of having dialogues and honest communication with our daughters is to understand them better to effectively guide them, and to instill self-confidence, and empower them.

Contempt Breeds Contempt

One cold evening in December a few years ago, Kay and I entered a store in a big mall to buy her some shoes for church. In the shoes department was a medium-built blonde lady with two young girls. The woman and her daughters appeared to be a solid upper middle-class family. The blonde lady tried to behave responsibly, but one of her daughters who looked distinctly taller and older than her sister remained loud, commenting on everyone who passed by, and laughing without cause. The other daughter was calm, and stayed close to her mother. After trying-on several pair of shoes, the teenage daughter told her mother the store had no shoes she liked. She asked that they try another store. The lady was talking to her younger-looking daughter when the teenager yelled out, "Move, Mom, I'm talking to you. Move, let's go. Didn't you hear me? Move!"

The woman appeared embarrassed and asked her daughter to be less loud but the young girl responded, "I don't care. I am a teenage girl; I should speak up. Let's go now, Mom."

The woman immediately told her child, "You are as bad as a rotten egg—fat, mean, rude, and useless. You are good for nothing, speaking to me like that. You are no good and will go nowhere with that attitude. You see why you have no friends, and no one likes you? My daughter's eye caught mine as I wondered if she was following that conversation. Feeling embarrassed, I immediately asked her if she liked what she had on, and she said she was still checking it out.

The older daughter had a repartee for her mother as they all walked away from the shoe department. "Whatever, Mom. I don't care. You are mean and stupid, Mom. I hate you. I hate you a million times...."

It was a loud, angry but cold exchange between the two of them. This left me with the understanding that people from any level of the social rung can be confronted with issues of verbal abuse and that some parents and their young girls have trouble relating appropriately to each other. I have no understanding of why the girl got to speak so rudely to her mother. I did not contemplate what gave the woman reason to trash her own daughter so badly—and in public for that matter. But I thought as the adult, she ought to have held herself better but firmly contain her daughter's naughtiness either by asking her to behave herself more appropriately and speak respectfully or by simply agreeing that they should leave. Besides, I do not believe there was a need for the woman to respond to her daughter's rudeness with insults. Is the behavior something that the girl got from her mother constantly bashing her? Or bashing other people in front of the child? Or is she just a provocative child? Does this mother understand that verbally abusing her daughter may negatively impact her self-esteem? Could she have restrained herself in that situation? Where is her emotional intelligence and is this for real? Where did she leave her self and social awareness? Did she understand that perhaps her daughter is frustrated because she has not found the shoes she is looking for and needs mom's empathy? These and several other questions ran through my head as we witnessed the incident, but I could hardly answer any of them. This situation helped convinced me that several other children and young women in this nation and around the world confront verbal abuse daily from their parents which may or may not complicate their interactions and relationships.

Building strong, confident girls entails a lot, and children may tempt you, tease you for the fun of it, and test you in different ways. I am not saying the girl's behavior was exemplary or that her mother should have condoned with her rudeness. No matter the extent of the attempt to have you lose your cool, fracturing the psychological well-being of a young girl by telling her she has no friends and no one likes her can only have very negative impacts on the child. What I am saying is that as a mother, you have the power to whirl your daughter's behavior. It may be best to steer away from a war of words with your daughters because in some situations, when you strike them verbally, they are more likely to strike back, sometimes even harder because that is often what life is; contempt would breed contempt because for "every action, there is an equal and opposite reaction," as I learned in my middle school physics class. Contempt breeds like itself, contempt.

That wasn't the first nor the last time we were hearing raw and insulting verbal exchange between mother and daughter. On an elevator going down to the lobby of a nice hotel in New Jersey, a woman told her daughter she wasn't appropriately dressed for the occasion they were going to attend by telling her, "You are dressed like a prostitute, or should I say a slut, Dana. You know you look just like a pig in that dress!" Her daughter's response was "Mom, not again! Stop! Just stop! Whatever, mom!"

The mother fired back, "Dana, did you look in the mirror before leaving your room? You are screaming to everyone, 'I am a slut, I am a slut, I am a pig!'" Dana did not respond to her mom's insults but she sniffed and cleared her throat a few times while her mom's verbal attack continued till we got to level one where we all got out of the elevator. It was awkward. The man who accompanied both ladies never uttered a word during the verbal altercation between the women. He appeared younger than the girl's mother but not old enough to be the young lady's father. He was apparently accompanying the mother rather than the daughter. It was a beautiful summer evening, but I wondered if the young lady would enjoy the occasion she was going to attend after submitting to her own mother's verbal bashing.

Bridge to Self-Confidence

It may be an understatement to allege that many parents are experiencing challenging behaviors from their teenage daughters and their harsh responses may not always be anticipated or premeditated. But parental verbal abuse, degrading language, insults and humiliation of any type equally impact teenage girls like physical abuse. To raise self-confident and empowered young women devoid of the feelings of shame and embarrassment that are secondary to such abuse, the principles of **Restraint, Emotional Intelligence** (EI), and **Emotional Support** have proven to be outstanding for my family. Together, these three are known as the **REE** principle. Restraint, Emotional Intelligence (EI), Emotional Support (REE) are some of the principles that could have helped the moms in the difficult shoe department and elevator incidents with their respective teenage daughter. As crucial characteristics when raising girls, these three principles may not be innate but could well be cultivated and practiced to help teenage girls to gracefully transition to adulthood. Mildly introverted, I naturally exercise great verbal restraint in challenging situations with our daughters but I am not inoculated against occasional emotional display. However, I have cultivated emotional intelligence and learned the domains to help me guide our daughters the best I can.

For a mom or parents, EI is her ability to understand her emotions and that of her daughter, and to exert emotional self-control in order to appropriately manage their relationship. Restraint is being able to self-control or to hold back in a tempting situation with a child. Emotional Support is when parents communicate either verbally or non-verbally in a manner that is comforting, and conveys their compassion, understanding and love for the child. The REE principle is wonderful because of the bottom-line similarities among the three concepts.

Considering the four domains of EI which are self-awareness, self-management, social awareness and relationship management, restraint and emotional support fit-in perfectly with EI as principles for guiding teenage girls. Parental skillful management of personal emotions and demonstration of REE towards their teenage daughters in-turn teaches them understanding, respect for the other, self-control, and self-respect which are highly required skills for successful friendships and professional relationships beyond teenage years and into adulthood.

Although endemic in a multitude of families and cultures, some have argued that physical punishment does not appear to be a part of human nature. However, if it were human nature, that is sure an element of human nature that abusive parents should rid themselves of in favor of the REE principle. Raising children is challenging. Having raised two girls provides me an excellent understanding of the matter. There is no one size fits all parenting model, but surely, smacking your daughters or verbally abusing them is not the acceptable way to correct, teach or guide them, and definitely not the quintessential model for guiding or empowering teenage girls.

There are several alternatives to smacking children. In some families, including mine, norms and boundaries were established at a very early age. The norms and boundaries are being respected by our children because they have been taught and believe those norms and boundaries should be respected rather than because they are afraid to receive a senseless and callous smacking from us for noncompliance or nonconformity to established boundaries. Should your daughters remain naughty or ill-willed and very tempting even after boundaries are established, let them know you are not happy with them and explain why. This is my favorite way of dealing with upbringing challenges. Alternatives to beating, as explained by other opponents of child smacking such as Jo Frost, include the use of social sanctions such as sitting in a corner for a brief period of time, no hugs for a day, time-out, grounding, no playdates for a defined period, no dessert, no sleepover for a defined period of time or take away one of highly valued personal items to dissuade your younger daughters from deviant behaviors. For teenagers, social sanctions such as not seeing friends outside of school, no birthday bash, phone-grounding etc are very effective.

Notwithstanding, it is also not right to only focus on misbehavior. If a rebelliously naughty daughter who habitually tempts your patience improves on her behavior, show appreciation for her effort. My bridge to raising self-confident ladies entails not only keeping a check on my emotions, but also felicitating our daughters for demonstrating good behavior and using the principle of **positive reinforcement** as a bridge.

A solid bridge to instilling self-confidence in our challenging daughters entails making it an important point to reward good behaviors, praise them for ceasing unacceptable behaviors when asked to, give them hugs, treat them to their favorite dessert, give them a loving pat on the back, use encouraging and congratulatory words such as "Good job, darling," "Excellent, lady! Wonderful teenager" "Well done here, little one," "Come on for a big hug," and wrap them in a nice warm hug and plant a loving kiss on their cheek or forehead to acknowledge and reinforce good behavior, show excitement and give a high- five, and say "Thank you for being good." Provide an allowance for older girls, or surprise them with their favorite store's gift card, or simply give her a special treat to reinforce good behavior. These are self-esteem boosters that would make any PETD child or teenage girl more responsive and nice. Trust me, these work amazingly!

The principle of Positive Reinforcement has an advantage in that it boosts the self-esteem of our daughters and provides a sense of accomplishment at home, which builds the confidence they require to affront the world outside the warmth and comfort of their homes. Positive reinforcement as a principle for guiding teenage girls into adulthood is invaluable and highly empowering!

The focus for correcting our girls should be their behavior rather than on their person or body. If you intend growing strong, graceful, and self-assured women in your family, consider raising your daughters without lifting your straps or belts to their bodies and avoid raising your big adult hands on their buttocks, backs, thighs, or faces. Consider a challenging daughter as a PETD child and may be leverage the savvy of Jo Frost, the Supernanny who successfully assisted some American families to deal with their PETD children and the principles shared in this *Compass* to help as your guide.

Interviewed after the Texas family court judge's scandalous beating of his teenage daughter, Jo asserted that the judge's behavior "is not justified behavior. There's alternatives of disciplining a child that allows you to have a healthy relationship with your children, trust for you to be able to build your family dynamics in a way that is functional." Insisting on her work with "families who have been raised to think that corporal punishment is acceptable and fine," she persuaded, "Parents have a choice to elect alternative discipline that allows bonding at the same time—that was a sixteen-year- old—there were several things that this judge could have done to discipline his daughter. That was not just abuse. That was humiliation." Jo encouraged families to grow with their children, to bond and to also set clear rules and have expectations that are understood within the family circle. That is excellent advice that I thought to share in *Compass*.

As we close this section of the book titled "The Backdrop: A Lesson" and proceed to discuss education in the next section, I would like to insist that the foundational lessons for our daughters begin from home long before they enter the general social environment, which includes educational spaces.

Their experiences and lessons learned from home could impact how they fare at school and beyond. Every child's backdrop and lessons learned from their cradle has accompanying effects that endure through teenage years to adulthood, no matter what. Kris's backdrop and lessons learned have formed the cornerstone or part of her personality, as she confessed it.

Understanding that hitting girls might cause them significant emotional repercussions during their teenage years and into adulthood, it is important to turn the page from reacting with physical and emotional abuse, to reacting by using the principles for guiding them into adulthood.

The principles shared in this section are: (1) **Understanding** which means being aware of your daughters' feelings of frustrations, be tender, sympathetic and sensitive in dealing with their issues. (2) **Tolerance** which is parental willingness to endure their child's unacceptable behavior and deal with it in a way that teaches and empowers the child to behave better in the future. (3) **Dialogue** which entails holding conversations with the child to understand the reasons for the behavior in order to appropriately manage the situation without the use of physical force, physical punishment, or verbal abuse. (4) **Open and honest communication** and the insistence on having **consequences for unacceptable behaviors.** Further in the book, I explain how I communicate with our daughters in a manner that is fully engaging for all parties involved in the communication, and making it especially beneficial for our daughters. (5) **Restraint, Emotional Intelligence (EI),** and **Emotional Support** also known as the **REE** principle. (6) **Positive Reinforcement (PR)** which is a positive and rewarding action by a parent after a child's good behavior to encourage and strengthen the behavior and boost the child's self-esteem. Worth understanding is that providing girls with emotional support makes them feel optimally safe, and that safety has several psychological and educational benefits for them. Such educational benefits include the potential to work cooperatively with their siblings at home, with peers at school, as well as the courage to assert themselves in any new situation of learning without fear of any kind.

SECTION 2

EDUCATION

There are several questions surrounding education such as, what really is education? As I interact with friends, family, and peers, some of them ask questions such as, what is the importance of education? How do young girls learn? At what age do young girls start to learn certain basic skills? Who is responsible for educating our young daughters or young girls? What is the difference between parental education and educational institutional learning for our daughters?

My responses to these questions emanate from the lenses through which I view and consider education. There is nothing more important to me than the type of education we give our children because I personally believe that high **quality education** is the only way to secure their future. Education can be viewed through several lenses, including life's experiences, community service, activism, feminism, and a lot more.

The education in discussion here is good, quality, synchronous, or asynchronous education. That is the importance of learning arithmetic or mathematics, geography, English literature, theater art, or art literature, history, chemistry, sciences, economics, civics, and other disciplines that converge to enlighten us on globalization, social justice, information management, critical thinking etcetera. When it comes to educating young girls, questions abound and perspectives vary. It is important to remember that very early in life, our children develop several cognitive skills that are foundational contributing factors to how they learn and, ultimately, who they become. Skills such as attention skills, memory, thinking, reasoning, and understanding skills are part of your daughter's innate capabilities at a very early age making them capable of learning at the highest levels possible later in life. The importance of educating girls from a young age cannot be underscored enough and our undivided attention to it as mothers should endure.

Having these and more in mind, providing high quality education for girls is a solid principle for guiding them from a young age through teenage years and adulthood.

Shared Responsibilities

Early education begins at home with parental instruction. Therefore, in the modern society of the twenty-first century, parents retain the primary responsibility for educating and socializing their daughters. While it is important to note that every child needs the presence of his or her loving parents' guidance to understand the fundamentals of education, this is particularly true for young girls. Collaboration between both parents in a healthy family setting is critical in raising and educating fine, strong women.

Notwithstanding, children's education is widely considered the joint and concurrent responsibility of families, schools, and communities at large. Additionally, teachers assume a significant role in guiding our children's social learning. An important element to remember is that families and schools represent two of the most powerful social institutions where young girls such as our daughters are educated and socialized.

The roles that communities play in the lives of our daughters can never be overemphasized. This translates to the need for family-school-community partnerships in educating young girls. Ensuring access to education for girls is probably the most certain way to arrest or reverse poverty and disease. History and experience have both demonstrated that there are myriad direct and indirect benefits of educating young girls. Oprah Winfrey demonstrated to the world that educating young girls in South Africa was as important as educating them in the United States because the bottom line really is that providing young girls quality education and preparing them to be confident leaders of tomorrow's societies is crucial to our communities and the world. Ms. Winfrey's gesture in sponsoring those young ladies was a voice so loud in favor of educating our daughters—and girls or women, in general—that it still resounds in my ears today, several years after she first introduced all of us to the girls she called her daughters. She would sponsor their educational journey to limitless destinations.

Kay, Court, and I were speechless as we watched her amazing generosity and powerful contribution to the lives of young women she hardly knew at the time. Instead of buying them Barbie dolls, American Girl dolls, Gucci shoes and purses, she gave them the most tangible, priceless, and timeless gift: the gift of education—the most important gift for any girl or young lady.

Educating our daughters rests foremost and primarily on us, their parents which further explains why providing quality education is a fundamental foundational principle for guiding teenage girls into adulthood. However, communities and our academic institutions have shared responsibilities to make quality education for our daughters' a reality.

Right Here at Home

It may come as a surprise to some around the world that in this country, the USA, some girls sell their bodies to sex traffickers, have not attended high school at the age of eighteen, do not understand the importance of education, and lack the basic information of the benefits of going to school and furthering their education in a college. From watching the news and subsequent research and information gathering from several sources on youth education, including Strong American Schools, New Information on Youth Who Drop Out, Eric Education Information Center, and the Department of Education, I gathered that 7,000 (seven thousand) American high school students drop out of school daily. Is your daughter, your granddaughter, your sister, neighbor, your niece, or a friend part of this statistics?

What is her alternative to education? Does she have one? Has she verbalized it either to you or to a close family relation? Is her alternate plan reasonable and objectively attainable? Is education important to you and your family? Have you considered the importance of education and how life changing it can be? Have you thought of how you can encourage her to rethink her decision of abandoning the train of books and studying hard for success? Would you wholeheartedly consider her decision premature, hasty, and unreasonable? Then begin building an action plan of intervention because our daughters need the adults in their lives to help them obtain quality education. While the government, some schools and its teachers might fail some of our daughters in the realm of education, *Compass* is focusing on parental involvement and individual responsibilities to help our daughters receive sound education, improve their graduation rate and their chances of professional and career success in their adulthood.

According to the 2010 fact sheet of the Alliance for Excellent Education (AEE), nationwide, about seven thousand students drop out every school day…Each year approximately 1.3 million students fail to graduate from high school…This statistic may not have been noticed fifty years ago, but the era during which a high school dropout could earn a living wage has ended in the United States. By dropping out, these individuals significantly diminish their chances to secure a good job and a promising future. Sometimes the reasons why students drop out of school are difficult to pinpoint and explain. According to the Alliance for Excellent Education, while there is no single reason for why students drop out, research indicates that difficult transitions to high school, deficient basic skills, and a lack of engagement all serve as prominent barriers to graduation.

The first and most prominent reason advanced by the 2010 Alliance for Excellent Education is that most dropouts are already on the path to failure in the middle grades and engage in behaviors that strongly correlate to dropping out in high school. Various researchers have identified low attendance or a failing grade as specific risk factors.

Should you consider yourself a parent or a relative of a young girl who is in this category of academic truancy and apathy, you should begin strategizing to maximally help your daughter. You may wonder aloud, "But how? How can I help her? She does not listen. I have tried. She now has a boyfriend with whom she spends most of her time. The teacher does not help her. The teacher discriminates against her. It is a low-performing school that does not encourage their students. The teachers do not encourage their students. The school does not challenge its students…"

I have heard all sorts of reasons why it may be highly challenging or somewhat difficult to assist some girls. And I presume some parents believe they have many reasons that explain why their children drop out of high school, and therefore, they can go on and on enumerating the reasons or explaining the whys for their child's dropping out of school for a very long time. Another assumption by me is that some of these parents have good reasons to believe their perspectives are legitimate.

The January 2012 *Caught in the Crisis* fact sheet corroborates the reasons forwarded by the 2010 AEE for student dropout:

Nationally, millions of students in grades 7–12 are at risk of dropping out of high school because of low literacy skills, poor attendance, and class failure.

It concerned me, especially as I have two young daughters, one of them currently in high school, to learn the following statistics about student dropout rate in the nation. I share it to create awareness and to forewarn you that this is an epidemic, and you can prevent it from attacking your loved ones.

- More than 1.2 million students drop out of high school in the U.S. annually.
- Over one-quarter of high school freshmen do not graduate from high school in a timely fashion.
- An average of just 58% students in the 50 largest cities in the nation graduate.
- Minorities are disproportionately affected in that over one in four Hispanic students drop out, and almost half of them leave by the eighth grade. Besides, Hispanics are twice as likely as African Americans to drop out.
- Dropouts make up nearly half the heads of households on welfare and high school dropouts commit approximately 75% of crimes in the nation.
- There is a likelihood that the dropout issue will increase substantially through 2020.

- America ranks 19th in the world for high school graduation rate.

Whereas the reasons why some students drop out of high school may not pertain to wealthy and upper-middle-class children, it is worth noting that several children who come from underserved and underrepresented populations or groups such as minority students, children from foster homes, students from low socio-economic status, and low-income students are at high risk of dropping out. In my humble opinion, what you should tell yourself and your teenage high school daughters is that without appropriate quality education through college, their situation of poverty and social stagnation or immobility will endure, potentially causing them to remain disenfranchised in a nation that provides limitless opportunities and possibilities. It is part of our responsibility to ascertain that our teenage daughters receive quality education in order to succeed, enhance their status, and become privileged in many ways and in varied quarters in their adulthood.

As you read on, remember that in high school, our daughters are already teenagers. So, I would like for you to think about these: How would you deal with something that you determine is hampering your sister, niece, granddaughter, or daughter's graduation from high school? Where is your child's particular issue? If she does not have any issues, can you use what you know and what you learned from *Compass* to help other individuals at your church, your neighborhood, your youth center, community meetings, bible study group, where you volunteer, or someone you realize needs help? How can you help some high school kid or teenage girls even in the smallest way possible?

Ordinary Recipe, Extraordinary Results

Believing in the principle of providing quality education for girls just like my mom did, I wondered how to approach it with our children even before their birth. Determined to prevent the issue of deficiency in basic skills as part of the foundation for learning, I concocted my own recipe for prevention. It entailed considering an early start to educating little but curious minds as a fundamental ingredient for success. To enhance our daughters' basic learning skills, such as listening, attentiveness, memory, and understanding skills, from their cradle, reading to our daughters and the use of storytelling at a very young age is key. Not only does it teach them the importance of learning or the fun and significance of reading a book and enjoying the story, it also helps them establish and strengthen their cognitive skills at a very tender age. I understand this first-hand from my experience with both of our daughters.

When I was pregnant for our first daughter, Kay, I read every issue of *practical parenting*, a parental magazine publication in England. I enjoyed each topic that I read, so I began telling myself my unborn child might enjoy some of the fun things that some issues suggested such as reading a fun book with your child. As my pregnancy evolved monthly, I started buying the most inexpensive children's storybooks. I was going to prepare my unborn daughter's nursery, but I was also going to dedicate time to read to her before birth. When I entered my second trimester of pregnancy, I decided to begin executing my plan. Most evenings, I'll read her a story from a book, then we'll listen to music, and I'll fall asleep. We listened to lullabies each night from my second trimester until she was born. The amazing thing I discovered about this is that the songs we listened to prior to her birth were those that calmed her the most and sent her to sleep from infancy through her toddler years.

Reading to her and then reading together and storytelling became part of our daily routine after she was born, and as she grew up. As soon as she was capable, I'd ask her to pick a book for us to read either during our quiet time, playtime, or at bedtime. When I wanted to teach her something specific, I'd choose what to read, but often, she'd say to me, "Can we read this one, please, please, please?" From three years and older, she'd sometimes ask me to tell her a fun story. Often, I'd pick a story from one of the children's books we read. On several occasions she'd say, "Mommy, tell me a fun story that is not in a book, a good, fun story from the sky." Although she often perplexed me and made me think hard, I realized the little girl was asking me to be creative. I told her stories from the Bible, stories that my mom told me or stories that I read in a book we didn't have. She'd listen keenly, and then as we continued our routine through the years, her little mind became quite inquisitive after a story, and she started asking me questions about the characters in my story and what the story meant.

After laying her to sleep one night, I thought of the story we shared before we kissed good night and the questions she asked me after that. I realized that my daughter was demonstrating very basic but fundamental learning skills such as attentiveness, memory, thinking and understanding. It was exciting to me because not only was I teaching my daughter, she was reciprocating in a highly meaningful way. She had listened keenly, remembered details about the stories I told her, thought about what she didn't understand, and there she was, asking me questions about the characters I had presented to her. She not only wanted me to be creative, to make it fun, she was also asking me to determine what lessons I wanted her to learn from the stories we read and the ones I told her.

When she became a big sister with a much younger sibling, I watched and listened to her read to her baby sister. She was more fun and exciting than I was with her, and as I watched her sister's response to her readings and her stories, which by the way were the ones I told her, I learned more. During story time, I saw her little sister giggling when she made funny voices, gesticulating motions, and excited, silly or funny faces when she told a story or read to her. I started copying her. So, when I read to them, I'd make a silly or a funny face or gesticulate to keep them entertained and interested. It worked very well! They remained attentive and engaged as always, but they were also very excited, with beautiful glimmers in their eyes as they giggled or laughed. What they also took great interest in were the questions that followed our reading sessions. Each one of them had to respond to basic questions about the stories we read. We called it *"the shining moment or the tell mommy time."* They took pride in responding to simple questions such as, what is this story about? What are the lessons we can learn from it? Who is the protagonist of the story? Who are the other characters? What do you believe happened and why? Could the story line be different? How would you have been or made it different if you were the protagonist?

When she turned six, Courtney my youngest daughter began requesting that her father drive her to our local library over the weekend so she could check out books to read after homework and during her free and quiet times. Now a fourth-grader, she was informed by the librarian at her school that she was named among the top 5 kids who had checked out the most books in third grade. Her older sister challenges herself to read a certain number of books each year.

While both girls were in elementary and high school, respectively, apart from reading after school and on weekends, during holidays, we created time for reading. We named it "our quiet time," and it occurred briefly but daily during holiday periods. We borrowed books from our local library and read them at home or during a trip. Manny or I read some of the books to assess the language, content, and the appropriateness for our children prior to allowing them to read on.

We selected books to be explored or analyzed after the girls complete reading them. We explored the books by asking the girls questions such as the ones above, but I also asked each girl to summarize the book, either in writing or verbally, and explain the main ideas and parts of the story. I often asked, "Have you experienced anything similar in the story? How did you handle it? Explain your rationale for your actions when you handled it."

Kay and Courtney enjoy reading and read over thirty age-appropriate literatures each, every summer. Providing them these basic learning skills have and is helping them cope with the rigors and demands of daily schooling during the academic year. After watching a movie, we engage in similar questioning strategies: What did you like about it? What didn't you like about it? What can you learn from it? By asking them such questions in a light-hearted and fun way, you not only gauge their understanding of the subject matter, you also analyze their attentiveness to details in the literature and storylines, their memory of the events that occurred in the story, and you can gracefully engage their critical thinking abilities.

Both of our daughters know the importance of receiving quality education. We have discussed it over and over, and each one of them set their personal goals at a very young age. Surprisingly, these young ladies wake up in the morning and want to go to school. During a parent-teacher conference, Court's homeroom teacher at the time, Mrs. Diana Davenport, whom she loves very much and who also influenced Missy's desire to go to school daily by being a loving, kind, and focused teacher with her students, told me, "It amazes me and the other kids in class when she raises her hand when I ask who wants homework. She is the only child in my class who wants homework. She is a delight to have in my room. She is one of my best students. She is truly a delightful student, very poised. You must be proud of her."

During a Christmas party hosted by a close friend at the end of 2012, I met our daughters' elementary school religion teacher at the time, Mrs. Pam. Stein, whom they both love so much and speak highly about. During our beautiful conversation, she said to me, "Your daughters are amazing. They are both so intelligent, respectful, and focused. You must be proud." I smiled broadly and responded "Thank you, it is the work of God." With my hands placed together and my eyes open and looking up toward the sky, I continued, "I give thanks to Him. It is and requires hard work with a lot of patience to raise them well." Mrs. Stein responded, "Well, you certainly have done an amazing job to have two wonderful girls such as Kay and Courtney. They are very responsible at their young ages."

During Court's seventh-grade parent-teacher conference I attended at her school, each of her teachers articulated their "joy to have such a student" in their class." Mrs. Patti Orchowski and Ms. Joyce Burke, together during the conference, were unanimous in stating that Missy is an "all-around excellent student. If every student were like her, our jobs will be very easy. There really isn't much to tell you about her, Dr. Bell. We are sure you know your child. She is an excellent student." As these two excellent teachers explained our daughter's academic performance and personality, they expressed the joy you see in the eyes of teachers satisfied with their job and proud of the students they are helping to mold. It was highly gratifying.

Manny and I went to conference with Mrs. C. Mitchell., and she articulated the same words as her colleagues while discussing Court's academic performance and general class behavior: "She is just an excellent student." Presenting her class work and scores to us, she insisted, "She is quite an excellent student all-round. She is one that I can count on to give me the answer to a question anytime. She is just an excellent student."

Manny and I looked at each other, happy and humbled to know that our daughter's teachers think very highly of her. We know Courtney is an old soul, focused and determined to succeed at every endeavor she undertakes, but we felt grateful to God that he had helped us instill in her the importance of going above and beyond academically, knowing that literacy and education are critical for future success. And also behaving responsibly, respectfully, and in an acceptable manner at school and beyond.

Kay's high school physics teacher, Dr. T., for whom our daughter has a very special liking told me and my husband during parent-teacher conference that "This is a tough class, and students are usually slow and reluctant to respond to questions, but Karen is always enthusiastic about us starting a new topic or lesson. She's the only one who says [the teacher raised her right arm, closed her hand, and waved energetically], 'Okay, let's go for it.' She doesn't stop to amaze me. She'll go places. I am serious. Your daughter will go places."

For simple, everyday parents such as us, and for a mom who has spent and continues to spend significant amounts of time reading to and with her children, it was beyond joy to hear these comments from our daughters' respective teachers. We have been paid countless compliments for the girls, but these were teachers, fine teachers commending their students.

We told Dr. T., the physics teacher, that we were amazed at Kay's excitement when she returned home and spoke to us about physics, her teacher, her experience, and her interest in the subject and lessons because so far, she has been academically very humanities or arts inclined. She loves fashion, literature, reading, writing, poetry, art, and drama. She once wrote for her school's yearly publication while in elementary school and has had to share her literature essays with her entire school two years consecutively while she was in middle school. In high school, she was the editor for the institution's online newspaper and started her fashion blogging business at fourteen. So we could hardly comprehend or even believe she would be complimented and commended by a physics instructor.

As Manny and I drove back home, we continued to wonder and discuss our children's education and how important it is to provide them at a very young age with basic but highly recommended foundational tools for educational interest later in life. We agreed that they are on a good path academically. My belief is that those reading sessions—which began while I was pregnant with each one of them, and continued in a simply structured manner at home and during vacation trips—have gone a long way to prepare them in a way that I never could have anticipated. We were happy and prayed that the interests would not cease at a later stage with more intense course work as upper-class students and in their teenage years. Understandably, upholding the principle of providing our girls with quality education which can begin as early as possible for each parent, with a basic foundation to love books was yielding these results. The simple, ordinary recipe of consistently reading to and with them was resulting in extraordinary interest in books, reading, studying, and academic interests of all sorts.

Transitioning to the Hill

A significant part of preparing children to further their education through high school entails building a solid elementary foundation that prepares them for an uphill climb to high school as teenagers, and college as young adults. Most high school campuses are bigger than middle school campuses, and they often "even appear intimidating," as a close friend puts it. Continuing education is an uphill climb, hence the importance of effectively helping our daughters understand and prepare for the leap forward and transition into a more rigorous academic setting in their teenage years. This brings us to the principle of engagement in our daughter's educational process which I will explain using various examples from my **engagement in the process** for both of our girls.

Learning from my personal history, growing up, I saw my parents and other family friends do their utmost to educate their children in the finest schools and keep them in school by all means. My mom believed every adolescent girl should be educated in a Catholic institution for girls, and boys should all attend Catholic schools dedicated to educating adolescent male and preparing them for college. My grandma would spend hours speaking to me about the importance of a girls-only institution and how she was determined to educate my mom through medical school. At the time, she was telling me her stories, my mom's dream of completing medical school and becoming a medical doctor had been cut short because she met and married a powerful and wealthy man who provided her with everything she needed or even wanted. He also took good care of her family. She was doing great by all the standards of their society and time. They had children, and she was dedicated to raising them right, and part of raising them right meant making sure they each had sound education.

In her endeavor to provide even her relative's children the same best that she wanted for her own children, she took Jerry in to live with our family. My father sent Jerry off to be educated in one of the nation's finest private Catholic boarding schools for boys, just like one of my older brothers was sent off to another prime private Catholic boys school. Jerry would have tremendous struggles at school and will ultimately be expelled from the prestigious institution. He was sent to another boarding school where he still was unable to cope. Although my parents sat down with Jerry to set his educational goals, he could not be helped enough to remain in that school. He was sent to another school. By this time, he had realized that my parents had his best interest at heart and, by making him stay at school, wanted to assist and contribute to his success.

My parents were not alone in their struggle to keep a child in middle school and better prepare him for high school. A close family friend whose daughters all attended a prestigious catholic boarding school experienced difficulty educating one of their daughters after she was expelled from the highly strict environment. After my mom experienced these struggles from within her family and her friends, she asked me how I'd cope in high school. I didn't know what to say because I had never attended high school. All I knew at the time is that I will be in school whether I liked it or not, and that I was going to be a lawyer if I weren't a nun. I liked school; it was somewhat fun, and I always passed my exams.

To prepare me for success in high school, my parents, even my grandma, made me understand they wanted me to be educated and successful. They had given me a lot to demonstrate their engagement in my education, and I wasn't going to let them down. My high school environment was small and tough because many students were very intelligent and many of the girls were too street-smarter than me. I was not street-smart and certainly not a tough kid, but I had been prepared to work in the environment. It was hard but my parent's engagement helped me focus. To effectively prepare me for high school, my parents paid some of my teachers for after- school tutoring in subjects that posed the most challenges for me. My parents consistently visited with my teachers to discuss my progress at school and learned about how I was coping. Our principal visited my family home on certain occasions to meet with my parents in private. The most important discussion centered on making sure that I received excellent preparation for the final high school test and college preparation.

The principle of engagement in our daughter's educational process is fundamental for guiding them through their teenage years in high school and into college and beyond as adults. Parental engagement in their teenager's educational process is the supportive involvement of parents in their daughter's academic learning and the process of the academic institution. Parental engagement in this sense entails having a high level of commitment to the teen's academic success by making meaningful positive contributions in her learning process. This can be done in multiple different ways including but not limited to: having discussions about her classes, grades, challenges, opportunities, her teachers, friends, by attending parent-teacher conferences and holding post conference mother-daughter follow-up, by articulating your respect and value for her education, and by being present during open forums to learn about her classes and meet the teachers...etc. Engagement does not apply when parents send their daughters to school and adopt a hands-off posture for whatever reason. Parental engagement in this regard entails taking ownership of actions in the teen's educational process with a goal of helping her academic success and graduation.

I engaged almost like my parents did, to prepare Kay for her high school freshman class in 2012. While in high school, I continued the support by leveraging the relationships with teachers and administrators. In high school, when she misses class work and appears to be behind, or when she has challenges in a particular subject, I make sure that she goes to school early for tutoring. After a math test that left her with regrets, she became a frequent early morning visitor to her math teacher. They met for our daughter to be tutored, and she has made immense progress. This delightful and kind math teacher, Mrs. Peggy Coleman, sent me an e-mail to explain precisely what happened with our daughter during her math test. Kay had already recounted her day to us the same day she had the test, so we were already aware of her challenges. Our e-mail discussions with the teacher were highly productive. We visited with her for parent-teacher conference and found her to know our child astonishingly very well. Kay made strides in math and ultimately succeeded amazingly per her teacher. Without engagement in her educational process as a principle to guide her, this would not have been possible because she felt paralyzed in math after her first high school math test and was ready to run away from the class.

Transitioning to high school can be challenging which makes parental engagement in their teen's academic process crucial for her success. It is worthwhile for you to invite your daughter to share her perspectives of high school and what she thinks her potential challenges might be. Each child is different, and so they all have different challenges as well. If she is in a low- performing institution or one that does not challenge her enough, then move on; change schools if you can. We have seen parents move from one city or county to another for the sake of having their children attend good schools. As parents, you want to pinpoint the issue that might cause your child's setback so as to confront it head-on for the sake of your daughter's educational success. Has your daughter or a girl you know dropped out of school due to difficult transition to high school? If your child's school is not helping to keep its students in class, you sure have realized by now that you are not alone in the world with this predicament, and you are probably acknowledging the fact that it is your responsibility, your moral imperative to educate your child.

Therefore, you must do your utmost to keep her in school even if it means relocating to another county or city with more promising schools or getting after-school tutors to prepare her for the rigorous high school work. Some children experience personal problems ranging from devastation caused by divorcing parents to peer pressures and mean-spirited peers. Sometimes, these issues are devastating to a young high school student, making it difficult or impossible for her to focus, succeed and graduate. For the girls who you know have similar personal problems, help them find a resolution to the issue after reading *Compass*. If you deem it necessary, seek professional help but do not desert your child or niece if you don't understand her challenges and concerns about school. Help protect her from dropping out of school and becoming a part of the startling statistics of high school dropouts. In some communities, high school girls assume important family responsibilities, such as caring for a sick grandparent or sibling while the mother goes to work. If this is your daughter's situation or that of someone you know, the advice is that the family members of that young girl should take turns in caring for the sick; schedule family obligations in such a way that your daughter has sufficient time to go to school and participate in the making of her future.

Watching Soledad O'Brien's *Latino in America*, it was heartbreaking to see that in some families, sending a young girl out to work and fetch money to feed her family is given precedence over her educational aspiration. I have since learned that in some cultures and families, young girls might be the sole breadwinners for their family. Such pressures are sometimes too heavy for the girl to shoulder or juggle with her high school work. The repercussion is dropping out of school to better shoulder the other responsibilities for the family. I can tell you that if you let her go through school and receive quality education, she will be a better family provider than doing odd jobs for meager pay because of circumstances. My very good friend and colleague, Hugo, and I had an interesting conversation about education and what some young girls really want. He explained to me that for some Latinas, the most important thing is to get married and have children. With a stern look in his eyes, he sniffed. "Ursula, I know this is sad to say, but ask some of them what they want the most, and this is the response you get—I want to get married and have children. Isn't that outrageous?"

I smiled. "Fair enough, but there's time for that. Education should be a priority on their agenda. You see, Hugo, these young girls need someone, an example, a role model or a leader in the community to clearly and boldly spell out the benefits of quality education versus the consequences of early marriage and childbearing. Childbearing or having a child is a blessing that we want to experience as women. However, that can be done after completing at least undergraduate college level education."

Hugo peered into my face. He was still wearing a serious look. I pursued, "There are certainly women out there that some of these young girls can relate to. These are the women who need to bring the message home if they have the experience, education, dedication, and care enough to impart them to such young and maybe ignorant women. They might be ignorant because of lack of awareness, information, role model, or mentoring relationships that proffer them the best ideas available to help them make more informed life choices."

As an adolescent girl who attended boarding school far away from home, my mom would hold long conversations with me the weeks leading up to the day I was leaving for school. She helped me fully understand that while she got married very young and early and quit her dream of becoming a medical doctor, that is not what she wanted to see happen to me. She said marriage should be the last item on my life's agenda because she made the choice of marrying and becoming a parent when she should have been focusing on school. She said, "The consequence of making such choices is that you fail your courses because you no longer focus on them, and that is what will affect your ability to complete school and graduate with your peers. You fail your courses, or you behave badly and you get expelled from school. Then what? What? Your education is disrupted. Be good. Focus on your schoolwork, and you will succeed."

Mom had my back so much I could not have felt more energy after each of our conversations. Each time I was dropped off at school, I cried from missing her, but I knew I'd be fine. God! Mom is the best mother any child can ever dream of having. Her words kept me carrying on at school, and I tried to make her proud with sometimes very good, often excellent grades and a brilliant report card.

Transitioning into high school requires parental engagement. Each student wants membership on the large high school campuses, but they also want to know that their parents are fully supportive of them as they move into a more complex academic environment. Parental engagement and a solid transition preparation, plan, and execution are the ultimate sine qua non for girls' successes and desire to stay at school.

Truancy is known to be a cause for some students' dropout of school. Academic truancy is prominently unpopular with teachers. A student with low school attendance cannot expect to pass all her exams. With a degrading grade point average (GPA) or an unsuccessful academic year due to truancy, your adolescent cannot feel like she is a member of her high school. Consequently, she will be suspended or expelled, which further compounds the attendance issues, or she will want to drop out because of poor attendance and academic failure to thrive. When your teenage daughter fails to complete high school on time, or struggles to stay in school, she misses the required foundational and fundamental skills and knowledge necessary to meet the rigors of college attendance and course work. To encourage their academic success and empower them to achieve the best academic results possible for their situation, collaborate with them to establish educational principles that comprise **zero tolerance for her poor class**

attendance and class work failures. For this principle, parents need to be outcome-oriented, disciplined, and determined about encouraging their daughters' educational outcomes; adopt participatory strategies in all her school endeavors and let her know that you are doing this because you have her best interests at heart and want to see her succeed. Such strategies might include checking in with her for test days, test results, teacher feedback, her reaction to test and examination results. By so doing, she will feel understood, supported, encouraged to perform at a higher level, and empowered to dream of success and work hard to achieve it. Additionally, you would decrease her risk of dropping-out.

Constructing a family foundational principle surrounding education early in life is critical for success. You might begin doing this by simply visiting your local library to look at the bookshelves, admire some books, and then begin borrowing some to read for leisure and analysis, like I did with Kay and Court (Missy). Articulate your vision for your children's education clearly and unequivocally. Build a firm understanding early in life that academic failure and dropping out is not acceptable but emphasize that they can succeed at school and anything else if they are determined and work hard at it. Explain what GPA means and how crucial it is to have above 4.0 or at least 3.8 GPA even if you are from a low socio-economic class, or a downright poor family.

One morning on my way to work, I listened to the story of a young girl, homeless or almost, who would ultimately make it into Harvard University under unimaginable circumstances. I thought to myself, Huh, a prestigious educational institution such as Harvard University has opened its doors to some young lady who could never have imagined she will attend such a prime university as a result of being born poor and unconnected. You want to know why or how? It is the result of her hard work at school, outstanding grades, and excellent GPA. Nice! I shared the news with Manny and the children that evening when I returned home.

Having read this part of *Compass*, can you begin to visualize how to more effectively help your daughters succeed at school, graduate from high school, and further their education through college and post-graduate school? It is possible, so get to work and learn the principles established to guide them through.

LEDD—My Blueprint

Sometimes I can hear myself thinking aloud to a group of underserved mothers, "Don't be afraid to ask about or explore educational opportunities for your young ladies." This nation has several different types of colleges to accommodate each family's financial situation and their student's academic capabilities. There are uncountable community colleges in the nation, many public universities, as well as countless private universities where girls can obtain undergraduate degrees and thrive as professionals thereafter or further their education and excel at their chosen career paths.

As a parent, I tried to make sure I understood when and where our girls' academic strengths and opportunities lie as early as from elementary school. When Kay was in elementary school, she was challenged in math. She received math tutoring in the summer prior to entering fourth grade and worked hard at improving her math scores during the academic years. Although she was in all the advanced classes, she consistently lacked either two or three points in math to navigate from honors to Eagle Excellence through her years in middle school at Overbrook School.

Realizing early that we had an issue in a particular subject so crucial in life, I developed a plan of action for success not only in math, but in every other subject moving forward, and in every other concern they wanted to chat about. I called my action plan the **LEDD** principle and prepared a template for it. As our children grew or evolved and matured, we began confronting some of the normal issues in life as social beings interacting with the contemporary world of the twenty-first century. Between school, our community life, and the rest in between, as their mother, I needed a strategy to help them succeed in math but also beyond their classrooms. **The LEDD principle** is what I have utilized with Kay and Missy for several years now. It entails **listening (L)** actively to what the academic concerns or general issues are, **engagement (E)** in the process of investigating the root cause of their concern and assessing it appropriately, **dedication (D)** in responding adequately to their query by finding a satisfactory resolution to the issue, and **devising (D) effective strategies** to prevent a recurrence of the issue in order to foster their academic success and personal growth.

Children need a willing and active listener daily. I am amazed at how some of us get buckled down by so many activities and are always on the go, so much so that we often miss dedicating quality time listening to our girls in order to appropriately assist in guiding them up the right path, whether it is academically, socially, or otherwise. Giving them all they need or want, providing them material luxury is one thing, but spending quality time with them and intimately discussing with them regularly to know and understand them is another.

My daughters and I agreed that each day either Manny or I pick them up from school, we shall start a conversation about their day at school. We call it *my student's day at school*. I'll ask one of them to "tell me about my student's day at school." Or I'll listen to whatever story they bring with them into the car after school and then after the discussion, I simply ask, "So aside from that, how was my student's day at school today?" The narratives continue as we drive home, knowing that once we get home, we shall change from our uniforms, eat a snack, gulp a drink as the desire might be and start off with homework after some minutes of downtime. Or set out for dance lessons, piano, track and field, or volleyball.

We've always had long rides to and from school, so we are rarely short of time to listen to each child's story. Further, I dedicate an hour or more every Saturday for *mommy-daughter conversations* using the LEDD principle. The initial plan was to spend an hour with each girl, but Kay, my teenage and high schooler uses up the hour easily, so she and I sometimes go well beyond an hour. During these times, each girl will either room in with me or I room in with her to discuss her school week. We laze around in bed, relax, and talk away. We engage in discussions of their choice. I ask questions relating to their friends, their peers, their teachers, administrators, class subjects, homework, group or individual projects, the playground, activities of the week, their class chores, Friday mass, and any challenges they may have. I let them share their individual perspectives on any other topics of their liking.

Also, I engage them as a team to discuss matters that can widen their reasoning and understanding especially ones that are education focused. Such conversations could be centered on interesting topics such as national education discussions, activities in schools to promote students' attendance and graduation success rate, your student's perception of her school district, her particular school and class policies, their teachers, and so on. I challenged them and they just spoke from their hearts. I learned a lot from them. Our discussions are often highly insightful and provide me with a landscape of their personal appreciation of their school and its environment, as well as the quality of administrators and teachers they have. We conclude our conversations by discussing lessons of the week. These lessons of the week help each girl determine and share one thing that was particularly striking from the week's experience, why, and the lesson she gathered from it.

Both girls know that my door is always open for them. We agreed that their questions and desire to speak personally with me precedes the time of day and/or my activity at any given time. They both understand that they can interrupt me anytime, and I will be available to them as a supportive and caring parent. I called it *mom's* **open-door principle**. My explanation to them in regard to the open-door principle is that they have access to me whenever they desire it. The girls and Manny were sometimes reluctant to interrupt me when I was studying for my healthcare doctoral degree. Noticing that my hectic and busy schedule was creating their reluctance to come and speak with me at certain times, I decided we were going to continue working together no matter what it meant to my healthcare educational experience. They saw how much time I spent studying, researching, and attending residencies in order to successfully complete my educational pursuit so, they understood how tiring and difficult it was for me as a wife and mom to continue going to school for over ten years. Hence, they decided to relegate some aspects of our communication to the back burner. But I made it clear that although my courses were brutally tedious and my workload was immense, I would discontinue the educational journey if it was affecting our communication, and I was not included in conversations about their daily lives and activities. Understanding the intensity of my studies and my desire to accomplish it, they supported me in this way by agreeing to our open-door principle, and resumed coming to speak with me about anything even when I was studying behind closed doors. The open-door decision made them understand they could walk into the study anytime and speak to me without a feeling of awkwardness or of disturbing me. I told our girls, "First, there are both of you girls. Then there is this scholarship pursuit. Okay? No one except God comes before the pair of you and Dad. Consensus?" We all agreed to it, and have kept it that way since.

My open-door with our daughters still endures after over a decade of initiating it and it is immensely beneficial to me and the girls because it is our time to connect thoroughly in a safe space, for me to give them my undivided attention, attentive ears, genuine advice, and share laughs or tears as the situation may be. The open-door gives me the required time to help guide both girls in the best possible and available directions that lead to an empowered adulthood. As our experiences together evolve daily, I realize that the great benefits of the open door which is the forum for me to use the LEDD principle are evidently uncountable for me and our two young ladies. Both girls have taught me that there is nothing more important than the dedicated, attentive listening capabilities of their mom and the EDD that ensues. Try it with your daughters. It works amazingly. Both of my daughters look forward to our open-doors weekly.

Make the Mark—the Gift of Time

Educating our daughters does not only entail sending them to a great school, it involves many other factors. As a parent dedicated to the education of her daughters and engaged in the process, I determined that the principle of **involvement in the institution** and its community life was also important for guiding our girls. To be involved, I decided on the degree of importance that voluntarily contributing my time to assist their school had for them and the school community. I became a voluntary ambassador for the school community but also for my children. I was a frequent visitor at the school to consistently take my gift of time to the community where our children spent most of their time during the week. I volunteered countless number of hours at their school, Overbrook School in Nashville, Tennessee. I started off as a room mother, something I had never done before. I made an error on the job and was admonished for it, but I learned from it and was honored to be allowed to continue serving the community.

At the school, I belonged to almost every committee or board that parents were invited to be members of or participate in. I was invited to co-chair the diversity committee.

I belonged to the institution's strategic planning committee and change management, the annual fund campaign. I participated at the Sally Foster wrapping paper sale events, attended every bake sale, and cake walk. I welcomed potential new families to the school and lent my voice at open house events. Besides those, I attended every back-to-school night and participated in every school event within and outside of the school campus. It was where our children went to school, and we were a huge part of the community. You name a committee at the school, and I was right there, present and volunteering for it and having fun with it.

The fulfillment gained from these activities is multifold and beyond imagination. I was an actively involved member of the community, giving it all that I could for the benefit of the community and our girls, but I especially got to see them on campus so often that our girls frequently said to me, "Mom, it feels great to see you at our school almost every day. It feels like you attended school with us because almost every day we see you at school. "We considered the community second home to not only our daughters but home- annex to us as well. I often saw my daughters in the hallway while I was volunteering in one capacity or another.

The teachers at the school are very attentive, kind, caring, and understanding. The school required families to call and notify them when a student was absent for the day. When any of my daughters were absent from school and I was a few minutes late to call and report the absence, I would receive a call asking me if all was well with the kid because they hadn't seen her at school that morning. I would also be informed that her homework and the day's learning material would be ready for pickup either at the receptionist's desk at the end of the school day or after school with a family of my choice. Communication between school and home, between our children's teachers and our family was timely, honest, and open. Consequently, I was often enlightened about anything I wanted to know regarding the girls' progress long before conference day. I knew all their teachers, the principal, the dean, and all the other administrators with whom I worked closely during some committee meetings at the institution.

I was not only interested in manifesting utmost, genuine interest in our daughter's academic pursuits, I was also determined to remain a big part of social activities at our daughters' school community by assisting in organizing social events such as teacher birthdays, teacher lunch appreciation day, and also by attending school social functions including Mardi Gras, back- to-school party, and the auction dinners. Attending the annual fund dinner was an honor, which I believe was the school's way of appreciating my presence and participation in the community life. That felt great. But frankly, what I was doing equally involved an active and fervent contribution of my time and other resources for our girls to see the level of importance accorded to their education and my involvement in the community where the education was being received. Seeing my involvement at their school taught them that going to their school was critical not only to them but to their parents as well, and it made them understand that it was a safe, great place to be, and that even their parents liked being there. Kay said to me, "Mom, you really like my school. You are there a lot. I like going to my school." That was OS, but my frequent visits and my gift of time was also for the benefit of our daughters. I was educating them by doing that as well as assisting the OS community. When she made the above comment, my understanding was that giving our daughters' school community the gift of your time as a volunteer encourages them to also want to be present in that same community. By all indications, my gift of time to the school was important to our girls, to me, and the community, and an importance part of my principle of engagement in their educational process, and my support and involvement in the institution as permitted by the school.

Traditionally, teachers had a wish list at the school's annual book fair. I had the girls sign books as gifts to various teachers from the book fair. This action taught my daughters that books are important and are cherished by their teachers, and since they look up to their teachers for example, they should also cherish books. I said to them, "See, I am not the only one with book wish lists. Your teachers also have book wish lists, and so should you. It is very important. Your teachers use theirs to help you and your peers. You should use yours to know more than what your school and I teach you and also help someone else. It can be real fun." They agreed and have since cultivated the habit of preparing their book wish lists. We get books from their wish lists either from our local library, school book fair, Barnes & Nobles, Amazon or from a local bookstore. This was my way of reminding them of the importance of books in education, self-reliance in reading and learning, and respect for their teachers as educators requesting assistance with books to help our children.

I was everywhere at our daughters' school, as a very involved parent. This further taught our daughters that their education meant the world to us and that we would be there to see that they are provided quality education. My actions at the school couldn't have been more transparent and evident. Each time our daughters saw me at school, they were happy. They smiled and waved and sometimes simply giggled among their friends. They understood my presence exemplified my incessant support for their community and their goals in providing prime education for them.

Potential solutions to help teenage girls against truancy is to demonstrate your involvement in her educational institution by being present at activities and functions at their school, as well as by volunteering some of your time at the school. I learned that when our daughters know we can be at their school at any given time of the day for a good cause, and when they see that their mom or dad supports the activities at their school by their involvement and participation, they are more apt to believe in the school system and more likely to want to go to school. It also lets the school administrators and teachers understand that you support their mission for our children, and that you have a vision for your child. I share this personal story to underscore the importance for moms and parents everywhere to cultivate the aptitude to liaise with their daughter's school administrators and teachers, to build effective mutually supportive home-school environments where your daughters feel free and safe to learn, present their queries, and explore their world with impunity. This is attainable through a principle of active involvement in the institution and its community life.

Partnering for Success

Manny and I consider ourselves our girls' partners for success on their personal journeys. Their education being at the top of our success wish list for their journey, I make it a priority to partner for school assignments, as mentioned earlier. After school, I spend time with the girls on their homework. Whether my fourth grader needs help or not, either her dad or I spend time reviewing with her to make sure she has done her homework appropriately. When she has to study for a spelling quiz, she revises, and I quiz her. The same happens in religion and other subjects. Her science book is quite voluminous, so I read it after her and explain the concepts before she responds to the questions. When a word is difficult for her to pronounce, I assist. If she does not know the meaning, I send her to a dictionary and have her define the word, give me a synonym and an antonym of the word when possible and also construct a sentence or two using the word.

Kay's high school program is challenging, and she likes it very much. She elected to take French as a foreign language in high school, and though she loves it, she has to work very hard at it. I also studied French at school and I speak it fluently, so I sometimes help her study and prepare for quizzes and tests. When the need arises and I can, I spend time studying with her for other subjects. I let her know I am committed to her success and devote time to help her succeed academically. When she has to work in a team at another student's home, I make certain that I am available to take her there and bring her back home. First, I call the student's parent to confirm that she agreed that the team project be completed at her house, and then we agree on drop-off and pick-up times. One Saturday, we spent over two hours at Farmers Branch, a historic park in Dallas where her team met to complete a French assignment that involved making a short video to create student awareness about the importance and benefits of learning a foreign language. When she studies for her finals, I am there to answer questions or quiz her in preparation. Although she said she didn't have to study for the PSAT which she took, I encouraged her to read through her packet and do some math and English revision. Partnering for success means that I am supportive, encouraging at my best, and collaborative when required to help advance them on their scholastic journey. She may not have seen the need to study for the standardized test, but as her partner on her educational journey, I thought she needed to, so I encouraged her to attempt revising, and she did.

Devoting time to assist them with homework benefits them substantively. Math is neither Manny's nor my forte although I had to know medication and infusion calculations for my healthcare professional success. It is Courtney's best subject, and it is where her sister struggled until high school. Not being able to help her at home used to bother me. After several email exchanges and a meeting her math teacher, we strategized for her success. Currently I am at peace because her high school math teacher, Mrs. P. Coleman is amazing. She is the best math teacher Kay has had since Overbrook School. The teacher is very experienced, knows her students, their strengths and weaknesses, and finds the best way to help the student eliminate the weakness in math. She encourages and tutors her two days a week, and communicates with us about the progress made, and the opportunities she has in the subject. Kay did an excellent job in math at the end of her freshman year, and remained in math honors for her sophomore year and continued the tutoring. She insists that she couldn't have been happier with Mrs. Coleman as her math teacher for giving all the time she needed to improve and enhance her math skills.

It is essential to devise a strategy to assist your teenager where challenges and opportunities are present because by so doing, you manifest your desire for her to succeed and also show her that you've got her back, and you are partnering with her for her own success. Kay finished freshman with an academic award in French. She placed ninth in the nation in the national French exam. She did all the hard work, studying and understanding the subject, knowing that she had all the support she needed to succeed. She ended the year promising herself to work even harder in sophomore, knowing I will be up at night to study with her and to make sure she realizes her personal academic vision. The lesson here is that as parents, giving our daughters a necessary rope to climb is good, but it will be great if we explain to them the essence of the ascent and let them know that if they become wobbly on the rope, we will be right there to help stabilize them, provide them new energy to move forward, and cheer them on. It is almost worthless to give them a magnificent new golden coin and not explain to them the noteworthiness of the coin. Show them the way to educational success by being engaged and actively involved on their route because this will prevent them from getting lost, confused, careless, and ultimately drop out, is what I am trying to say.

Remain engaged, whether you have a daughter who completes her homework easily, attends school regularly, and has no problems with the school administration or a student who has challenges at school. Some students get in trouble at school because they are helpless, and are crying out for help. They need our attention and want our help as parents. Be perceptive and receptive. If the school reports an irregular behavior from your daughter, be prepared to openly discuss concerns arising from the school or teacher, hold serious conversations with your child, and ask her the hard questions such as the following:

a. Why didn't you complete your homework?
b. Why were you absent from class today at 10:45 a.m.?
c. Let's discuss your behavior at school today. I learned you were rude to your teacher today.
d. I want us to discuss the reasons you didn't have your books ready for class this afternoon.
e. I learned you were involved in a fight at school today. Tell me about it. How can I help you avert situations that cause you and all of us negative attention at school?

Listen, listen, and listen again to their responses at this stage and remember the LEDD principle. I heard my dad say often to me and my siblings that he has two ears so he can be a better listener to his children. As stated above, my personal strategy with challenging situations has been to use LEDD as a framework for understanding and resolving my daughters' concerns and challenges. Remember that LEDD means *listening actively to the academic concerns or social issues presented or discussed by your daughter, engagement in the process of appropriately responding to them, dedication in resolving them, and devising effective strategies in response,* in order to foster your daughters' academic and/or personal success. While using LEDD, be sensitive to her but remain firm for her own good. It is not advisable to yell or use any type of parental powers to try to correct her, scolding will not help, and is not the right answer when your intention is to understand the issues she faces in order to encourage her to make the right choices.

Believing that our children are our most precious gifts and resources; our future and our life's capital, we should fully commit as parents to utilizing our education, experiences, wisdom, and knowledge to help them get the best quality education we can afford. Providing them education does not only mean sending them off to school daily and allowing them to fight it out for themselves after school. Educating our daughters requires more than that therefore, helping them all the way through with the issues they confront, and seeing them through their struggles with school is critical for their success.

As children between the ages of thirteen and nineteen all over the nation encounter deep and complex issues that contribute to their school dropout rate, the first place to start brainstorming for solutions is at home, in the family. Questions we can ask ourselves in the family may include: Am I a problem at school? Do I adhere to my school's rules, policies in the school handbook? Do I consider myself a very good student? What does a very good student mean and look like to me, my parents, and my school? Do we have a problem at school or with the school system? What is the problem? What are the potential solutions for the problem? As you will read later in another section, we determined how we wanted to confront the issues we encountered and kept our children going to school and thriving as we expected them to do.

After Kay experienced challenges with her first math test in high school and reacted in a way that sickened her and prompted her teacher to send us an e-mail about it, we sat down and analyzed what happened, why it happened, and what her reaction would be if confronted with a similar situation in the future. At the conclusion of our conversation, she took a deep sigh while looking at me straight in the eyes with a look like that of a puppy needing a hug, and she said, "So where do we go from here? What do you want me to take away from our conversation? I understand that I should not seek perfection because it does not exist. But I also know that I cannot miss the same shot twice, right?" She perused my face and my body language. I smile and hugged her. She smiled back, hugged me tightly and summarized, "I am at a great school where the math teacher is awesome. I love her so much. In a good way, she is nothing like my former math teacher. I just didn't know where to begin. It is an advanced class, and I thought I wasn't ready for a quiz. But I know I was wrong. I deserve to be in the class, and I knew several of the answers. I am ready for another math quiz."

Taking both of her hands and looking straight in her eyes with a twinkle in my eyes, which I know usually provides the boost she looks for from me when need be, I responded, "You are not required to be perfect for me to love you. Our expectation that you do an excellent job does not mean that you cannot have a hard time in a subject or miss a shot. Contrary to what that one student at "open house" said about her classes being a breeze, I want you to be prepared and understand that school is not always a breeze. You might encounter difficulties one way or the other. Sometimes people stumble and fall. As a student, you have to expect to stumble or miss a shot sometime. If you fall, do not stay on the ground for two seconds. I will not let you. You must not let yourself. Pick up yourself very quickly, dust off any dirt, learn something from the fall, and move on as a more experienced and enhanced young lady. Okay?"

Serious-looking big hazel eyes peered into mine as she responded, "Yes, Mom. I agree that anyone can make a mistake. This is my first and last. I am already up and moving again." I smiled broadly, extending my right palm high up for a high-five. More firmly but with a sweet smile, I pursued, "You and all the freshmen in your class are on the same platform zero. All freshmen are on platform zero right now. Do not allow yourself to be defined by any misses at school. You are a very intelligent student, you know it. Believe it and forget about what happened today. You'll do better in your next math quiz. You might even become a math whiz! How's that?"

She laughed and exclaimed, "Oh, Mom, you are cool. I am never freezing again. I am confident." Her big hazel eyes shimmered like a million shooting stars on a very dark night. "I love you, Mom. Thank you for always being there for me."

We hugged again, and before she left the room, I assured her I will always be there for her. Then I thought to myself, I cannot forget that as a student, although I excelled on many subjects, I gave up math, chemistry, and physics too early. I was focused on becoming either a nun or a lawyer so much that I forgot I could be an engineer, a pharmacist, chemist, or a physician.

When I later embarked on a scientific tour with health sciences, I realized after my undergraduate years that I shouldn't have given up those three subjects that early in my student life. Besides, not every student or teenager will have an impeccable educational path without any litters of errors and mishaps on her route. As a student, I don't remember having any free falls, but I tripped on my way to college. Generally speaking, students will stumble, trip, or fall, so I wanted to help her understand that she might fall but she should not waste time on the ground. She must get up as fast as lightening, dust off at the same pace, and move forward as a more experienced student. It is partially our responsibility as parents to help our daughters recover from any academic stumble, trip, or fall. Her increased self-confidence was palpable when I spoke with her the next week to know how she was doing in math. Besides, after a few weeks of the incident, her math teacher sent me an e-mail confirming that her self-confidence had heightened in math and to tell me she was helping another student understand and solve math problems. I emphasize this to highlight my assertion that the relationship between school and home, parents, teachers and administrators, as well as parental involvement in, and support for school activities are cardinal in guiding our teenage daughters in school and protecting them from dropping-out. And to insist that partnering with our children and the educational communities of our choice will result in our children's academic success.

A very friendly couple at my former church in Tennessee appeared excited one evening in Lent when I arrived at church for evening mass with my daughters in their school uniforms. Immediately after mass was over, the lady walked up to me and greeted me. "I see your children came to mass in their school uniform. You must have been so busy they didn't get a chance to change into church clothes for evening mass."

I was courteous and smiled back "Their school is very far away. We have to drive forty-five minutes, and there is usually traffic in the evening—you know, rush-hour traffic on the motorway. We got into Springhill late and didn't want to be late for mass, so they agreed we should come here straight."

She continued, "Where do they go to school?" I responded slowly, "Oh, in Nashville."

Her husband who was greeting other church members at another end of the room now walked up to us. "How are you, ladies?" He extended his right hand for a handshake, and I reciprocated by extending mine as well. "Where are you all from?" he inquired.

"We live here," I responded, smiling mischievously. "Do you mean where we are coming from tonight, where we moved or relocated from to Tennessee, or where we were born?"

We all laughed while he shrugged. "Oh, I see how you understood my question. We ask that when we meet someone that is not from the south. We can tell from the way you speak. I just meant where you came from this evening. I see these young ladies are in school uniform," he said, looking at both of my daughters with a fatherly smile.

We all laughed again. I was flanked by Kay and Court. They both giggled. "From Overbrook School in Nashville"

He asserted, "Very good! You drive all the way out there for the children to attend school? We also drive for our children to attend school in Nashville," he said. Nodding his head up and down and looking at my daughters, he told us what school their children attended.

The conversation continued for a few minutes more, and we said good evening to each other and parted ways. We became kindred spirits and chatted after mass on several occasions. Americans from the deep south of Tennessee, they were proud to share with us the benefits of educating their children in a school where the population was diverse. Both of them dentists who were born and bred in the South, they had several valuable lessons to share with us regarding the importance of educating minority children in diverse educational environments. Later when we became close friends, the couple shared many of their personal educational experiences with us. They shared with us that a significant number of black American students attend high schools made up mostly of black students. He told my husband and me that such highly segregated schools hardly promote diverse learning environments that are socially and academically beneficial to the students. He said, "When a school is populated with more African Americans or minority students, there is likelihood to have fewer resources, more unprepared teachers and low graduation rates, which mean the students are less well prepared for college."

What I gathered from the couple is that parents of black and minority children should not hesitate to explore the possibility of having their children attend schools with a more diverse population of students, schools with a reputation of excellent teaching models, effective teachers, comparatively high student scores on standardized tests, or blue ribbon status and high graduation rates, even if that means covering some distance to attend a good school.

To Each Their Own

Each family has certain preferences when it pertains to where to educate their children. What I mean is that electing to educate our children either in a single gender or coed institution, in a public or private school environment is a very personal choice. For some parents, it is important that girls attend all-girl institutions and boys go to schools that are dedicated to educate only young men. Some of our family friends prefer to educate their daughters in coed institutions for valid and plausible reasons. My parents, especially my mom, believes that young girls need an *educational environment that is dedicated to educating them in faith and Christian values, as well as orienting them to be confident and independent future leaders.* I forged my inspiration and educational perspectives from the backdrop of my mother's educational ideals. She forwarded reasons for her ideal educational environment for girls, which I thought at the time were just because she had dreams of seeing me become either a nun or a lady like no other.

Although I had unanswered questions regarding her educational penchant, I fervently believe in my mom's ideals. She is very intelligent and often made it a point to give me plausible reasons why she wanted things a certain way while I was a young girl growing up. As a staunch proponent of educating adolescent and teenage girls in a girls' only environment, I found myself looking for more reasons why that was the best choice for my daughters. In the course of time, I'd confront a few challenging situations as my daughters experienced difficulties with some boys in their classrooms.

As a fourth-grade student, Kay experienced challenges with some of the boys in her class at OS. They had a reciprocal dislike for each other. She'd say to us, "Some of the boys in my class are badly brought up. They are disrespectful and mean."

We would tell her, "That is harsh to say a kid is badly brought up. Why would you say that? What do you mean? Please tell us more about that. What happened? What did the boys do or say to earn that?" Her teacher was very much aware of the issues between her students. According to the school's policy, parents received notes explaining confrontation between students whenever such incidents occurred, so we received notes from the teacher explaining incidents that occurred between our child and another student. A particular boy made things worse one day after they received results of their quiz. On that day, the boy targeted her, followed her to her locker, and gave her long braids a name. When Manny and I met with the teacher to discuss our concerns, she did not mince words telling us what she thought about the issues between the two students. Mrs. M., a very gentle and soft-spoken middle-aged lady, unequivocally stated what she perceived as the reasons for the boy's poor choices and negative attitude toward Kay.

"The boys do not like her because she is a very intelligent girl. She is challenging to them. They are not used to girls challenging them. They are not comfortable with her because she is challenging. This particular boy is difficult." The teacher paused and looked at us.

I was dumbfounded hearing this. Manny and I looked at each other without uttering a word. With my eyes dimmed, my lips tight, and a frown on my face, I looked into her very meek face and inquired, "So a girl has to be stupid for the boys to accept her and not be that nasty to her? She has to shut up in class and answer her questions wrongly or fail her quiz in order for her hair to not be called a name? She is being called a name by the boys. We hope this is not acceptable behavior. It is horrible and you know what this is."

Whether she knew how we felt or not, hearing what she had to say about the reasons our child was targeted, we understood she had voiced it, and it was her truth. The truth was coming from an experienced teacher who knew what she was talking about.

"I am so sorry about this. I know it is a difficult situation. We are working with this family to help improve the boy's behavior. I am very sorry," she insisted. She was very professional and sincerely apologetic.

I asserted, "That little boy is growing up as a bully. I hope he stops the behavior today because we would not like to hold this conversation again. We are here today because we want the best educational and social experience for our children while they attend this school. His behavior is despicable. Our daughter is strong because we encourage her. She is feeling terrible with this name-calling by the locker. We expect her complaints to cease after today. We want her to be very comfortable in her class, in this school. And we do not want to force her to go to school each morning."

We all agreed our daughter will no longer have such complaints. It was a productive meeting. After that meeting, Kay had no further complaints. The school took immediate serious steps to put a stop to what had happened. Following our meeting with the teacher, Manny and I asked ourselves several questions for which we had no ready responses. I had just learned that when some male students feel "challenged" by a female student's academic prowess and capabilities, they may behave negatively toward her. The resultant action from me after the meeting was to find answers to certain questions such as:

(1) Do male students feel intimidated by their female peers who exhibit superior intellectual potential?
(2) What would push a young boy in middle school to feel so strongly about a female peer who is just as bright as he is to the point of calling her names?
(3) How could the teacher have been so certain about what she said were the reasons for the young man's poor attitude to my daughter?
(4) How much more does this teacher know about boys behaving badly toward their female counterparts who challenge them academically?

My attempts to provide reasonable answers to these nagging questions reminded me that my mom always said, "Let girls attend Catholic schools for girls and have the boys educated in all-boys Catholic schools." My quest to have a better understanding of what I thought was mother's theory would lead me through a very enlightening journey of Qs and As. Determined to have our daughters experience education as a fun activity, I invited Manny to help me find five reasons to educate our daughters in a coeducational institution and five reasons to have them attend a single-gender school. "Are you simply looking for the advantages of coed schools and single-gender schools, or do you want to know if intelligent female students do thrive in coed school settings?" Manny, asked looking curiously into my eyes. "You still appear absorbed by what the teacher said to us the other day," he pursued, wearing an astonished look like a fitted garment. He understood I wanted answers to some simple questions, so he immediately reassured me that he will help me understand the advantages of the types of educational systems I had asked for.

"Do you remember the days when some people said boys are more intelligent than girls? Would you agree with me that this student evidently believes that boys should outperform their female peers at all times or that men are born to outperform women?" I asked him, biting my lips.

"That was several years ago. You are talking about twenty-first century children now, today, and right here. Times have since changed. It is a very long time since women began succeeding in what was known primarily as masculine turf. While I believe the thought that boys are more intelligent and know better than girls still exist in certain arenas, it is shocking to hear that the minds of some elementary school kids are tilted toward such an erroneous belief," he said, looking at me excitedly.

"You understand why I say our daughters should start studying and understanding what feminism entails at an early age? With young men such as some of those in Kay's class, our daughters need to understand that boys and girls have equal but may be diverse intellectual gifts that they need to tap into at school. I think our girls have a lot to learn," I insisted. He agreed.

I continued, "If a middle school boy thinks he should outperform female students, then I want to know if the old assumption that men are more intelligent than women is true or if men outperforming women in sciences such as math and physics is just a result of boys bullying girls into submitting to their whims and onerous attitudes at school. Maybe the educational environment is a moderating factor of girls' performance at school?" My unanswered questions were many.

Several ideas and thoughts were going through my head. I had to think hard and come up with why growing up, I heard conversations and arguments that men had to be educated and women had to be homemakers because men were more intelligent and more liable to succeed in whatever career than women.

Well, the exception in the arguments I heard was that women had to be nurses and men physicians. It was all coming together in my head. I was finally piecing the puzzle pieces together to better understand what mom was trying to tell me as a little girl regarding education. In her society, there was open gender-based discrimination against women in education and career aspirations. Astonishingly the assumption of masculine supremacy in the field of education appears to still be alive and kicking in the twenty-first century, as remarked by my child's classroom teacher. I became even more determined to educate my kids in a Christian environment for elementary education with the hope that for high school, they would attend a Catholic all-girls institution.

I have heard some people say things such as, "What a man can do, a woman can do even better." Each time I receive an e-mail from Kay, I am reminded by a quote at the very tail of her mail page reminding me of what Brigham Young famously said, "You educate a man; you educate a man. You educate a woman; you educate a generation." The gist of this is that our daughters need to be provided quality education no matter where they reside in the world or their circumstances because they can do as well as their male counterparts, and they have the potential to impact countless other women and lives with their knowledge.

However, to each their own. Therefore, not every parent or family might like or simply want to educate their daughters in a Christian girls' elementary or high school. Every family makes their decision depending on different factors. What we all need to understand is the importance of educating our girls wherever they are, and whatever it takes, period. It is incumbent upon each family to know their daughters' personalities intimately in order to make the right school choice for them. It does not matter what part of the world you are in or what community you belong to, the main goal of educating your daughters is to empower them, arm them with knowledge, and enable them to assume their rightful place as leaders who make significant contributions to their communities. Educating our daughters should be a priority, knowing that their destiny, as well as that of their future children, could forever change as a result of their level of education.

Far from the Truth

As a young student in health sciences, I decided to work on a project that necessitated several visits to a shelter for adolescent and teenage single mothers. It was an eye-opening experience for me. Some of the girls were just fifteen years old, had dropped out of school due to pregnancy, lack of educational interest and truancy, while others had an interest in furthering their education but were unable to do so due to their circumstance at the time. The shelter director informed me that the place was full and needing to take in more young mothers who needed their services.

I interacted with most of the mothers and gleaned their perspectives regarding the importance of education. Nonchalant attitude toward education is what I gathered from most of the young women in that environment. It felt sad that some of the young girls had no understanding of how their circumstances could dramatically change because of quality education.

Although research has it that the birth rate of females between the ages of fifteen to nineteen years old in the United States has steadily decreased over the last two decades, teen pregnancy rate is still dramatically high in America compared to other industrialized nations. The consequences of teen pregnancies include withdrawal from educational pursuit to raise the newborn baby. Often the teenage mother does not continue their education even after the first pregnancy. Discussions surrounding the prevention of teenage pregnancies are not embarrassing at all. Rather, it is a critical conversation that mothers should have with their teenage daughters.

When an adolescent interrupts her education as a result of pregnancy, the probability that she will return to continue schooling after staying at home for a long time to raise a child becomes highly unlikely, especially when there is a cloud or mist surrounding their basic ideas regarding education. Self-consciousness about, and attentiveness to female education should be a priority on every woman's mind, whether you consider yourself a poor woman, a working mother, or an uneducated female.

One sunny Sunday afternoon in May, I went to the shelter to deliver some clothing and other items to the young mothers. We sat around the table in the courtyard and talked about the importance of education.

"So will you return to school, and go to college after some time?" My eyes moving from one young girl's face to the other, I asked anyone who wanted to talk about school. Pat, an adolescent single mother I met at the shelter, was wearing a somber look. Although her eyes were red and baggy from sleeplessness, her young forehead furrowed from consistent frowning at nature and her experiences, she smiled with tight lips "I will not go back to school. I want to go and look for a job when it's time. School does not matter. The money I will make is what matters. I can use it to feed my children and pay my rents. Even if I complete high school, I can't make it to college. No one in my family went to college. What good to go to college? How will I pay for it even if I wanted to go see for myself?"

Bria, the brass of the group, laughed loudly, looking at me straight in the eyes. "When you are a poor girl like us, you don't go to college. You were born poor, and you will die poor. My mama always says that. There's no money to send you anywhere to college. After high school, you get you a good job, make some money to pay for your roof, and eat some."

I was concerned and uncertain as to how to continue the conversation because it involved what her "mama always said." I felt like a fish out of water sitting there with them, trying hard to make conversation that they would consider good and meaningful to them. I was not in my element, and my mind felt uncertain about how to positively impact these young women. I took a deep breath and mustered courage. "Why did your mama tell you that you will die poor because you were born poor? It is not always true!"

Without mincing words, Bria frowned and then smiled briefly, insisting that her mother knew what she was talking about and asserted her personal belief in what her mother had told her about poverty and education. "Don't question what Mama said. You think it is easy for all of us here to go to school because it is easy for you? School is not my best topic of discussion. No money, no school, I know that."

As brave as a lion, and knowing how far from the truth this was, I pursued without regrets, "I don't believe it is easy for any of you to go to school. But I am not here for me. I am here for you, to visit with all of you and to talk openly about the things that might interest you such as high school and how fun it was before you left. After high school we can talk about college." Her face became plain, like she suddenly wore a mask. She sat still like a corpse. You could have heard a pin drop.

"I am here for you because I care," I insisted, looking straight into her face. She folded her arms and ceased to speak.

"I understand if you don't want to continue talking about that now. We can discuss it another day when you are ready to talk about it." I later understood that her mother died two years prior, leaving her and her younger sibling. They were ejected from their family home following their mother's passing. To compound her heartache, she and her sister have since been separated, one living over a hundred miles from the other. They never knew their father and had a grandmother who was in a terminal condition in a nursing home. I impart this story to underscore the centrality of encouraging your daughters in their educational pursuit.

Long-term benefits of educating girls include but are not limited to economic independence for the girls, gender equality, social mobility, self-confidence, increased self-esteem, and empowerment. Evidently Bria's mother passed on to her daughter her personal belief that their poverty will perpetuate despite education and that there was no reason for her to dream of getting college education. How far from the truth was she? Do you think she is alone to believe that? Well the news I have for you from my experience is that whatever your circumstances are today may not determine your future, especially when you are resolved to succeed, have great dreams, have established a clear vision for yourself, and work hard to obtain your goals. Education is the surest route to success, and poverty is not a criterion for getting quality education. The America system of education might be imperfect, but it is built in such a way that no matter your financial or socioeconomic background and reality, there is an educational institution that can respond to your individual needs. The ideal is not to tell your daughters that there is no way out for them because they were born into a certain disadvantaged community. There are public high schools in every corner in each state, although high school education or the GED is no longer sufficient as an educational certificate to procure anyone a good- paying job.

It certainly will not provide your daughter a career path, but it is where a student must start if she intends going to college.

There are a few things to remember when discussing education with your children: The first one is that currently in this country, jobs requiring two-year college degrees are disappearing. Secondly, grades are important to get your student to a great high school or college. Great schools are admitting more intelligent students than the average student. The implication for this is that excellent grades could determine where children from low socioeconomic groups obtain their degree. Remember that I heard on the radio news about an almost-homeless girl who was going to attend Harvard University because of her scores and GPA? Well, the same may apply to any other hardworking and very intelligent girl from a disenfranchised background. Additional great ways that the American educational system is set up to assist very hardworking, determined students is the availability of the Advanced Placement (AP) programs for highly motivated and hardworking high school students in, two-year community colleges in several states and cities, four-year colleges that are state-associated, and possible grant, loan, and student aid programs available to students and families on needs basis. Ask the educational institution of your interest to explain their student financial aid program to you if you determine that you might need it to obtain a college degree. The sad reality is that as state funding for college education shrinks, the cost is increasing at lightning speed.

Secondly, another critical piece that determines success nowadays is technological knowledge or tech literacy. Encourage your daughters' interest in technology because we are in the technological age, and technology currently drives the educational engine for success.

You may ask the question, "What doesn't technology drive these days?" And my answer is, "that is a great question. It drives everything – or almost!"

The other thing to never forget is that the path to success is through DHPPR. The first time I told my children this, they both asked me to speak in English. "What exactly is DHPPR, Mom? Please speak in English!" they both spoke simultaneously and emphatically. My response was determined and brief. Smiling, I declared, **"Determination, hard work, patience, persistence, and resilience**, **DHPPR**, certainly will take you to your ultimate destination of success." This simple but evidence-based theory is applicable at school, at work, and anywhere you focus positive energy and hope to reap benefits and success. Whether your daughter is academically gifted or not, an elite or not, upper middle class or not, you should feel compelled to provide her the opportunity to pursue education and to do so in a safe environment. Bria's mom was very far from the truth when she told Bria she would go nowhere in life because she was unfortunately born into poverty.

Women should not be the ones to discourage girls to go to school given the tremendous transformation of modern society in recent years. Instead, women should use every opportunity to promote and extend the benefits of educating girls, and firmly lend their voices to female audiences regarding the need to unleash the potential of young girls through education. Bria's mother died, unfortunately, but my intuition tells me there are many other women in our world just like her—women who believe there is no way out for their children due to their socioeconomic status, lack of connection, ignorance, disability, or other. Some women still believe that when one is born poor and unconnected, they live and die unconnected. That cannot be any further from truth and reality. I am confident in stating my conviction that quality education is the single most essential killer of social-economic stagnation. You may have been born underserved, but make excellent grades and gain admission to a top, prime, or prestigious college and perhaps with scholarship! Now, see what future you would have, the friends you would make, the peers and colleagues you would collaborate with, and the consequences of that. Quality education has undeniable potential to ultimately create economic and social migration for anyone. that Bria's mom told her is very far from the truth, at least in this country.

The circumstances of one's birth are not factored in their eligibility for success in America. Those circumstances might be very humble, but they should not be allowed to define you forever since you have a long trajectory through life. Your personally crafted vision, the route you take to realize it, and your destination are what should matter to you. And you have to be willing to change your circumstances in order to build your own vision. America offers uncountable opportunities for every girl to move forward in life and reach limitless horizons through education and *DHPPR* - *"Determination, hard work, patience, persistence, and resilience."* **Determination** means being resolute to accomplish something. For example, being resolute to succeed at school, go to college and graduate, have a great career, being an outstanding leader, build something, denounce, report, and stand-up to school bullies, resist victimizing peers, not succumb to peer pressures, etc. One has to be determined to succeed at doing something, or to accomplish their goals in life. **Hard work** is being diligent in completing assigned tasks while putting in the nest effort required to accomplish the task. Examples may include hard work studying at school to maintain good or excellent grades, and pass exams. Hard work requires diligence, assiduousness, and an understanding of the value of hard work which incites work ethic, and quite an essential ingredient for success. **Patience** in the context of *Compass,* is the ability to tolerate a difficult situation or a delay without frustration and anger. It is the ability to gracefully wait with hope. **Perseverance** is persistence in achieving a goal despite challenges. It is being steadfast, and not throw-in the towel or give-up, but to keep the eye on the price with the goal in mind. Perseverance is an indispensable quality for success, and a predictor of achievement according to research. **Resilience** is the ability to cope well with stressors, and bounce back from tough experiences. There are four kinds of resilience namely: Mental, social, spiritual, and physical. Mental and emotional stamina are required to be resilient, therefore for our teen daughters, parental and social support are key to their resilience. Resilience is a highly beneficial trait to have because we never know what life may throw at our children, and at what age. Suicide stats for children between 9th and 12th grade in the U.S. is alarming – a good dose of resilience will be beneficial for these teens who may have been bullied, taunted or pressured to the grave. DHPPR (*pronounced dehpr*) is a critical parental principle for guiding teenage girls transitioning into adulthood because it doesn't only teach them diligence and work ethic, but it strengthens and prepares them for real tough, rough and rainy days in the big, wild, wide world.

The Exceptional Nation

One of the exceptional things about America is that it does not care about your financial origin to allow you to become a great success story and do amazing things with your life, and in your community. In January 2012, I was traveling to and from a leadership meeting at the corporate office of the healthcare organization I worked for. I arrived at the airport a few hours before my return flight and sat in a very quiet corner all alone. I paid little attention to my surrounding as I intently focused on reviewing the material I had to summarize and present to my colleagues upon returning to the hospital the following Monday. As I read through the pages of the literature I received at the meeting, I occasionally raised my head and looked left and right to flex my muscles and not stiffen my neck. After over an hour of sitting there alone, a young lady walked by and asked me if she could sit down next to me. Not understanding why she would avoid all the many vacant seats in the area to come sit where I was, I assured her she could. She sat down and apologized to me about her selected sitting spot. She explained her need to use the electrical outlet to charge her computer, which she needed to do some work. I understood and agreed she needed to sit by me and welcomed her again, insisting I was glad to have company. We chatted for a little while about our flight destination, faith, kids, modern society, and education. She amazed me with her energy, determination to succeed, and ambition.

She was born and bred in India. As a newly licensed professional registered nurse working in India, she responded to an ad in a magazine she was reading at work one night, and it ended up changing her life forever. Two years after responding to the ad, she began planning her legal migration from her home country to the United States to work as a registered nurse. In a total of two and a half years from the day she responded to the ad, she relocated to the United States as a nursing professional to work for a nursing agency that placed her at a hospital in Dallas. "My two-year contract at the hospital ended quickly, and I learned very fast and enjoyed working there," she noted, smiling.

Sunita was beaming as she spoke. After three years of working as a registered nurse in a major hospital in America, she insisted that she had learned quite a lot to allow her to decide that she wanted to become a medical doctor.

"I noticed there were less physicians in my area of town to serve all the patients' needs, so I thought I could become a family doctor and serve the patients in my region," she asserted.

"Although I thought it was a very ambitious idea and maybe a long shot at the time, I was determined to take advantage of what America has to offer me in terms of education," she continued, smiling as she spoke.

"Of course, that was a brilliant goal and quite unselfish of you to want to help your community in that kind of capacity." I smiled back, looking directly in her eyes with utmost interest in our conversation.

"I studied fiercely and took the MCAT and passed. I kept working as an RN to make enough money to assist my family back home in India. I have a sister and a brother. My parents worked very hard to help us. Anyway, I had to continue working as a nurse because I could help them better. I was told that as a student in medical school, I will not have much. I basically lived off the student loans I took out. If you went to school here, you understand me. Did you go to school here?" She asked inquisitively.

"Oh yes, I did. I do have some student loans too," I agreed.
She was focused. She pursued, "It's all worth it. I finally decided I will follow my heart because I passed the MCAT and proceed to go to medical school. To summarize, since we are talking about the importance of education, ambition, vision, and determination, I wanted to share with you that I came here from India as a nurse. I am now a medical doctor, a professor at a university hospital medical school, and I serve my community in many ways and work with board members at the city council on projects. I happily serve my patients every day I go to work, and I'm helping other students succeed in their career path. I also have a very good family life, and I am very happy here. America has given me everything. This country has endless opportunities for everybody who wants to succeed. It is an amazing place," she stated categorically. And I couldn't agree with her more...

"Yes, America is an exceptional nation. It has given countless number of people their hearts' desires and continues to change the lives of many. You see, when you know where you want to be tomorrow afternoon, you do what it takes to get to that place, right? You must have a goal, a vision, a certain drive to accomplish those. You must have a dream, nurse an ambition, and work to see your dream materialize. When you do, in this nation, nothing, and hardly anyone can hold you back. I know a near similar story to yours," I responded.

My point here is that America is a country where countless people have emigrated to from the four corners of the earth to find success through education. Sunita is a good example of that, and there are countless stories like hers in America. I have told my daughters numerous times to understand that the quality of education we are providing them is part our legacy to them and they should make the best use of it.

After discussing with Sunita, I thought to myself, Wow, this is a lady who came to America from India and has utilized education to transport herself and her family to a very different socioeconomic status than prior to coming to America.

Most of our conversation kept coming back to me long after our first meeting. Her story was uplifting and encouraging. I thought she exemplified a person who came from very humble origins but did not let her challenges dampen her ambition and determination to succeed. She carved a plan for herself, built her vision, and used DHPPR to obtain it. It is difficult, if not impossible, to successfully complete a five- to seven-year doctorate degree program without using DHPPR. I know this firsthand, and I can attest to it because of my personal experiences. I imagined she had to put in her all to get to her current destination.

She smiled. "This is the place where you can find the things you are looking for." I nodded in agreement. "It sure is an amazing country in every sense of the word. Sometimes the road to what you are looking for is very hard for some though because some people put barricades in your way to prevent you from progressing. But exceptional, yes it is."

The Choice

My lingering questions about coeducation versus single-gender education induced, and permitted me to examine the subject of high school selection for girls a little bit deeper. I reminded myself that the preservation of single-gender education is firmly established in the minds of many, including my conservative Catholic mother and many others. I began creating reasons in my mind why that was so important to many. I realized my child's experience with some of the boys in her class was helping me piece together critical parts of a puzzle I always thought about but did not think deeper to understand the importance of the parts. I used Kay's experience to educate myself further and attempt to respond to the questions that kept lurking in my mind.

One of my good friends suggested to me that "girls can thrive better academically in institutions that do not have the physical presence of boys, especially in middle and high school." I kind of interrogated her after she affirmed that viewpoint. She vividly described a situation with a young female student whose close friendship with a male student kept her from making it to honors through her first two years of high school. The student is her niece. My friend recounted a moving story that culminated in moving her into a single-gender school. The school transfer made a huge difference in her grades and how she completed high school. After hearing her experience with her niece and listening to several other parents who shared similar stories, one evening while discussing the subject with Manny, I wondered, *does that explain why some institutions proudly maintain a long history and tradition of educating girls in a girl-only environment?*

I was sure several people share the perspective that boys could be a distraction in a school environment. Kay had just experienced a situation of distraction by some boys in her class, and it was concerning to us. Her grades had not been impacted in any way, but she was affected enough by what happened to her, and her highly experienced teacher attributed the reason for her experience to be "because she is challenging to the boy(s)." My resolution to educate our girls in a single-gender high school was absolute now more than ever.

My quest to know more about the facts of the matter oriented me to research the subject. Material was sparse, but available extant literature providing the reasons for single-gender education was enlightening. I hardly found a clear-cut conclusion that girls who attend single-sex schools versus coeducational institutions were more focused academically or more likely to thrive academically. However, it was evident that this was a topic that many parents, scholars, and researchers had exploited and analyzed in an attempt to find answers. It was comforting to understand that I was not alone with questions such as the ones I mentioned earlier, questions about the potential distractions our daughters may encounter in coed schools and the archaic belief that the male students outperform their female counterparts especially in science subjects.

While it might be difficult to evaluate and compare scores of girls attending coed versus single-gender schools to determine which environment is better for our daughters, I learned that the standards of education are pretty high in single- sex schools. As a parent with a daughter in an all-girl Catholic high school in Dallas, UA, I understand that the school is highly selective with respect to not just the students it admits but also its teachers. Admission into the institution is primarily based on academic merits. Kay says here is *"where young girls go to thrive academically, accomplish their individual scholastic goals and be themselves in the absence of boys."* She says at her school "girls are very competitive but collaborate on team projects and build sincere and genuine friendships that go beyond the high walls of their classrooms."

After her first semester at school, she concluded, "A school environment of only girls is academically inspiring and much fun at the same time. In all my classes, every girl strives to be the best. We take turns leading class and team projects. We go to study hall and discuss our challenges and opportunities, and learn how to grow individually but also as a team of leading girls. We know each one of us is a potential leader, so we discuss our chances at different leadership roles, even when we go to the chapel and pray together. We do not think of, or discuss boys, or worry about critique in the morning when we arrive at school without makeup or earrings. We each focus on our grades and how to be successful."

Then smiling, she says, "we can also be sassy, haa! We can be sassy, successful leading ladies, ha! Mom!"

She insists that all the girls in each of her classes are very intelligent and want to be the best, which makes it fun to compete since each one strives for the golden grade. The funniest thing she said to us one evening at dinner is, "You know I don't have boys looking at me in class or making fun of me because I answer most of the questions, or always have my hand up ready to answer my teachers' questions. Those boys who make fun of intelligent girls and called me a nerd are not in my school, so I am very comfortable and happy. My friends and I think some boys just can't stand to deal with it when a girl knows better than them. My school is perfect for me."

During the annual fund campaign dinner offered to freshmen parents of the school, the principal asked my husband and I how our daughter was enjoying school and if she liked it, and we narrated our daughter's ideal to her. We told her our daughter believes she is in the best school, a school that has eliminated any possible distraction from the presence of boys. We all laughed about it and agreed that our daughter's viewpoint is valid. At the dinner, all the parents we spoke with shared similar thoughts from their daughters. Interestingly, we noted that the young ladies at Kay's school preferred an educational environment without boys because they were considered a distraction to their success.

The question of whether boys and girls should be educated together or separated by gender in an effort to reduce perpetuating gender differences in academic performance is still highly researched in the field of education. A 2011 research conducted in Germany used 252 German student participants between eighth and twelfth grade to respond to the questions pertaining to the performance gap between girls who attend single-gender schools and their same-sex counterparts attending coed schools when solving a mental rotation task known to produce substantial gender differences favoring males. Results from the test showed that all the students completed the mental rotations test, and that twelfth-grade girls attending a single-gender school outperformed girls attending coeducational schools.

For women who have not considered educating their daughters in a single-gender institution, whether it is a Catholic school or not, my experience is that there are several advantages to it. However, parents should examine their daughter's fit in the institution of their choice. Remember, to each their own. All single-gender schools do not necessarily uphold the same ethos, and one girl's experience might be different from another's. Research the institution you are interested in and make your selection based on your daughter's and school's characteristics. Great institutional and personal characteristics fit are required for your student to thrive and evolve in any academic environment.

You do not want your daughter going to school and being miserable because she thinks she is a misfit among her peers. Also, consider her prior academic achievement and her determination to succeed.

The research findings I read on this matter indicates that the girls who attend single-gender schools are often success-driven and highly motivated. Prior to making such an important decision, ask yourself pertinent questions such as the following: What are your daughter's characteristics? What are the characteristics of the school? What is its reputation? When doing your analysis, remember that contrary to the portrait that society has painted about girls and women as individuals who are constantly bickering and cannot work together, it is in such an institution where lifelong friendships are formed between our daughters. This is where young girls go to learn how to be independent in their studies and pursuits, effectively collaborate with peers for the good of the team, and also learn to be strong leaders in their communities.

The all-girls school environment crushes stereotypical conventions such as "boys are better than girls in math and consistently outperform them in math tests" because girls in Kay's class at her high schools are going above and beyond in math. She is in Algebra I, which is advanced math. One evening, I was driving her and some friends to a school party, and during the trip, they focused their discussion on math, their recent test scores, who made the highest scores, their present challenges, and how to improve their individual scores. It was amazing for me to listen to their conversation and to realize that these girls were doing very well, but their goal was to be excellent and great at math. I do not know what boys in other schools are scoring in math, but I sure know that these young girls' scores are well above the mark, although they appeared only partially satisfied with their performance. Evidently these young ladies were not competing with boys. Their benchmark was excellence in math, and there was no one telling them students of the opposite gender were performing better than them.

Their self-esteem and spirits were high, and they were encouraged and united in their determination to attain a certain goal in math. At the end of the fall semester, their conversation shifted from a sound focus on how and why it is critical for them to excel in math and physics to their grade point average (GPA) as the reports for the semester came home and they were all in honors classes. The discussion of very successfully crossing the finishing line at their highly challenging high school started.

The important thing to note here is that these young girls' conversations were neither centered on male students, dating, how many Kendra Scott jewelry they have collected, and facial makeup, nor their physical appearance at school. The discussion focus was often on academic success. My thought is that the absence of the physical presence of male students in their daily lives at school provided them an environment to thrive academically without the criticism and stereotypes that male students perform better in certain subjects than their female counterparts, as well as without the distraction of boys in their daily academic life.

Peer Pressure, Fitting-In, and Vulnerabilities

Adolescence is a sensitive time as our daughters continue to develop psychosocially, mentally, as well as physically. It is a time when friendships develop and blossom between our daughters and their peers, creating at times a desire for the adolescent to act independently of her parents. In my experience with my daughters and their peers, belonging to a peer group at school appears to be a very important characteristic of adolescence. Traditionally, peer group is a group of close friends of the same age and with similar activities. My personal experience is that peer groups usually form at school, although it may form at church or Sunday school. Some children are prepared by their parents to tackle school and life, while others are prepared by the life experiences they gather growing up in the general communities they get involved with. If you are a student or have been a student, then you will agree with me that many things happen at school that prepares us more than anything else to face life.

Reviewing my experiences from some decades ago, I can assert that our daughters learn from socializing and gaining insight into the norms and values of their peer group and social milieu while in that community of friends. Girls attending single-gender institutions and those attending coeducational institutions all learn from their classes, as well as from the hallways, dorms, locker rooms, after school activities, and peer groups. School environment is where most of our daughters will be tested by peers for the strength of their characters and personalities. As feelings of acceptance, belonging, and connectedness to their peer groups strengthen and easy identification with the group is complete, the level of influence exerted by the peer group might equally intensify. When one succumbs to the influence of a peer group, it may or could result in peer pressure.

Generally, *peer pressure* is when a person is motivated to think and act in certain ways because she was pressured, challenged, or urged by peers to do it. Conformity and a desire to fit in are results of pressures that some of our daughters' experience from tender adolescent ages at school. Having experienced the girl environment at boarding school, listening to current experiences of some of our daughters and the sometimes sad consequences engendered by peer pressure, I determined to take stock of our daughters' vulnerabilities on this issue.

Mel

Mel is from a very Christian family we have known for several years now. She is an only daughter among two boys and has been raised very sheltered. She is highly jovial, polite, very responsible, and intelligent. During her first year in high school, she made friends with an effervescent group of young adolescents her age. Her parents decided she'd go to a high school very close to their home because both parents commute to work daily. She can easily walk to school, which is across the street from her house. It is a coed school. Mel telephones Grace, her mom, daily during her lunch period to tell her she got to school safely and let her know how her day is going. Her effervescent group of friends asked her why she has to take a few minutes daily to call her mom, and her response was, "This is our daily routine. It gives her peace of mind since she works away from here." Her friends laughed and asked her to "grow up. You can't possibly do that daily. You are a big girl. Take care of yourself and your own business. Tell her later if she wants to know."

Mel responded, "My mom deserves the peace of mind my phone call gives her. I must call her first thing during my lunch break."

Her friends pressured her to quit the habit, so Mel went to Grace with the suggestion one Friday evening. "Mom, I have to stop calling you daily because my friends think I am not grown up enough and independent enough."

Grace laughed it off. "Well, ask them to call their moms during their break. If you each do that, you will keep your parents informed and give them the peace of mind I get when I hear from you and know all is fine with you. You are in high school, and I care about you, so I need to know you are all right at school."

Mel, an obedient and very sweet girl, agreed with Grace. Her calls continued daily for six months until she was told by her friends that she needed to act like a big girl and quit calling or she was no longer welcome to the group. Mel succumbed to the pressure and quit calling her mom per their long-standing routine. Nothing her mom said made sense to her because her peer group mattered more to her than the few minutes she used daily to notify her mom of her safety at school. Grace explained that was the first time she thought, "Who are my daughter's friends? What are their values? How can they possibly influence her thought process and beliefs to this extent?"

Mel explained to her mom, "I have had a difficult time adjusting to the school after spending eight years in a Catholic school. My friends at my high school do things differently than my friends from my former school. They have been a source of support for me at school while I struggled to fit in. They helped me adapt, and I have settled in the school now with their help."

Grace acknowledged the advantages that belonging to a peer group has provided her daughter. "I can appreciate that you have adjusted to this school and have adapted to a very different value system here. I am aware that socially, you feel the importance of recognition, value and acceptance by your peers."

She was also concerned, and she expressed it by saying, "What I'd like to see your friends do is also learn to tolerate the individual differences you each bring to the group. Yours may be a daily phone call. You certainly tolerate things about them. You each need to understand tolerance as peers. You must not let them influence you the wrong way."

After Grace intimated this to me, we agreed Mel was under peer pressure to appear like an independent adolescent.

I concurred. "Individual differences abound among friends and should be recognized and respected. Your peer group might want to test how different you are or can be from them. Be yourself. Do not deviate from your values. Personal responsibility results from the responses to peer group tests."

During her sophomore year, Mel's friends actively encouraged her to have a boyfriend and try a first kiss, which they had each experienced. A boy in the junior year wanted to befriend Mel. He insistently tried charming her, but Mel resisted, stating that it was not time for her to engage in boyfriend-girlfriend relationships. She told Grace, "We are friends. We see each other at school and say hello in a friendly way. That is enough for me but apparently not for him. I don't want anything more than that, but all my friends keep giving me his messages and encourage me to say yes to him because their boyfriends are in his group. They make fun of me, saying that I am not adventurous and want to be like the "Virgin Mary."

When Grace inquired what they meant by "wanting to be like the Virgin Mary." Her daughter informed her that all her friends were dating boys from the junior year and had been to their various houses to watch movies and had exchanged kisses and gone further during an outing at one of the junior student's home in the absence of his family. Grace was furious about the new details Mel provided her, but she was reassured and happy that Mel had not succumbed to the current pressures.

Mel promised her she will not give into the pressures from her peers to start an "amorous" adventure. Mel assured her mom, insisting, "Mom, you can trust me. I will not do that. I told them I have a lot of homework to focus on, plenty of chores at home, extracurricular activities, and other family and church engagements that keep me pretty busy. I will never have time to go watch movies with the guys. I create time for the girls and that is enough. Trust me, Mom. The guy is polite and nice, but I don't like him more than how I already like him. Its platonic." Grace lit up at the conclusion of her narrative to me. "Mel's group of friends continued pressuring her daily to date a boy at school, but she firmly resisted until she graduated from high school. Her friends later professed respect and admiration for her values, personality, and her strength of character. She is now a junior in college, and Grace says she is dating a nice Christian friend in senior year." I smiled when she took a deep sigh at her conclusion.

I was very happy for her and Mel and responded, "Peer pressure could be direct or indirect. Indirect peer pressure occurs when an individual unknowingly modifies her behavior to mirror that of her group. Direct peer pressure is when peers actively urge their friend to join the activities of the group. Mel was tested directly and indirectly. The fact that her friends dated boys in high school and they all socialized as a group while she did not is a testimony of how strong our daughters can be if they are determined to do the right thing for themselves.

Adolescents can be easily influenced by their peers' opinion of them. Mel socialized with friends who all had dates, but their opinion of her as unadventurous or wanting to be like the Virgin Mary by not dating a boy while in the group did not bother her. You must be proud of the strong lady you have raised."

Grace confirmed she was humbled. She said it was through the grace of a more powerful being than her teachings that helped her daughter not fall prey to the pressures of her high school peers. Mel's mom, Grace, was tense while sharing her daughter's experiences in high school. Mel successfully handled some of the peer issues she was confronted with at school. Although she gave up her telephone calls to her mom, she was a strong girl and was able to stand up to her peers and respect her personal values regarding dating at a certain age and other temptations she faced. While Mel's story has a tinge of success, what she witnessed is not always the experience of several other students. Some peer relationships are healthier than others.

Ingrid

Ingrid, an outstanding senior in high school, shares her apartment with her mom and brother. She studies hard at school and dreams of making her mom very proud of her by going to college and becoming a pharmacist. She and her little brother knew their dad only briefly before he abandoned the family residence for an adventure in the big, wide world. He has never returned to them since the morning they last saw him in the spring of 2009. Ingrid and her friends had known each other for a while after she and her family moved to the area and she started attending high school. She never imagined she was hanging out with the wrong crowd. She ignored several warning signs, as well as her mom's wisdom, natural motherly instincts, and advice. Her mom, India, wouldn't quit cautioning her that she was being influenced by her group of friends. Ingrid brushed her remarks and paddled on with her friends. They did many things together but studied less. Ingrid sometimes returned home late, long after school was closed for the day. India was invited by the principal for a chat because Ingrid, a very bright student, was suddenly failing all her classes. Her principal reported that she got to school unprepared for class and was friends with a wild group of students who are rude and take nothing seriously, especially their education.

India was livid after her meeting with the principal. She thought Ingrid had it all together because she spends a significant amount of time coaching her on friendships, the importance of personal values, the importance of education, and her hopes for a better life for her and her brother. India affirmed to me, "I know what role her friends can play in shaping her life course from here.

I try to help her safely transition from adolescence to adulthood. She is not independent yet and is still learning her own values as an individual. She cannot give them control of her life. She must understand who she is, what she really wants from life, and have a personality with set values."

I concurred because she was right. Then I added, "This is the time for mistakes. School is the time when students are tested, make mistakes, and become more responsible after learning a certain way, which is sometimes the hard way, right? Speak to her about it. If you realize her challenge is mastering certain life's skills at this time, help her out. She is yours. It is your duty, your responsibility to see her excel at school and in life. Calmly dialogue with her about the issues raised by the principal and discuss your concerns. Do not allow her friends' attitudes and behaviors to influence her. She appears to have a problematic peer relationship. Yet, let her know you trust her to make the right judgment call, or ask you if and when she needs your input. Tell her you believe she is strong. As an adolescent, she would like to know you have a high opinion of her. Wave the stormy discussion style away and use reason and charm so she can listen to you very keenly."

India frowned. She leaned forward. "There is more," she stated categorically. "Although she denies smoking," India asserts, "I sometimes smell cigarette from her breath and clothing when she returns home from an outing with her friends. One Friday evening after work, I stumbled on Ingrid and her crew in a supermarket. I was stunned to see my child puff off smoke from a stick. I could never have imagined that my child was smoking cigarettes without my knowledge."

One Saturday evening, Ingrid asked India if she could attend one friend's birthday party that had not been previously planned. She set a time for Ingrid to return home. Ingrid agreed to be back home at the set time. India said Ingrid had never missed her curfew, although she had begun adopting the behaviors of the company she kept. She did not respect the curfew on this occasion. After several failed attempts to get hold of her daughter on phone, India decided she'd go to the birthday girl's house and bring her child back home. "I knew we were having difficulties with honest and open communicating after I saw her smoking cigarettes. I want to keep her safe. My children are all I have.

Ingrid is succumbing to the whims of her peers, and that can be dangerous. If she was out there doing the wrong thing, I wanted to protect her by bringing her back home with me. I was worried and scared for her. I just felt it. I felt something that pushed me to go bring her to safety." She sighed and was silent for a few seconds. Then she continued "When I got to her friend's house, I saw ten young boys and girls downstairs." She continued.

"Upon entering the home, I immediately asked to see the owners. I was told the parents were out of town. Then I asked where Ingrid was. The only girl who was courteous enough to respond to me pointed to the stairs. I looked around me. There were several bottles of alcohol on the table and the floor. The music was deafening. Some of the boys and girls were making out, some were smoking, while others were just hanging out and talking. I made my way through the stairs and got to the landing. There were five girls standing beside each other, talking and laughing hysterically. I recognized all of them. They were Ingrid's group of tight friends. I asked where Ingrid was, and I was shown a door. I looked around and peered into the eyes of the young adolescents drinking alcohol. Then I slowly walked into the door of the room where I was expecting to find Ingrid. There were three girls in the room. I recognized all of them. They all appeared drunk. Ingrid laid in bed, drunk, and appeared too weak to even speak to me. I helped her into the car and took her home. Then I called the police and sent them to the birthday party. I returned to Ingrid's room after placing the call to the police. What I noticed almost drove me crazy. She was grunting and foaming through her mouth. I immediately dialed the emergency number, and an ambulance came right away." She was teary.

"After spending hours at her bedside in the city hospital, I was told her lab results were concerning. The physician called me into a room and told me that my daughter had taken ecstasy drugs. Two other girls from the party were later transported to the emergency room that night. One of them did not make it after spending a week in intensive care. Ingrid was hospitalized, and we spent six weeks in hospital. She remained unconscious and unresponsive for two weeks in the intensive care unit. During the last four weeks at the hospital, in addition to her medical treatments, she also received both mild physical and psychological therapies. When the physicians in her care deemed it right, she was dismissed from the hospital, and we returned home. Once at home, she continued receiving both physical and psychological or memory therapies, which helped her recover fully. We moved away from that school district to give her a fresh start elsewhere. I can tell you, I know something about peer pressures and its dangers."

Stunned at the turn our conversation took regarding the issue of negative peer pressure, I remained lost for words for a few seconds and just looked at her.

Then I realized I had to say something to her. I was admiring her for several reasons. I could simply say, "Oh dear. I am sorry you and Ingrid had quite an experience. I admire your motherly intuition, instincts and the way you set out to ensure your daughter's protection. You were right on time when you got her out of that party house. Someone more powerful was watching over you all."

She quickly agreed. "Oh yes, some bigger, mighty person was right there to shake me into action. I am thankful to him. I think I got there just in time for her. It might have been too late for her like it was for her friend," she concluded firmly and sadly. Tiny furrows appeared on her forehead. Her eyes were still wet.

I smiled. "Yes! Adolescence is a period of life when experimentation of new behaviors, and vulnerability to risky behaviors can significantly impact life's journey for some girls. Some adolescents are easily persuaded into conforming to behaviors of their peers or their group. We have to continuously dialogue with our adolescent and young adult daughters and make them understand that they do not necessarily have to make personal behavioral adjustments in order to bond socially, feel a sense of belonging and acceptance by school peers. Peer pressure is responsible for myriad of ills suffered by some adolescents including but not limited to criminal behaviors, drug abuse, unhealthy sexual behaviors and exploits, teen or immaturity pregnancy, unsuccessful academic pursuits, and school dropout secondary to failing grades. Some peers are very influential in their persuasiveness to instill bad attitudes in others, and some girls are not strong enough to say, 'I need new friends because the ones I have make bad decisions and unacceptable choices.' Research suggests that students with healthy peer relationships thrive socially and academically more than those suffering from negative and problematic peer relationships. This is part of the struggles for our young girls in many academic environments. We cannot and should not ignore this. High school can be a pit fall for some girls, especially those who drink and/or smoke."

Eve

Eve is a young girl from an upper middle class family. Her friends belong to the same social milieu as her family. Their families are friends with each other. Eve and her high school pals are considered to be the popular juniors at their small-town high school. Some of the girls think they run the world because they drive fancy cars to school and boys seek their attention. Eve remains very levelheaded, polished, and well mannered. She is an intelligent student, makes excellent grades, and is dreaming of attending an Ivy League university, much to her family's pride. She is the only girl among her peers who has not attempted cigarettes, vape and alcohol. Her mom, Betty, is very proud of her daughter. But things were about to take a different turn for Eve, who began feeling the pressures of her pals because she would neither drink nor smoke when they hung out or attended parties. Her friends had been persuading her to smoke and drink, but she had been firmly resisting their pressures. Suddenly she decided she was old enough to do her own thing and forget mother dearest's advice. She was invited by one of her friends to her beach house party during spring break. Betty says, "There was food, snacks, assorted beverages, and the children had smuggled in lots of alcohol, cigarettes and drugs. We do not know where the drugs came from, but the girls believe some of the boys brought them."

That is where Eve was initiated and introduced to drugs. She had never tasted alcohol but drank some because her friends made fun of her for not drinking. She said she was even called names and asked to leave if she didn't try. She just wanted to stay in her usual circle of friends, so she tried everything that was offered her. She also learned at the party that her friends had given themselves away in bed to their boyfriends. It was a rotten party by all standards. By the time they took her to the hospital, she had thrown up several times, said she was having palpitations and was later unable to speak. Her system had certainly taken too much of substances that were foreign to it.

Her parents were out of town but returned immediately and went straight to the hospital. "She told us all about the party after we got home from the hospital. Her friends had refused to tell their parents what really happened at the beach house party that night. I learned that the children often lied to their parents, to us, me included. None of the parents knew our daughters were at such high risk for alcohol and drug intoxication. You know, you never imagine these things will happen to your own daughters. Things took a different turn for her since then. She is a senior now, but she continues to struggle academically. She attends all the parties her friends want her to attend. Some of the boys in their group have access to drugs. We have gone from dialoguing about the dangers in their behaviors through warnings to cut her allowance, to threats, and arguments. I do not want to continue fighting with her. She will soon be going to college, and we want her memories to be what she wants them to be. She is a reasonable adolescent, approaching young adulthood. She should know what she wants in and from life. We laid the foundation. She is responsible for developing the end result. She appears to prefer the ideals of her social group than our old-fashioned education. She has a strong bond with this group of girls, and she is unwilling to give it up. It is to her detriment. Her grades have suffered immensely since she signed in as fidelity member of the group. We see her scholarship dreams being crushed under her own feet and before our eyes, and we are powerless," her mom said, looking very sad.

"One of her friends is three months into her first pregnancy. I wonder where her hopes for college will be kept while she has the baby in her parents' home, and try to provide for it and herself. Those that do not listen to parental counseling often end up deeply regretting their actions, don't they?" She sounded and looked bitter with this discussion topic.

I submitted that "when as a parent you have been actively involved in your daughter's holistic education and provided her the necessary tools with which to arm herself for social life as adolescent and adult, you find a certain degree of peace of mind knowing you did all you could to make her a successful lady."

There are millions of girls with healthy peer relationships. There are those who consciously remove themselves from relationships with peers who exert negative influence on them, but these are rare. Peer pressure is becoming a serious infectious ailment for adolescents in school communities. Family and friends are the two main sources of information for adolescents as their cognition matures, and they try to exploit their personal abilities in all the spheres of life—socially, educationally, spiritually, you name it.

Parents should consistently scan the quality of social relationships and bonds their daughters have and mold their thoughts to always elect to do the right thing for themselves at all times by providing them relevant information about peer relationships. Students with healthy peer relationships experience positive educational and social outcomes according to researchers. Our daughters see their social bonds in and out of the school community as very important. I agree with them. I have encouraged mine to create a personal list of acceptable and unacceptable things about a peer's attitude, a list of personal expectations for the future, and their personal goals and aspirations in life. They know that these have to be based on their personal experiences, values, and environmental influences. I asked them to imagine and create their own processes to deal with, and navigate the issues they confront as young women. I make them understand I will be there to assist them, but they must have and use critical thinking skills for every situation encountered in life and develop an excellent process to deal with contemporary issues such as this.

"You have done all that any reasonable, loving, caring, and supportive parent would have done if they were Eve's mom. I respect you so much for sharing this with me."

She did not wait for me to complete my last word. She quickly stated, "You are a lovely lady. I am glad I could share some of these with you. Peer pressure is a serious issue in schools. Our children are at risk to take drugs, alcohol, bully other kids, engage in premature sexual activities, and become pregnant at a very young age because they feel the need to belong to a social group of friends who are doing these things. We have a lot of work to do to help our girls out of this. Is this part of education? Is this part of the education we were supposed to give them at an early age? I thought we educate them according to their ages and maturity level."

I agreed and added, "There is scholastic education, and there is parental education, and family values, and then we also have community and relationship influences. These culminate to teach our daughters a lot of stuff. She is receiving a strong foundation for excellent scholastic education as she proceeds to college. But you are right about the consequences of peer pressure. Truancy, delinquency, scholastic underachievement, sadness, depression, and suicidal risk can also be added to the list of potential consequences of all that. I believe that parents and school communities should be working together to help these children.

The good news is I read in an article that several schools in the nation have devised systemic strategies to prevent student risk behaviors on issues such as drug and alcohol use. Besides, I know a lady whose daughter is on 'a positive peer impact group' at her high school. Her teachers provided her with training on appropriate listening and communication skills to have one-on-one discussion sessions with her peers on issues such as teen pregnancy resulting from premature sexual activities. You see, she got herself in trouble as a teen, and experienced hard times from having a baby and leading a very rough life after that. Now she mentors and tutors her peers, providing them with highly positive messages to help them resist pressures from their friends and instead do the right thing. She is now a role model. She is a junior. It's not all grim in every school, with every situation, and with all our children. There are stories of positive peer pressures coming out of very many schools around the nation. It behooves us parents and moms to persist in discussing the issues facing the youth population in our communities and beyond, and to teach them how to handle such situations."

She nodded. "Very encouraging, very encouraging to hear that. I want to hope, just hope that…well, just hope." She took a deep breath and continued: "Just hope that the positives come and stay, you know uuhh uuhh…there is college too and that is a big place uuhh you know." I nodded and smiled.

Transitioning to College: Mind the Gap!

Several high school students dream of going to college, excelling academically, and graduating with an excellent GPA, then move toward a career path of interest. Most well-rounded students that I have come across have articulated furthering their education to postgraduate levels. I have heard the high school students I know excitedly make plans for college in spite of just commencing high school. These teens are working hard to obtain entry into good colleges and are exhibiting excitement about the prospect of embarking on a new phase in their lives.

One of my colleagues and friends' daughters graduated from the girls' Catholic high school my daughter is attending. She was instrumental in the writing of this section of the book in that she graciously gave me a series of lectures on how hectic it is to prepare a girl for the transition from high school to college. As Catholic women and mothers with two young daughters each, we spent most of our lunch breaks from work talking about our children's education. I was eager to listen to her during our discussions so I could learn more about the high school we had selected for our daughter and also gain her perspectives on college preparation. She had two daughters in UA, the school Kay would attend, and her oldest daughter was a senior at the time. Our conversations, which I have dubbed her lecture series because she mostly talked while I listened and asked questions, were highly beneficial and motivating. Her oldest daughter had been in the school for four years, and her younger one was a rising sophomore in the same institution. She knew the academy very well, and loved it wholeheartedly for the quality of education her children were receiving. She explained the benefits of having her daughters there, the differences in the personalities of her two girls and how the institution, through its amazing college preparatory program, had helped metamorphosed her youngest daughter into a gracious and studious young lady.

As a senior, her older daughter, a well-rounded young lady applied to several colleges and received scholarships to more than three colleges. She and her parents thoughtfully and meticulously considered all the college options they had and then selected the university she would attend after a thorough family debate on what was best for their daughter and her probability to succeed in the college of their choice given all the advantages of the college. She asserted that the preparation was hectic and stressful for the entire family, especially for her daughter who was leaving high school, her friends of several years, and her family, for a bigger campus out of state, with new and unfamiliar students from all over the nation.

"It is big world out there. She is going into an unfamiliar terrain with excitement, fear, uncertainty, and caution all at once. The academy has done a great job preparing her, and we are also doing our part. We would have liked to but did not choose the colleges that offered her scholarship. We examined many things about each of the colleges before settling for this university. She is going into an independent Catholic university that we like so far. It is in Indiana, close to Chicago, where we have some family. However, we acknowledge it is still a big deal, you know, for her to go out there. I tell you I don't know what to say. It is hard for all of us right now just preparing her," she explained.

I looked on with not much contribution to make except to share memories of when I went to college, and that was almost two decades ago. "Hmm! Dealing with the academic and social demands of university require special coping skills that our daughters must possess prior to entering the university campus. It is a big deal. Leaving home is a big deal. College is an even bigger deal," I concurred.

We discussed the practical issues and possible stressors that she mentioned before, such as the loss of high school friends and the formation of new relationships, having roommates you never met before, and being solely responsible for your daily activities away from trusted family.

"Before she leaves home, she must graduate in increased RIA" I said smiling. She smiled too and said to me "I don't know what RIA is, please explain because we need excellent perspectives to help us guide her appropriately." Smiling, I responded "It is a simple principle I learned from my mom before leaving home for college myself, the principle of **Responsibility, Independence and Autonomy (RIA)!** Again, prior to leaving for college, you should make sure she has a diploma in increased *responsibility, independence* and *autonomy,* in life, as well as in her studies. And she must take those certificates with her into college. I applaud you all for refusing scholarship offers from some universities, and instead chose a university with an environment that you believe will continue enhancing both her Christian moral values, and the intellectual abilities of your child! To turn down scholarships for out-of-pocket payments or student loans elsewhere is amazing and highly commendable! Good for you all!" I paused.

"I assure you that is not an easy thing to do. That choice was not easy to make, but we have to look at a whole lot of things before we make such serious decisions. We believe that as a UA graduate, she will feel more at home in that university. So tell me more about **RIA**" she concluded with a brief smile but her stress level was palpable. My personal experience made it easy for me to understand and empathized with her.

The principles of **responsibility**, independence and autonomy (RIA) are quite essential in guiding teenage girls in high school transition to adulthood in college and beyond. **Responsibility** means acting independently and making decisions without parental authorization. It includes taking actions and being accountable for them, when need be, and not postponing doing things that can be done now. Part of being responsible is being dependable, own your words, be honest and trustworthy, be accountable for your actions —In the context in *Compass*, it entails things like guiding the teen to drive responsibly, and to respect speed limits. Stepping-up to help in the family, church, community and school environments, keeping to time, being organized, avoiding excuses for not doing what is supposed to, could or should have been done, and earning your own very personal trust to handle simple things well. Responsibility as teens or even from an early age has myriad benefits down the road as an adult. It earns them respect within the family and friends, and raises their self-esteem as they earn respect from others.

Independence in *Compass* means thinking or acting for oneself, and the ability to do things without relying on other people. This goes hand-in-hand with autonomy; however, with independence we could still have some parental influence over our teenage daughters, but we leave them the opportunity to be able to think for themselves, make their own choices and decisions with limited to no parental influence, depending on the situation.

In *Compass,* **autonomy** is contextually being able to make informed, free-willed decisions as a child still under parental guidance. Examples include making autonomous decisions about what is right or wrong in social situations with peers and friends such as having a fake ID, serial partying, underage drinking or abusing alcohol and getting drunk, vaping, have inappropriate relations and sending nude pictures, etc...

Autonomy here means that parents leave their teens the room to be self-reliant to make the right choices in certain situations, in preparation for their departure from home to college, away from the immediate access to parental decision-making skills. Giving teen girls the autonomy to make certain decisions is important for their self-esteem because it lets them know that you believe that they are a grown-up... they have a choice... and their parents trust them to make the right choice or decision on their own in certain situations and be their own person. Autonomy must be accompanied by accountability, and it it is important to explain that to our kids while guiding them.

RIA is a significant principle for our teens because transitioning from high school to college means that they will have to undertake the giant step of living away from home, which entails limited parental oversight and almost complete independence in prompt decision-making and time management for all daily activities. Away from the network of friends and family support that is usually at their doorstep while in high school. Going to college is essential for personal enhancement and growth since our daughters migrate into higher educational opportunities, career prospects, and build personal lifelong relationships. However, they may be potentially at risk for college-attendance-induced stressors that would receive utmost parental attention while in high school. Fundamentally, the risks involved in our teens' transition from high school to college without adequate preparation must be considered by every parent and affronted squarely with strategic principles such as these to enable a smoother, easier, and more successful college séjour for our daughters.

Another colleague recounted her daughters' transition from high school into college. She affirmed that "the transition is not always a breeze or smooth sailing for girls who move away from home, especially when they have been very close to their parents and family who are always around to help them with everything."

Hearing these made me nervous and concerned, and so I asked Manny if we were doing enough to prepare our high school freshman for the transition into college in four years. In response, he looked at me with blank eyes as if to say, "There is plenty time for that. Not yet!"

He argued, "She has just begun her freshman year, and you are going to start preparing her for college? Take it a step at a time." I was quick to unmask my worries. "I am learning from colleagues at the hospital that transitioning their daughters from high school to college 'is not a breeze.' I understand that preparation must start early because some high school students are successful at high school but fail to successfully attend college for the required four years until graduation. I have heard that even good students can drop out of college if they are not well prepared to transition smoothly from high school to college."

Smiling ardently, he said, "Fascinating, but leave it alone till next year, can we? Let her enjoy her first year of high school." I agreed but would hold casual conversations about college with Kay from time to time. Understanding that there are potential challenges for her ahead of the high school curve, I wanted to make sure she began understanding what going to college entailed even though it would only happen for her in the next four years. Learning that several high school girls don't make it through the four years of college prompted the questions and conversations, and sent me to search for root causes of the failure, and solutions for our daughters.

I listened keenly to the response that my colleague had to offer. She based her perspectives on personal experience because her two daughters were juniors in a renowned college in Texas, but she had to change their college after the first year. She had a difficult time making them settle into college life in the first college. They were home every weekend for the entire first year.

"I don't think my girls were ready to embrace the new environment they found their college campus to be," she said regrettably. "They would return home often, and that got them very tired because of the long drive. The school was a wrong fit for them. They both focused on sciences, and selected a major that they realized was not what they wanted in the end. They later focused on engineering, and so they had to move into this renowned engineering school. Another concern they had was their class sizes, which they insisted were too large for the professors to effectively manage the students, and provide them individualized attention. My daughters fell through the cracks in the overpopulated class. They returned home after the first year and refused to return there. We had to start searching again and eventually moved them into their current college. They share their room and like it better in class. Their current college has been a more positive experience for them." She smiled.

One of Kay's godmothers, a very good friend, sent her daughter away to college, but the first year was very challenging in several ways. Her student returned home after her first year in college and refused to return. Her parents had to start over and relocated her to a different college. Her daughter's roommates partied often, returned to their room late on weekend nights, or rather, early Sunday mornings, and made much noise upon returning from their weekend parties. She was a misfit, according to her roommates, because she studied hard, watched her grades, and did not attend weekend parties. She was lonely during her first year, although later in the academic year, she became friends with another girl who also attended an all-girls Catholic high school. She called her mother several times a week to express concerns about many issues including the workload and the stress that engendered. She had not been adequately prepared for college workload, and the community life on a college campus. However, she worked hard and successfully completed her first year there, and her parents packed her out at the end of the academic year, and into a different Catholic university in another state. Her mom stated to me that once transferred, she enjoyed the Catholic university very much, made several friends on campus, and excelled academically. Her daughter since completed her undergraduate studies and postgraduate studies at the same university.

Academic unpreparedness is one of the several reasons why some college students drop out. This explains why parents should be selective when choosing a high school or college preparatory school for our daughters, and remain attentive to their progress in high school. When a high school does not sufficiently prepare its students for the rigors pertaining to college course work and schedules, the students' unpreparedness manifest itself in their failure or inability to cope with the workload. Besides, some students slack off academically during their high school senior year, and that results in academic unpreparedness in the first year of college and potential subsequent dropout.

While discussing the concerns about the transition from high school to college, one of my friend's daughters insisted that some colleges do not offer the personalized guidance, attention, and mentoring that her high school offered her in preparation for college, so students do not have a place to go seek advice when need be. Consequently, they return home to seek more parental assistance.

For main street folks like us, concerns about the education of our daughters are vast and diverse. The transition from high school to college is an issue of high threshold. I believe parents do not want to see their daughters drop out of college due to difficulties adapting to the pressures and demands of college curriculum, workload, and social interactions. Hence we need to make the college mountain low for them to climb by providing them with the necessary tools for success in post–high school institutions. Armed with the awareness that transition into college might be tedious for Kay, I read about what her school offers its student as preparatory tools aside from the quality and challenging curriculum they offer. Then I asked her about her perceptions of the varied elements that could influence her transition experience. She said she wasn't thinking of a transition yet since she is just finishing her high school freshman year at the moment.

I called one of my mentors and asked her how her daughter coped with transitioning from high school to college. "You start by selecting a quality high school with known academic intensity and quality curriculum that challenges the students to use more critical thinking skills than memorizing material and regurgitating it in tests. Such a powerful foundation in high school is critical for academic success in, and smoothly transitioning into college and the rigorous academic schedule. Is your daughter ready for college yet? I thought she is a freshman?" Dr. Mindy is always ready for my calls. She is used to me asking her never-ending questions, and she responds graciously at all times, as a typical mentor would.

I assured her my daughter was still a freshman and four years away from transitioning to college. "So, who is going to college tonight or tomorrow morning?" she asked, laughing on the other end of the phone. "Did you hear something in the news today that I missed?" she pursued, sweetly laughing again. "The news I got was not broadcasted on a network you are familiar with." I laughed. "Let's imagine this is a telephone survey, and you are responding to my questions—very open-ended questions because I need all you can offer on the topic," I continued, sustaining the laughter and looking at my watch. She does not like to stay on the phone for more than thirty minutes at a time. It was a brief call. She was succinct and terse in her responses to my questions.

"Many of the nation's students are at risk for experiencing difficult transition to college, and several students are not at risk because of factors such as what Iris experienced. High schools with great teachers, college guidance counselors, academic advisers, and college-linking strategies better prepare their students for college. This underscores some of the nuances between a great high school with effective college preparatory strategies and high schools that are void of such blueprints. The other thing to remember is that parents are joiners in their daughter's educational journey and transitional success stories often hinge on parental presence and support. *Parental support is the highest type of social capital for their children. I leveraged that capital to ease Iris's transition into college. My relationship with Iris results in obligations and expectations that shape her attitude about college.*

Some colleges offer orientation programs and freshman seminars. Your daughter must attend those because they facilitate understanding of the campus, the institution, its academic requirements, and it is also a medium to meet other freshmen and socialize. Iris was academically and socially involved from her first day in college, which helped make her transition a lot easy. We were there for her anytime she needed us," she eloquently summarized her daughter's experience of transitioning from high school to college and at the same time provided invaluable advice on how to obtain a successful transition for our daughters.

I knew **parental support** was quite important for children and it was one of our family's principle, and Dr. M. confirmed by mentioning it in our conversation so I noted it during our discussion. I had a last question for her, and I hastily asked, "What type of course or courses, if any, did Iris take to further enhance her coping skills prior to entering college?"

She paused for approximately three seconds, then insisted that "time management course, coping and study skills are important for transitional success. I enrolled her for these courses at her high school during the summer of her junior and senior years. Those proved to be fundamentally invaluable to her and contributed to her ease with settling into college campus life after high school. Going to college is a giant step in a young lady's life. I expect your daughters to transition with a certain degree of ease just like Iris did. You have to assist them in this. I guess you called me tonight to ask me how you can help your Kay prepare for college." She laughed again and assured me we could continue the conversation the following weekend because she could go on all night on the importance of time management and coping skills from high school to college and beyond. We spoke for a few more minutes about what was novel in international education, and how mystifying it is to see where the American educational system and student success rate places in comparison with other industrialized nations. Her emphasis and perspectives sealed **time management skill** as a fundamental principle for guiding teenage girls through high school to college, and beyond as adults.

"What role do teachers assume in high school students' successful transition to college, if any at all? You would be the perfect person to tell me about this if there is something I need to know, right? My head is just spinning with many questions Dr. Mindy" I inquired of her. "Are you asking me all these questions because I am a university professor or because I am parent to a female college sophomore student, or is it because I am available to you?" Dr. Mindy is often gingery and sometimes nicely spicy. I like talking to her, and although she does not like to talk for over thirty minutes at a time on phone, we always have a great conversation. She makes me laugh a lot because when I ask her questions pertaining to female students, she often throws in a stubborn statement having raised a lovely, intelligent young lady, Iris, who has not given her a second of a hard time.

While discussing the importance of educating girls, she once said to me "If Iris gave me a hard time, I hardly know what I'd do, but she understands my values. I am more interested in understanding the coping mechanism of students who do not have responsible parents to count on all the time," she asserted. Then she responded to my question, saying, "Let me see how I want to phrase this because I know educators are an important part in determining our children's academic success. You see, teachers, quality teachers play a significant part in a successful and seamless move from high school to college. Do not forget that quality teachers must be given the training, support, and the right tools to be able to accomplish the job of mentor and counselor for rising college girls. This conversation is a major one, and we can continue next weekend. Remember, the kid is yours. Be all hands-on and make sure to guide her through where nobody else can. Her teacher might not be prepared or capable of helping her to the extent that her family is capable of assisting. However, if the school provided rigorous curriculum and her teacher maintained the rigor in every aspect of their academics, then your daughter is partially prepared. As parents, we partner with our daughter's school and teachers to prep them for college. We all remain accountable for their experience and success at all levels of education," she concluded brilliantly.

My call to Dr. M. the following weekend was met with some serious questions about my personal intervention to prepare Kay to go to college and remain focused on her education while there.

"Have you identified any challenges that your daughter might face during her transit to college? How are you preparing her for

Section 2: Education

the big move in a little over three years?" She sounded anxious and excited to listen to my perspectives.

"I understand that college is a different world than high school, and unprepared students would be the ones facing all the disadvantages, so while we discuss her high school course work, her academic achievements, and her extracurricular activities, we also discuss college preparation. Although she is a high school freshman, college goals are foremost on our minds. She understands the importance of college education, developed a college mindset before entering high school, and has a highly positive educational outlook. We agreed that taking as many honors classes as possible in high school will enable her to better prepare for college. She is currently taking some honors classes and will apply for more in her sophomore year. Honors courses are fast-paced and challenging, and she told me she wants to take all the honors classes available to her in sophomore year including English, math, et cetera. I believe this is preparation in itself because of the rigors involved in honors classes. We have discussed college in real terms and plan to visit and tour a college campus before she starts her junior year. This will allow her to visualize herself on campus and provide her initial understanding of what college life might practically entail. She has identified her major and believes her scholarship goals are attainable," I stated confidently to this highly seasoned and intelligent college professor and hospital executive who has mentored me for almost five years continuously from the day I enrolled and started the healthcare doctoral program at the University.

"From what you are telling me, I understand that your Kay already has a bourgeoning college-focused mind-set. Does her school have college counselors? How does her school prepare its students for successful transit into college?" She queried. I affirmed that the school does a fabulous job preparing their students for college through experienced personal and college counselors assigned to each student. Typically, college counselors are assigned during junior and senior years, but parents can request that their daughter have one during her sophomore year for precocious preparation. Most students and their parents begin making appointments with the institution's college counselors during the junior year.

"As a freshman, she visited her personal counselor to request more information and guidance regarding college. Informing her that it was not time yet for her to begin the procedure did not quench her thirst for more information, so she got me involved. I made an appointment and met with her college counselor during her freshman year. The program flows very smoothly through the senior year." I took a breather.

"College nights begin during the girls' sophomore year. College nights entail the visit of various college representatives to the school to talk to parents and students about college, curriculum, etc. College night informational sessions occur every few months, and all sophomore families and their daughters are invited to attend, receive critical information, and ask representatives from the colleges present, their sixty-four-thousand-dollar questions.

"During the junior year, parents and their daughters also attend organized college nights similar to the ones attended in the sophomore year. From the junior year, students are authorized class absences when they travel with their parents or family for scheduled college day visit. Such visits are highly encouraged and considered advantageous. During the visit, students and their parents receive a campus tour and explanation of the history and highlights of the college, its position in the geographic area, its accolades, the campus and class sizes, and also discuss with administrative personnel, with a chance to ask all their knotty questions. Such visits usually last for a day or two and provides parents and their daughters the opportunity to look and feel a personal attraction to the college community, its environment, and what it has to offer. College plans become the main focus and are more vigorous in the senior year during which college nights continue for senior students and their parents and also for juniors who want to get a very good head start." I continued.

"Our daughters are allowed up to three days' absence for college visits with their parents prior to completing their college applications during their senior year. In addition to touring the college, talking with teachers and administrators to learn more about the institution, our daughters could spend a day shadowing a student to experience what I call—a day in the life of a college student. We plan to make excellent use of the institution's well-cut college preparatory strategy to Kay's utmost benefit. And we plan to speak with her college counselor when the time is right. She attends UA, the only independent all-girls Catholic high school in Dallas. Her teachers are of great quality, their college preparatory program is very rigorous, and it is a highly challenging school. She will be well prepared at least from that standpoint," I concluded breathlessly.

Dr. Mindy is a very thorough professor and expects questions to be answered to the fullest, so she or anyone else listening can grasp the full picture the response paints.

"Oh how excellent!" she exclaimed with a sharp, intelligent voice. "How *excellent!*" she exclaimed again, insisting, "with the appropriate preparation, college is a realistic goal for most of our children. You have placed your daughter in a splendid institution with prime strategies in place to secure a first-class success rate of college graduates from the school. When an academic institution meticulously designs a transit path to college for its students, such as the one you just explained, there remains little or no room for errors either from the parents or their daughters. The consequence is high college success and graduation rate for those young ladies." She sounded very excited, stating her viewpoint about the college preparation Kay's school provides its students and their families from what I told her on the call. She said she was proud that although I was busier than a bee, I had created time to familiarize myself with the institution's transit strategies in spite of having my daughter in the school for less than a year. She said most families waited till sophomore year to start delving into information acquisition for college prep. I emphasized, "The earlier we start the prep, the more chances we have to better understand the program and succeed in making the college journey easy for everyone." Her voice dropped, "That successful preparation and journey is what every child need. Otherwise, they drop out of college and return to the community or the society as failures—parental, institutional, and national failures. College experience and education helps our young people in a myriad of intangible ways, and the benefits go far beyond career and income. My daughter Iris has undying love for knowledge as each day she learns that there are several things she does not know. She has developed inquisitiveness beyond my wildest imagination since entering college. I would encourage you and other parents, and families I know, and our institutions to do whatever it takes to solidly prep their students, especially young girls, to seamlessly move from high school to college. A seamless transfer provides our students better chances at success and increases graduation rates."

My smiles on the phone could be felt on the other end of the line. Dr. Mindy told me she felt I was smiling and wanted to know why. She is a very funny lady, too intelligent and full of intuition. I responded, "You made my day. Your contribution is priceless, and I want to thank you for always graciously taking the time with me." She was not ready to say good-bye because she had an unanswered question for me. "Before you go, please tell me about the college application process at the magnificent high school that your daughter attends."

I shared my understanding of the process at the school and also provided general knowledge pertaining to college applications. "Parents and their daughters can elect to apply to college during their student's junior year. This is a personal choice and decision. "Notwithstanding, PSAT scores and academic grades for the second semester of her junior year will be sent to the colleges we plan to apply to. Pragmatically, during the first two years in high school, some parents and their daughters construct a provisional list of colleges or universities that interest them and request admission application packages from them and sometimes, go for a campus visit, tour, or information session at the institution. Acquainting oneself with the application procedure earlier rather than later provides upgraded awareness of what a college application entails for more informed decision making and planning for a successful transfer. College application forms are the best way to understand what our children are required to obtain either course wise or in terms of extracurricular activities that might assist in showcasing them as attractive applicants for the specific institutional admissions board."

I added "as a freshman, my daughter has received invitations to attend summer school at some universities. We are excited and will select one of them after gathering sufficient information about her major at the specific university. Should her summer school experience at the chosen university be good as anticipated, the university will remain one of our college choices for her. We will begin applying at the end of her junior year. Prior to submitting her applications, we will schedule three days' visit to various selected universities for a personalized experience on campus, understanding what a day in the life of a college student entails." I affirmed.

She agreed there couldn't be a better way of getting firsthand information about life on a college or university campus than personally going there for personal experience. "And tell your student you all must trust your gut feelings when you go on those visits. When we did same for Iris, she trusted her guts, and we did too. She is very happy we did and abided by what our guts told us. Her academic progression at the university is what we expected. She is doing very well. We do not expect her to drop out. She was well prepared for college both academically and otherwise."

I was impatient to articulate what went through my head in a rush. I interrupted her, something I had never done because we have the rules of mentoring down to the tee. She is highly well mannered and educated, and I have immense respect for all that she always has to offer me, so I usually do not interrupt her when she speaks. Impatient this time around, I cried, "There! There, Doc! That is where I am driving to. The type of scholastic ammunition given to high school students, the college preparation they receive from parents and school college counselors' help prepare them for what lies ahead. By giving them a sneak peek of college life during visits and tours, we the parents help them briefly experience what to expect as a student on a college or university campus. What I would like to see is the reduction of college dropout rates for girls even if they were not adequately prepared for college experience. Parents of college preparatory students from every stratum of the society must become aware of the importance of those visits. They must be armed with the information that you and I have to prepare our daughters for college so they do not drop out for one reason or the other. Funny how you said you do not expect Iris to drop out. Bingo!!! Point be made with my numerous questions! Ha~! Doc, how do you think we can attain such a goal if we set our minds to it?"

She paused for a minute. The silence fell harshly on my ears. I wondered if I had said something wrong. I suddenly became mute. She was thinking. Then she exclaimed, "Great question! Hmm! The university helps a lot of young people stay in school through counseling etcetera. Nevertheless, I understand that college and university attrition and dropout rates are pretty high and on the rise. I know you are going somewhere with this question, so I want you to work on it alone. Consider this your mini project assigned by me. The next time we talk, I would like for you to share with me what options you have to disseminate what we know to other parents who might need the information. How is that for a plan?" She laughed repeatedly as she spoke these last lines to me.

One of the numerous fascinating things about my mentor, Dr. M. is that she is highly transformational. She uses intellect stimulation often, and rarely gives direct answers to questions needing deeper and more critical thinking. I enjoy my relationship and conversations with her. She often talks of the level 4 teaching methods, so I realized she was using that here with me. I had my answer for her, but I was not ready to share it yet. I had asked myself the same question and internalized potential responses to the issue of information dissemination, lack of sufficient information, or illiteracy. She was very delighted when I shared my views on the topic when next we spoke. She listened attentively as always and then asked me impatiently, "What about your daughter's own views on where she wants to go to college? Does she want to be closer to home, far away? How does she feel about it right now? What are her own thoughts on all of these preparations?" Although highly maternal, Dr. M. is neither an overpowering nor overbearing mother to Iris. She has often insisted that she considered college preparation for Iris, her daughter, as something that impacted all parties involved because her young adult was taking a huge step, heading into a new unknown adventure in the big wide world to begin a real fight for her own future; and her parents were anxious, very anxious as they tried to prepare her for the real world, accept that she is now an adult, let go, and take a back seat. She remembers her preparation for Iris as "an emotional time for all of us."

I responded decisively. "My daughter Kay is just finishing her freshman year in high school, so I am not sure yet where she will go. She wants to attend a college where she will fit in nicely just like she has in high school. But she will visit a few colleges when she becomes a rising senior and hear their stories, feel the impact the community and its people may have on her, and then go with her gut feeling of it being the right place for her. She already knows what she wants to major in, but we will help guide her to the right college. Her involvement in the preparation will be key in the decision-making process. Questions I have for us to answer include, does the college have a strong faculty in your major? What is the school's reputation in that field of study or program? Any alums in your field that you can point to? Where do their students complete their internships? Do they have study- abroad programs in your field? What is the general reputation of the college, and what is the institution best known for? We hold college prep conversations now and again, and I feel great about it because she is all in and participating amazingly." In typical Dr. M. style, she congratulated us for being ahead of the process. "Awesome," she said. "Great job starting the discussion early. Keep the conversation going. Her choices may change over time, but from all I know about her, she will select a college where she will feel right at home giving her values, personality, and educational foundation, after visiting the campus and interacting with teachers, peers, and administrators. If the atmosphere of a college campus feels right for her or any of our children, their excitement will not hide from you, from us as parents. That is a very deep feeling, and she will articulate it right there. And that is where they feel like they can live for four or more years, adding more bricks onto the building of their future. When it all feels good, and it is precisely the way they want it to be, young adult college students would thrive in the milieu.

Now, one last thing before we part for tonight. She paused. She spoke emphatically by insisting that "young women, students, all of them should seek a mentor, an admirable person with strong personal and moral values, one who values education and can support them in different ways. It could be a parent, someone admirable who is willing to further help even if it is only periodically, to answer questions and give guidance to help them progress with their educational and career goals in life." I hastily said, "We are not done yet. It is not even twenty minutes yet since we began our conversation. We have eleven more minutes, Doc, right?" I smiled. She coughed lightly to clear her throat and said, "Okay. Iris will call me in fifteen minutes, so what is your point?" I laughed. "I believe there is a gap between high school and college. The gap could be causing college dropout rates to increase for some of our children. I imagine the gap may be ineffective preparation of our daughters for college. I am thinking of how effectively I may contribute in helping Kay and other women prepare their daughters to go to college and stay there, hence reducing the college dropout rate for our girls." She agreed and forwarded her last thoughts on the topic, concluding our conversation fantastically by stating, "that is a very noble thought. Journal K's preparation and share it. You see, we need to help the community of parents and initiate a mother-daughter forum for discussion of hot topics such as this. I mean it. Mentorship is important. Become a mentor, hold open forums, and spread your experiences. When you have a good story of effective college prep to tell, share it, and we will all learn from it. It is a terrific idea."

She insisted, "Let's all mind the gap between high school and college! The gap you just mentioned!" She was categorical about it. I expressed my gratitude for her time and the excellent insights shared. I also sent my best wishes to Iris, and we bid each other good night after she reciprocated by sending her regards to Kay and Court.

When Dr. M mentioned parental support and time management in our conversations about "all things college preparation for girls", I knew that me and Manny were excellent parental support for our two girls because that was part of our principles, to always be there for our daughters. But I also knew that we hadn't discussed time management as a couple or as a family with Kay and Court. We knew it was very important to use our time wisely, keep to time in our multiple daily engagements etc. I make a to-do list often, and have a planner to stay organized, so we consciously respected time but had not discussed time management. It was time to consider helping our teen understand it as she was in the preparatory stage for college, like Dr. M. said. So we did, and happily registered Kay for a time management summer class which she took in preparation for college. **Parental Support** and **time management** as important principles to help us guide our teen daughter into adulthood has had our continued attention since.

Parental Support is being readily available to our daughters in time of need and providing them with consistent emotional presence. According to research, it positively impacts children's self-efficacy, especially girls, and it is cardinal to their overall well-being. **Time management (TM)** means managing one's time in a way that is efficient and effective. It entails allocating time for the right activities and accomplishing them in a timely manner. Time is often considered a limited resource as we all parents often say "oh how time is passing-by so fast" or "where did time go" or "come on guys lets go we are running late" …. effective time management skills are critical to have, and an important principle for guiding teenage girls into adulthood as it teaches them how to be organized, prioritize, plan, and do things in order of importance. TM skills are so important for teens in the adulting process, especially when going from high school to college so much that my mentor Dr. M. sent her daughter, Iris to learn about it in a summer school class before college, and I did same with mine.

Crucial elements of **TM** as a principle to guide teenage girls in high school, and on their way to college includes **(1)** setting goals in a prioritized fashion. For example, you have to accomplish your first goal to be able to achieve the second one. For instance, your goal is to finish high school first, then go to college and graduate, and then start a good career, **(2)** Planning – get a planner and write out the plans for the day or the week. Create a to-do list in order of priority and cross or check-off items as you accomplish them. I still do this and cannot imagine stopping because it is an outstanding technique that has helped to keep me being productive at home and at work for decades, **(3)** set deadlines for accomplishing tasks and goals, **(4)** Build structure around your work including time-block for your work, and track your time to stay on schedule or adjust your time as warranted, **(5)** Avoid procrastination – make sure to engage and accomplish tasks in a timely manner, and do not leave any work that could or should be done today for tomorrow, **(6)** Create a balance – The saying goes…"all work and no play makes Jack a dull boy." You do not want this! Create time to have good fun with friends and the people you love, and enjoy doing the things that make you happy as a person, as well as do your required work in a balanced manner.

The benefits of effective TM are innumerable to include being organized and experience less stress as a result, being punctual in accomplishing tasks, meeting goals, and even in attending fun activities, and in being disciplined and self-confident. It is a prime principle for parents when helping teens transition to successful and well-organized adults.

To conclude, in this section we discussed certain principles that are critical for guiding girls into adulthood with the goal of building a strong foundation for them to ensure their successes in life. The principles include (1) Quality Education (2) Engagement in the process of their education (3) Zero tolerance for poor school attendance and class work failures (4) LEDD: Listening actively to their issues, engage in identifying the root causes of the issues, dedication in responding adequately to the issues, and devise effective strategies to prevent a recurrence of the issues (5) Open door (6) Involvement in the academic institution and its community life (7) DHPPR (pronounced dehpr): Determination, hard work, patience, perseverance, resilience (8) RIA: Responsibility, independence, autonomy (9) Parental support, and (10) Time management.

SECTION 3

BULLYING, INTIMIDATION, AND PEER VICTIMIZATION

I have heard some people say, "My boss is a bully" or "Bullying is going on at my school, on the playground, the locker rooms, in class, at my lunch table." My daughters and I have discussed this sad topic over several times. Each time they explain what is happening in their surroundings, we agree it is bullying but without the pushing, shoving, or beating that we have watched on national television news or seen in true life movies. We understood cruelty of various types entailed bullying, but still I could not provide them a clear-cut definition of the word. So that we all remain on the same page about what bullying really entails, I decided to work it out here for everyone.

Like us, some may wonder what bullying comprises of. My family is part of those who wanted a clear-cut definition of this ill. According to the National Institute of Child Health and Human Development, bullying is "being aggressive to another person in a physical, verbal, or relational manner." A 2001 Journal of the American Medical Association defined bullying as "physical or psychological harassment of one child by another who is viewed as stronger or more powerful. Physical bullying involves intentional pushing or shoving, kicking, slapping, punching, beating another person, or forcing them to act against their will. The verbal aspect of bullying entails name-calling, verbal threats of physical harm or beatings, spreading false rumors about another individual, verbal insult, taunting and teasing. Relational bullying occurs when an individual is made to feel left out, ignoring or not talking to them and encouraging others to do same."

A Nightmare

In 2006, a disease attacked a member of my family. It was an infectious disease that emanated from her school environment. We did not notice she had an entry port for the potentially dangerous pathogen. The good news was that it was easily curable since it was at its primary stage, and Manny, my husband and I were determined it would not leave any sequelae on our loved one. It first happened very early in her early school year. I sensed the initial symptoms immediately because of the abnormalities I was experiencing with her, and she reported the pain fast as it was occurring. However, our reaction was initially to wait and see if this disease was truly existent in that environment, how it would progress after the first report, if it had a pattern, and where it thrived.

Stupidly but honestly, we thought maybe we needed confirmation of what was a reality in the shades, or we weren't very sure how to react to the intruding ailment. We had not encountered an ill of similar nature in the past. Our children had experienced school life in other environments without any concerns or complaints prior to our introduction to this disturbing disease. When we had proof of the disease and a diagnosis to refer to, we decided to meet the teacher the next day after school to discuss the epidemic that we were hearing about from our four-year-old.

We had not been exposed to the disease prior, so we reacted rather slowly to the first few reports of slowly creeping incidents. Our meeting with the teacher was highly insightful. She was new to the class, the school, and the state. She had recently moved from out of state where she taught the same age group of children. She insisted she had never seen so many "out-of-control children" her entire life. She confirmed the existence of the ailment in her class. She said it was very infectious in the class environment. We proposed a diagnosis for it. This disease is called bullying.

A Surprising Early Beginning: Bullied at Four

The little four-year-old girl was standing in car line waiting impatiently for her mother's arrival at her school to take her home at the end of the day. The beautiful sun rayed on her golden-brown skin as she stood waiting. She was carrying her pink lunch box in her right hand, frowning and ready to burst into tears. A teacher was standing next to her. A car pulled up in front of them, a teacher opens the door, and she quickly jumps in and buckles up. Her sister who was picked up first on car line was in the car as well. Her sister hugged her but noticed tears running down her little pink cheeks. "What's wrong, Mimi? Are you not feeling well? Why are you crying? Awww, Mom, Mimi is crying."

I could hardly focus on my driving, but I had to for safety reasons. "Babe, what is the matter?" I inquired worriedly. She continued sobbing without uttering a word. She had been in the school for over four months now and still had difficulties adjusting. She wanted to be at the school because her older sister was in the school as well. She had transitioned from another private pre-K school that we all liked very much, but she wanted to join her sister in this school.

Prior to the day of this emotional outburst, she started insisting on returning to her previous school on grounds that the children in her class were "not nice and push a lot." I often asked her to explain what she meant by "the children push a lot." I had asked her if some child or children were intentionally pushing her, or they pushed in a rush to go out to play or be first to get an item or in line. We had agreed that no matter the circumstance, it was wrong for her or any other child to be pushed by another child. Now I was disturbed because it was unlike her to just cry her eyeballs out like this. I know she had been telling me she is not happy because the students in her class were "rough, loud, and pushed a lot." Some days she would cry and refuse to leave the car in the morning when we got to school.

On other occasions, she would say she has bellyache and will not be able to stay at school, requesting we return home. I usually pleaded with her and reminded her I will be early on car line to take her back home. She routinely gives me a rundown of her day after school. I know she was not happy at this school, but she had never returned to me teary-eyed.

On this particular day when we got home and she had settled in, she told us, "The children in my class are too rough. They have been pushing me, and today Riley hit and pushed me in the restroom after lunch. I don't want to go back to that school, Mommy. It's all because of Riley. She tells the other children to push me." Little arms wrapped me up in a hug, and I reciprocated. I held her tight in my arms, her soft voice resounding in my head over and over with the words she just spoke. I felt sad and frustrated to know that the pushing was intentional, there was a name attached to it, the pushing leader was ordering other children to push her, and that she was hit today by another child. I asked her again if she reported the incidents to her teacher and what the teacher did after she told her what had happened to her in the restroom. She said her teacher spoke to the girls responsible for the pushing and told them to stop doing that, or they will get kicked out of her class.

I met with her teacher the next morning to discuss my daughter's complaints. She acknowledged the issues in her class, deeply apologized, and promised she will make sure it does not happen again. The teacher's body language spoke louder to me than the words she articulated that morning. I sensed she had a difficult class and that something wrong was going on in that class. I told her I would go to the principal the next time I have a concern.

"My child does not want to come here. She cries before exiting the car every morning, and it is becoming ultra-painful for me leaving her here each morning. I hope you can keep her safe from the rowdy kids. She has been pushed and hit. That is very serious. I hope you all are doing something about this situation. Are other children suffering this as well? Are the parents of the problem children aware of what their children are doing to other kids here?" I asked firmly.

The teacher was young, professionally mature but appeared overwhelmed and unhappy. "This is a very difficult class. I have never seen what I am experiencing here. Most of the children are rule-less. It is a real problem. I promise you I will take care of her," she confessed.

Our daughter settled into calm in her class for another month. I communicated frequently with her teacher during the month, and it was going smoothly for her. Then one afternoon when I picked her up, she had one of her long tresses in her hand. "Mom, look at what she did to me today. She pushed me in the restroom and pulled my hair. This fell out, and she threw it on the floor. I picked it up and saved it for you. I told my teacher...Mom, Riley is very mean. She hit another girl [name withheld]. You know, she hit her hard on the face, and she started crying really loud and went to the teacher."

Courtney (Court, Mimi, Mi, Missy), my four-year-old daughter cried as she recounted the incidents of the day. I pulled up in the school parking lot to listen and think of an immediate action while still on the school premises.

"Has she resumed her demonic acts? Is she at it again? I can't believe this is happening among four- and five-year-olds. Sorry, babe, so sorry, sweetheart. Please don't cry. I'll speak with the teacher and the principal about this. She will be punished one way or another. I am not sure her parents know this little girl is so mean. She is a torn, badly brought up girl, the MRSA in your class."

I quickly realized I was bitter and that my language was harsh in front of the kids. This was becoming very emotional for me. I thought deeply of my little one suffering in the hands of some nasty, unlucky little brut. I helped myself and tried to console my Mi, who was sobbing in her car seat. Kay was devastated for her younger sister. She had her arm around her little sissy and wiped her tears as they ran down her cheeks. I asked her repeatedly if she was also experiencing similar issues with her peers. She denied having such an experience in her group. In fact, she made friends faster than expected. I got my children out of the car, left the parking lot, and returned to the class to make sure the teacher was aware that my daughter's hair was pulled out and she had physical evidence of bullying. We discussed the incident at length. Court mentioned the name of the student who was that cruel to her. I asked the teacher if the parents of the girl were aware of their daughter's attitude, and she affirmed they had been informed and will be informed again. I knew the kid's mom. I saw her at school daily. She was friends with a family we were acquainted with. I asked our acquaintance if she knew Riley's parents or mother, and she confirmed they were very close friends. I left it at that. I did not want to engage her in the issue. I thought maybe when Riley's parents are made aware of their daughter's issues and the complaints, they will call my family to apologize for their daughter's attitude and do their utmost to help their daughter face the truth about her behavior at school. That was wishful thinking. Besides, our family's preference was to wait to hear back from the school after reporting the multiple incidents. The week passed, and I did not hear back from the school.

Court had another peaceful week at school after that incident. The following week, as I drove both girls to school on Monday morning, my kindergartener said, "Mommy, I am feeling sick. My belly is hurting, Mom. Can I stay with you please, please?"

I assured her, "I will stay in the car with you for a little while and see how you do. If you feel better, I will leave you at school, but I will be the first on car line to take you home. If you feel bellyache in class, ask your teacher to call me so I can come get you. Is that a good plan?" I asked, looking into her sad eyes.

"I don't like going to this school. There are very mean children here, Mommy. I want to go back to my other school. Mommy, please may I go back to my other school? I don't like it here. Mommy, please don't leave me here! I want to go back to my other school, Mom, please!"

She refused to leave the car. I drove around and pulled up in the parking lot. In spite of her vehement refusal to go to class that day, I later walked her into her class after spending over fifteen minutes with her in the car talking about her concerns and fears and what her teacher and I were doing to arrest the bullying she was experiencing in her class. I went into her class that morning and spoke with her teacher again, explaining all what was happening. I went to the administration office, but I was told by the secretary that the principal was unavailable that morning. I made an appointment to see her the following school day.

That was a fateful Monday. In the afternoon, Mimi returned home with a squished and swollen left index finger with a broken fingernail that Riley had slammed against the door of the restroom. Her finger was swollen and had turned blue, the nail had turned black, and it was suspended off its nail bed. It was a very painful injury. The little four-year-old cried incessantly from the pain. We consulted her pediatrician, and she was placed on analgesics for the pain. The damaged finger and nail were also treated with wraps and ice for cool therapy.

After an extensive meeting and lengthy discussion with her teacher that afternoon, we gained more insight into the issues of the particular class and how the school was handling the issues. "From my understanding, there is no handling of these issues. You are left on your own to fix this jungle of wild, untamed, and ruthless four- and five-year-olds?" the young teacher who was new to this state and school said, looking sad with a frown on her face. I asked the teacher to make sure I understood her. She did not mince words and appeared very frustrated. She doubled down on her earlier statement.

"I have a terrible plight here. This is not what I expected to see when I signed on. My plan is to not return to this school next year. I have no support here, and no one knows how to deal with this bad situation. This is a very bad class; I am not sorry to say but I am very sorry this happened again." She intimated to me and Manny.

We had a clear picture and sense of what was happening in the kindergarten class among the younger children in the school. There was no note from the teacher informing us of our daughter's injuries sustained from Riley's physical bullying.

We understood this school was like the jungle. We knew what our next step would be. We were on time at our appointment with the principal, also known as the school director, the following morning. Court, our four-year-old daughter, was with us. During our appointment, we dressed the meeting room with all the issues suffered by our daughter, with a clear point-by-point narrative of times and agenda of our multiple meetings with the teacher. We asked our daughter to interject and interrupt us when it was necessary to correct us if we stated something incorrectly. The meeting was intense. I did well keeping my emotions at bay. We had suffered enough of the epidemic. Sadly, our daughter had physical evidence of the disease that had evidently been diagnosed but was still without therapies at the institution. Our kid was right there with her tress in hand, her painful, awful-looking finger, and fright on her face. Yet the parents of the students responsible for torturing her had not met with the school principal to discuss their children's behaviors and how to help them cease the horrific behaviors.

Those students were in class while mine was out sick, in tears from physical and emotional injury. The Principal, a.k.a. Director of the school, apologized but appeared cold and stoic even after our narrative and viewing our child's physical marks. She asked our daughter the name of the person who bullied her.

"Riley," the kid responded promptly.

This principal or director wore a telling blank look on her face when she heard the name of the student bully who represented the infection that was spreading like wildfire in the kindergarten class.

Looking at Courtney, she said plainly and simply in a quiet voice, "I am so sorry you had to endure all that. At this age, some children are very mean-spirited…"

I waited for her to pause. Respectfully but with a feeling of disdain, I responded to her "Thank you, ma'am. She does not and will never understand that there is a reason or an age that makes certain children behave in certain ways that totally and brutally hurt their peers. She's been hurt, and she has a name and a face of the child hurting her. She just wants her peace right now. She cannot get it here at the school. We are requesting that you release us immediately from our financial contract with the school. We are withdrawing her from the school, effective today. She has not been to class today and will not return. We also want this month's fees refunded as she will miss school the entire month."

This was an expensive school that did not care much about the well-being of its students. It also had very poor communication or rather absolutely zero communication between school and home. The principal verbally acknowledged our request. A week after our formal complaint and request for contractual relief, we received an official letter from the school relieving us of any financial obligations after withdrawing our child from the school. Included in the mail was a check with a refund of a month's worth of Court's tuition. We let her older sister complete the academic year at the school and then transferred both girls to Overbrook School, where our family found peace and happiness.

Another family moved their toddler son from the same school like us into Overbrook School that year. Currently one of our close family friends, Jules asserted that school is not where she would send her dog for a day. Patti, one of my good friends, suggested that we report the school to the board of Tennessee private schools for failure to appropriately handle the bullying crisis in Court's class. We also told our family friends Dr. Sami and his wife who were not surprised by the details. Although we had evidence, we elected to move to a better educational institution without taking Patti's suggested route. It was the first and only private school we visited when we moved to Tennessee and had ourselves to blame for not visiting the other schools in the city before settling on that one.

Bullying was the intruder that almost prevented Court from going to school every day. She was only four years old when she felt the hurt of bullying descended upon her little person like a sledgehammer. The school's reaction was inert. That school was a nightmare to our family and others like Jules.

The Amazing Sixth Grade Mom: No Place for This in Our Family

In sixth grade, Kay was also confronted with bullying. Though very briefly because it was tackled promptly by the school and the child's parent, Kay's coming face-to-face with verbal bullying was saddening. She was bullied by a male peer who, according to the homeroom teacher, "felt threatened by her academic strengths." As soon as his parents were made aware of their son's attitude, his mom called our home after 2100 and put her child on the phone to apologize to me and my child, promising to never again call her names and to be a better peer. That was highly commendable parental handling of the issue, and Kay never had to deal with him after we received their call. What the parents of the boy indicated to us was, "There is no place for this in our family, and we mean it. We are very responsible people and will not tolerate bullying either by our child or against him." And we appreciated their prompt tacking of the issue.

Bullying is an evil that has a potential of destroying any child. I'd like our daughters and granddaughters to understand the components of bullying and be ready to confront it squarely anytime in life. From Court and Kay's experiences, I gathered that bullying is not necessarily done by a loser, an imbecile, or a jerk that pushes his or her peers and other kids into lockers. It can be done by almost anyone at any time. Bullying can be done to children of any grade, culture or socioeconomic milieu. It can occur on campus at school, on the way to and from school, on the bus or on foot, at home, at a social event, in the dining room or cafeteria, or on the playground—you name it.

I'd like our daughters to understand what bullying entails, and be ready to confront it squarely whenever they recognize the ill at any time in their respective lives. This is an issue that has endured for too long, and it continues to rid several children of their personal happiness at school, on their way home from school, and even long after they get home from school.

Middle School Longtime "Friends"

When they were in eighth grade, Lilly, one of Kay's very good friends, faced bullying from some of her longtime peers. A group of girls had decided they were the "popular ones" at school and had "reference powers" endowed to them by the very definition of popularity. They called themselves the "power nine." Some of the "popular" girls belonged to the school's team of cheerleaders who had decided for themselves that only a student from their group could be friends with attractive male students.

Jason, a male student who moved to the school from Louisiana was said to have a cool accent, according to the girls. He was also an attraction to them because according to some of the kids, "he was easy on the eyes." To the disbelief of the "popular girls," he became very good friends with Lilly, who belonged to the "normal" group of students. The "popular girls" decided the friendship was unfortunate for Lilly. They could not fathom their Louisiana heartthrob would be friends with a "normal," non-cheerleading girl. Lilly is a well-rounded, soft-spoken, tanned-skin, intelligent, kind and beautiful girl who quickly became friends with the gentleman from Louisiana. It was unacceptable in the "popular" circle, so she became a target for bullying by the girls. Nessa, one of the group's favorites who thought Jason was hers, was unable to contain her dissatisfaction with the friendship between Jason and Lilly. She was neither shy nor discreet in expressing her discontent to her group of friends. "Jason is mine. He is my best friend. Lilly better back off."

In the school hallways, Nessa articulated these same words to Lilly, asking her to "back off from Jason or else!" She made the sign of a gun with her hands and shot at Lilly, insisting that if Lilly didn't back off, she would shoot her with a gun. Lilly endured approximately three weeks of her peers at school terrorizing her, asking her to "go jump off a bridge, go kill yourself, disappear from this earth." She was also warned to "sleep with one eye open because something bad will happen to you soon. We will bomb your house and you will die." Lilly became very frightened and reported the issue to her mother, who immediately contacted the institution. The institution's reaction was also instantaneous.

Lilly and Kay spent time on phone discussing Lilly's fears and concerns. Kay remained a great support to Lilly throughout the traumatizing incident. Kay spoke with two of the "power nine "girls and asked them to cease the bullying. The girls she spoke to affirmed to her that they were not part of the bullying and despised Nessa's reaction to Lilly and Jason's friendship. Kay was particularly close to the two girls from power nine that she spoke with, so she felt good that the girls she considered friends were not participants in the bullying of Lilly. Still, the incident bothered her because according to her, "It is wrong for any child to not feel safe at school. Lilly is the meekest and peaceful student I know and does not deserve this. No one does, but she has done nothing to deserve the meanness of these so-called popular girls. Mom, what would you do if you were bullied? Have you ever been bullied? Tell me, Mom, please. How should a student like me handle bullying?"

She appeared to be in a pensive mood. I immediately understood this was serious. Kay looked at me with sad eyes that begged for my perspective on the issue. I told her a brief story about me and a bully at my school and how her attempt to intimidate me ended. The case caused a deep divide in my school. A good majority of the students were for me while the school's administration and teachers were divided between me and the student.

I went to Kay and took her hands into mine. "The student was a notorious petite, blonde bully. She made very poor grades. I was a normal student. I had never been in trouble with anyone at school. I was very intelligent, unassuming, and well-liked by my peers and most of my teachers. We were in the same grade but in different homerooms. We had been assigned to attend the same hospital for clinical rotation, which we called pracs. During our two week's clinical practice at the hospital, she was often rude to me and commanded me around like I was her maid even though I always ignored her requests. Other students noticed her poor attitude toward me and asked her to stop being disrespectful to me. She was stubborn and ignored her peers' good advice.

I had warned her peacefully to stop sending me around, insisting she was not my instructor. On the last day of our clinical, she yelled at me because not only did I refuse as usual to obey her, I told her she was very badly brought up. Upon hearing me say 'you are badly brought up,' she said to me, 'You are a useless zombie.' Everyone who heard what she said turned red-faced. Some students told her right away that she was crazy. I said nothing to her. I walked away. Her words replayed in my head throughout that day. All the questions I entertained after hearing her went without answers. Once in the parking lot at the end of the day, I stood in her face and told her she was the zombie. I warned her to never dare try to push me around again or she would see that I am not one she can mess with. She tried to move away from me, but I told her to stand right there and dare not move 'when I am speaking to you, zombie.' I was mad, and all the students were gathered there to take our school bus back to the campus. Verna, the bully, started crying and coughing. Then I finished by saying, 'You, zombie! Now see how it feels to treat others with spite, certainly the way you do not want to be treated.'

"Our bus arrived. We boarded our school bus, and it drove off. She cried on the bus. The other students ignored her. I was with a friend who was concerned that I had yelled at a petite blonde girl and I might be expelled from school for that. I told her, 'So be it.' "The next day at school, the news had spread like wildfire. I had students who never spoke to me saying 'good morning' to me, some just saying 'thank you for what you did yesterday.' I was called to the dean's office, and all my teachers asked me what happened because I was a very quiet student, and very smart too. I did explain. There were no consequences for either of us, but one of my teachers hated me for being 'bold enough to stand up to a blonde' such as Verna. This was seventeen years ago, and it is a long story, darling. Your dad knows the story very well. My parents weren't there, or I certainly would have shared with them and sought their advice."

Refocusing the conversation on her friend Lilly, I continued, "In Lilly's case, she has done the right thing by telling her parents. Her mom has gone to school to discuss the incidents with the school administration, and the vice principal has handled it promptly. The students have been punished for bullying Lilly."

Kay was itching for a deeper response to the ill. "What else could the school have done? The students' punishment, which entails not sitting together at lunch as a group, was reversed today because their parents came to school to complain and protest it. So does this mean the parents support their children's bullying of other students? Is it not their responsibilities to agree with the school's decision to separate these girls for a while and educate them as to the consequences of their actions toward Lilly? Mom, you would have punished us even more by grounding us or taking away a favorite thing, I know it, Mom, you wouldn't condone your child trying to destroy another child's happiness at school like that. It's all just very wrong: the bullying, the school's funny punishment, the parents' reaction to the punishment, and the school's position after the parents' protest. Some of the parents say the children were just joking. You accept your child should joke by telling another one to go kill herself and die? As parents, do they not know many children have harmed themselves and died and are still dying as a result of bullying? Mom, I don't understand." She was upset. Her phone rang. She checked it. "It is Lilly. May I be permitted to speak with her now please, Mom? She needs me." I nodded my approval. She took the call and went to her room.

As a high school freshman attending the 2012 summer school at UA of Dallas, Kay had an assignment that required writing a persuasive speech about an ill that she would like to see disappear from schools. She selected bullying. "Mom, as my summer school project, I have chosen to present a brief paper about bullying in middle and high schools," she indicated as soon as she entered the car from school. "Each student has to select a topic dear to their heart and present an argument persuading her peers to join in the fight against the selected topic. I have chosen bullying because it is a terrible thing and affects students in the most horrific way. My best friend was bullied in eighth grade, Rudi called me names in sixth grade, my teacher demeaned me by pulling my hair in class in front of my peers, my little sister was almost killed by four-year-olds in pre-K. I don't know why children, hmm…ughhh…I mean some students are so cruel to one another. I want to persuade my summer school classmates that bullying is an evil so that as we all start high school, hopefully we are a better team, not bullies. And most importantly, I want them to be ready to intervene against bullying when they witness it." She sounded persuasive. "You do not have to convince me. That is an excellent topic selection. I agree with your choice. When is your paper due? Did your teacher provided you with an outline of the important elements your topic must have, or do you have to come up with one?" I inquired, trying to understand the rush in her voice."

It will be cool to do this. I have to figure it out all by myself and write my own speech from what I find and how I want it to look and sound." She sounded and appeared elated to work on the topic of bullying. Her theoretical outline of the speech she wrote and presented at summer school 2012 is appended to this topic.

My girls' experiences with bullying, Kay's dramatic response to Lilly's case, her reaction to her summer school project, her selected topic, her excitement to lend a voice against the morbid ill, and the sad effects of bullying on the lives of countless children and families around the world inspired me to write this section of *Compass*.

Cyberbullying: Cowardice

Bullying has migrated from traditionally happening environmentally, to include cyberbullying. Cyberbullying is mainly done electronically, on the Internet, using e-mail, text messages, instant messages, and all the cyber space venues. It is bullying through electronic medium. Cyberbullying is electronic aggression and has happened to several children, even adults. The heightened use of social media, e-mailing, and the Internet in general has seen an increase in cyberbullying. Electronic communication is a way of life in contemporary society. Majority of modern man use the Internet to conduct business, and we appreciate the progress that science and technology has made to improve lives and help us conduct business faster and more easily. Sadly, vicious individuals are exploiting this medium to assail and demolish their preys. My presumption about the increase in this type and medium for assault is that bullies no longer have to be face-to-face with their target to cause havoc and inflict pain upon them. Cyberbullying is as ferocious as the traditional face-to-face bullying, and I say it is done by the cowards of our world, out of their share cowardice.

Mary-Lou

Mary-Lou, a.k.a. ML, a very pretty freshman in a coed high school returned home from her first night dance and headed straight to her computer. She says, "It is habit. I log in as soon as I get home because my phone does not have e-mailing possibilities. I want to be in tune with my friends and know what is happening. I got home and turned on my computer, time to change into my jammies and eat a fruit, and it was already there—an animated picture of me, naked, with only leaves covering up certain parts of my body. They made it look like I was wearing makeup. The picture made me look fat at the bottom and my chest. Then they wrote, 'Ah pretty makeup for someone this ugly! You are so ugly, go to hell, die now. Hang yourself. He does not want you!'" She was in tears as she recounted the story that happened to her during her first two months in high school, eight months ago.

She cleared her throat. "The only thing I did wrong was to dance with a guy that evening. Dina told me last week that her brother says Jake, who is her brother's friend on the basketball team, says he likes me.

She also said I should not dance with him at the school party if he invites me to dance. I had laughed her off, saying I will dance if any of my friends ask me to. She was mad and said if I do, she will get all her friends to make fun of me.

"At the dance party, he asked me to dance, and I did. There was me on the Internet, I mean in an e-mail in a picture I never took, looking horrible and being asked to die…I went straight and got my mom and showed it to her. She saw it. The e-mail was sent to twenty other students. They had circulated the e-mail all over the Internet that weekend, and other bullies had sent replies with comments ridiculing me and the picture. When I arrived at school the following Monday, my friends and classmates started laughing at the sight of me. No one spoke to me except Jake and a few of his friends. Even my usual friends laughed. I was ridiculed at school for two days, so I refused to go to school for the rest of the week feigning a headache. My parents figured it out, and the next Monday, they were in the principal's office with all the e-mails and cyber stuff printed out. The principal had heard rumors and handled it very well. The whole thing took a toll on me, my class attendance, my grades, and my friendships of years and shook the school up."

Her sadness was evident. ML was visibly still shaken by the act of cyberbullying she suffered months back. Countless students have suffered and still suffer bullying in schools around the world.

Cyberbullying is even worse because it has no specific time during which victims could suffer humiliation. It can happen at night, and/or during the day. One can realize it in the middle of breakfast, lunch, or dinner if they have access to a cellular device and the Internet. Perpetrators of this type of bullying are mostly cowards who decide to bully anonymously making it a tough task to identify them. Aside this type of situation, cyberbullying could be done in many other ways using the Internet and social media.

Our daughters and their parents need to be vigilant about this. Parents should make every effort to monitor the appropriate use of the cyberspace by their children. Our daughters should understand that their parents must know what they are posting and writing on social media before it is done. It is irresponsible and not cool to bully anywhere, even on cyberspace, and parents should do everything to help their children avoid getting involved in this very wrong act, by using a principle of social media utilization **checks and balances** with their teens. Social media utilization checks and balances in *Compass* refers to parental supervision of their children's use of the various social media platforms to ensure their use and communication in such platforms are appropriate. Ensuring checks and balances with teens social media use and presence on the platforms may include controlling and limiting their use of any social media medium that may be negatively affecting them, or discontinuing their presence if they are involved in cyber-bullying or any inappropriate use of the platforms. I am not opposed to children using social media platforms because it is incredibly important these days to stay connected etc. However, it has its disadvantages, and when misused by a teen or any child, it is parental responsibility to no longer allow the teen unfettered access to the platforms.

Behind Professional Walls

Part of *Compass* is that our children should be able to identify bullies and their cruel act as soon as it begins to occur in its slightest form. It is important for them to know that bullying could be present at their place of work. Workplace bullying is very much similar to psychological harassment. It is adult behavior that occurs when someone with power at work directs vexatious attitudes toward you, treats you poorly, humiliates you, abuses you, isolates or ignores you, and bruises your self-esteem. Workplace bullying can be very humiliating, especially when an individual is taunted or abused in front of colleagues as well as subordinates. This is bullying which is different from discrimination that several individuals experience daily, and competent professional women and other minorities suffer from their superiors at decent organizations, offices and workplaces.

"Stop! Stop talking. I don't need your explanation. Time out, I say, time out!" With her left hand and fingers raised vertically in front of her face and her right fingers placed horizontally in the middle of her left palm, I saw and heard my manager warn the hospital's Chief Nursing Officer (CNO) to observe "time out" like she was a TT, also known as terrible twos. I remember telling my daughters "time out" during their TT years. I was befuddled as I observed. It was before 9:00 a.m. one day in April. We were just about to go into the boardroom for a meeting. Several other hospital directors were witnessing the scene, rather nonchalantly. After all, Sniffer, the boss, was talking. She was the CEO. I was less than a month old in my position as a director in the hospital. I was astonished at the CEO's words and behavior.

"Stop talking now, time out!" she yelled again at the CNO as I entered the waiting area of the hospital administration. I opened my eyes wide, and my mouth remained half open upon hearing and seeing what was happening in front of me. Danielle, the CNO, looked embarrassed and highly humiliated. She appeared sad. She became quiet. The room was suddenly quiet.

I said, "Good morning, guys." The CEO turned toward me, smiled, and walked off to the boardroom.

"Hello, how are you, Danielle?" I asked the CNO, who appeared mute. She nodded at me, lips pulled together in a tight grip, and walked off to the boardroom after Sniffer. We all followed quietly. Series of humiliating incidences for the CNO followed this one. A few weeks after I accepted my position as a director for the hospital, I realized the relationship between the two ladies was fizzling, and the interaction between them was increasingly uncomfortable to witness. The bullying from Sniffer continued for a month before the CNO resigned her position.

Some directors pulled me to the side and warned me about the bullying nature of Sniffer. "She is a terrible manager to work for. I am just warning you because you are new. Be prepared for her always. I have been here for seven years. She's the worse CEO I have seen here." My colleague said this to nicely put me on my guard. Sniffer's unprofessionalism and bullying attitude toward

Danielle reached its crescendo when she completely belittled and humiliated her in the presence of several physicians who attended the Medical Executive Council (MEC) for that quarter.

"What are you doing about incomplete care plans, Danielle? The report for the quarter says there are X number of delinquencies. Do you know how much money is lost per incomplete care plan? Let me tell you how much it is. It is X amount per care plan. Now I want you to multiply that by the number of delinquent records or charts without appropriate care plans and tell me the total," Sniffer charged at Danielle in the meeting. "Do you understand, Danielle? Do you understand what I am saying? When the care plan is incomplete, there are serious financial consequences. Now have you done the calculation? Do you want me to tell you how much it cost? The cost is $48,275 for the delinquent charts. How much does it cost? Hein? Do you want to say it so we can hear how much we are losing?" Sniffer asked, looking directly at Danielle.

"The cost is $48,275," Danielle, looking gloomy, indignant, and forlorn, repeated after Sniffer. "Would you like to lose that amount of money, Danielle? Do you understand what this means to my hospital?" Sniffer continued. Danielle was quiet, and so was the entire room. I was the one presenting during the meeting and reporting to the Committee for the quarter. I fidgeted uncomfortably in my seat. It was my first MEC in the boardroom. Although I had read some parts of the Medical Staff Bylaws for the hospital, I did not know the rules of MEC in this organization because no one had taken out time to appropriately orient me to the code of conduct for the meeting, but I learned fast by watching and listening to those around me. I maintained a sullen silence until Sniffer requested that I continue the presentation. The atmosphere was tense for several of us present. I looked at Ti, and she immediately winked at me. I continued my presentation. Charis, another director, was also present. She was the second colleague to warn me about Sniffer. She was the one director in the hospital that wouldn't condone with Sniffer's bullying. She was a seasoned, intelligent, and savvy RN director of another department for the continuum of care for the organization. She often made Sniffer appear stupid in meetings, and so Sniffer did not like her. Charis did not mince words when she spoke with Sniffer or responded to her questions in meetings. Charis was tall, with a tough-looking personality. She had a big golden heart and was a gentle but a firm speaker. She was a very intelligent director. Indeed, we were a bunch of highly smart professionals on the team. Ti's wink and Charis's smile spoke volumes to me. I continued with the presentation. I was physically stable, but I was suffering an internal bruise from what was happening in the meeting. The atmosphere was not collegial. It was an avant-garde for me, to be in a boardroom with such a tense atmospheric appearance. I was shaken. It was incomprehensible to me that with all the physicians present at their own meeting, this would be happening. And none of them uttered a word against the incident. I thought to myself, "how disrespectful to them. This is so unprofessional."

On her last day at the organization before she resigned, Danielle pulled me aside and said to me, "You are new to your position in this hospital and on the leadership team. You are also new to Sniffer's ways, and so I want to caution you before I leave. She is a complete bully. She has spoken to me like I was stupid and ignorant, with complete disrespect of my person, knowledge, experience, contributions, and position in this hospital. She has bullied me for an entire month, and I have had enough. Nothing I say is good enough for her. Nothing I do is good enough for her, although I used to be a star to her. She has humiliated me in front of the entire exec team, her assistant, my staff, and even in front of housekeepers. She is unprofessional and unethical, and you see it. You know it. She is a very unethical CEO. She is a crude bully. You are new here. I want you to know that she will turn on you someday, and for no reason. She might be mentally unstable or unsuited to lead mature, intelligent, and experienced leading professionals or nursing directors in a hospital. She knows the financial stuff in the business of the hospital but does not know leadership and has no people skills. She has silenced the voices of the professionals and adults on the exec team. She is a demagogue. Her leaders do not have a voice. She likes her own voice and her voice alone. That is how she operates. But do not stay here to be treated like she has treated me. You must leave as soon as you can. I hope you graduate soon so you can resign without her bullying you. This is your honeymoon phase. She likes only herself and is very pretentious. She has hurt me so much. I feel like I know nothing in this field right now. My self-esteem is suffering because of her humiliating me so often." She sighed and then continued:

"I have palpitations each morning when I wake up to prepare for work. Did you see what she did to me in MEC? Last week I felt numbness to my left cheek. That was from stressing out about her bullying me so much. I am tired of being treated like that, so I am resigning today. She did same with Charis because she is a very smart director who ran her department with excellence and was a challenge to her. Charis would not take this b—— she has given me. That girl will never change. She pushed your predecessor to the brink, and they both got to verbally fight, so she terminated your predecessor after concocting whatever she wanted to concoct as reasons for terminating her. Be careful and cautious. I wish you all the best at school. You are very intelligent and sweet. I know you will become a doctor and do great. I hope we can work together again someday. Be vigilant and be careful with Sniffer. I am going to resign now. This is it for me here. I will be happier once I leave this building. I am done. I must let go of this job and preserve my health. I must leave now. I am sorry. Bye." She spoke calmly but firmly, looking straight into my eyes.

We hugged tightly, holding onto each other for a few seconds. "I will miss you a whole lot. You gave me so much here. I appreciate you, and I love you. You truly do not deserve this malicious treatment you have received here. I am sorry. You will do very well wherever you go. You are a super smart professional. Best of luck! All the best, Dannie!" I concluded.

We hugged again and parted. I was sad for her because she had been dramatically bullied. Several individuals witnessed the humiliation she suffered. I was short of words each time I witnessed Sniffer's insanity toward this very smart and seasoned executive. It was psychologically draining for me to witness the disgusting behavior. And like my peers, I was guilty of inaction and my inability to help the situation.

Two weeks prior, she began telling me she was experiencing headaches and facial numbness due to stress from Sniffer. Sniffer's bullying was threatening Dannie's' health. Telling a mature, experienced, and seasoned nurse executive to "timeout" was like telling a three- year-old at home "timeout," I thought to myself. I knew Danielle suffered more than verbal abuse from Sniffer. She had mentioned receiving bullying e-mails as well.

Dannie and I worked very closely together during her tenure at the organization. She is one of the smartest CNO I ever came across. She had positively turned the hospital around and was very well liked by her staff. I was not surprised by her sudden resignation and I was happy for her. I was certain she had made the right decision to put an end to Sniffer's bullying cycle by leaving the organization. Yet it was heartbreaking for me to see her leave so suddenly.

Sniffer bullied me as well before I resigned my position at the organization. I had decided I was ready to move on before her bullying started. I worked long hours as a director for the organization, and Sniffer appreciated me a whole lot initially. On several occasions, she lavished praises on me and the work I was doing for the hospital. It was evident that I was loved and respected on my team and in the organization. I was doing an amazing job, according to Sniffer and my peers. Everything was hunky-dory until the political replacement for Danielle who resigned in May joined the organization's team from one of the company's hospitals in Penn State. The political replacement for Danielle took the CNO's office in July. I call her Dannie's "political" replacement because a month after she relocated from PA, she did not hesitate to explain that she was the true reason why Dannie was bullied and why she came to replace Dannie. From all her explanations, Dannie's exit and her entry were both politically motivated. It was sickening to listen to her stories—which were many—always. She asserted that she was the best friend of the director of human resources for the region and had been in the organization for many years. Consequently, she got whatever she wanted including Dannie's job. It was all so political ad nauseam.

By December of that year, the boardroom had become more of a place where discussions, mainly between the CNO and CEO Sniffer were more relevant to bedroom partners, sweethearts, lovers, couples and intimate family members than to me and the other directors present. The hospital's senior team meetings were a true waste of time for me. I had my job to do and I needed time to complete my duties than listen to indecent college tales of girls in nightgowns without underwear and confronting police officers on campus. In addition to the differences in values that were beginning to surface between me and Sniffer's leadership, or call it the organization, the boardroom was kinda sad after three directors with whom I had a great connection resigned due to poor leadership and bullying. I knew what I had to do by then.

My personal values made it hard for me to sit in the boardroom each morning for ops meeting. By January, I was made aware that Sniffer had asked some other directors to inform her of any questionable thing I do. Having always held myself to utmost ethical standards throughout my professional career, I reassured my peer informant, "You know she will hit a dead end looking for I don't know what to build a case. She must look elsewhere if she needs something against me. She can make anything up anytime if she wants to. I am not worried at all.

She does not have to ask you for help. I have been late faxing a report to corporate. She can hang on such a limited incident." My colleague and friend agreed, and we laughed about it. That same month, I realized that Sniffer began isolating me from the team. It was evident she was bullying me in that manner. Our team members noticed and commented on it. Some of the directors actually came into my office and apologized on her behalf. For example, she would greet everyone in the boardroom by calling their name, speak to them and completely "forget" I am there by omitting to either call my name too or speak to me.

I thought that was childish. I had been warned she was a bully. I was ready. I shared her bullying tendencies with my family. I did not care much for her. Our values were at opposite poles already, and I was preparing my exit from the organization. Further, during an internal audit activity, she talked down to me in front of the administrative secretary and other lower managers. She was actively looking for ways to frustrate me, and I knew it but always maintained my composure which frustrated her. I resigned in February. Two weeks later, Danielle's political replacement from Penn State also resigned as CNO for the organization. She had worked for the company for ten years intermittently and had relocated and spent less than seven months as the CNO at the hospital where we met as colleagues on the exec team. News of her exit did not surprise me in any way. I learned her personality fast after she arrived and understood her well. From the stories she told everyone in the boardroom, I believed and forecasted that she and Sniffer would not work together for a long time.

After her "shocking" exit, just when the hospital was expecting the Joint Commission's visit for their triennial reaccreditation survey, I thought "Bingo! I said it! But how odd is the timing of her exit? Understanding the importance of the Joint Commission's visit to the hospital could she not have postponed her resignation for a later date? Is anyone asking the right questions about the turnover rate at that organization? How many leaders will an organization lose within a period of one year before stakeholders start asking themselves real questions about the leadership practices at the organization?"

I was curious as to why instead of speaking up, some of my peers tolerated Sniffer's bullying and why others looked away while she bullied their peers. Thinking of the true implications of my personal philosophy MELP (Moral, Ethical, Legal and Professional), I started asking myself pertinent questions about professional environments and workplace bullying practices that go without being reported by internal stakeholders and hence go with impunity.

I relocated to my new state of residence a few years prior. This was the second organization in the state where I noticed bullying of employees was common practice by some managers. In my prior workplace, the bullies were untouchable and unstoppable. Some clinical employees suffered emotionally and psychologically due to the behavior. Many knew it was wrong, moaned about it under their breath, but said nothing about it. When I raised an alarm as I witnessed it, I was warned by an ethically upright peer: "This is common practice here. If you speak up, you will be gone from here faster than you can imagine. If you want to keep your job, suck it up and go with the flow." Prior to relocating to my current state of residence, I resided and worked in the same state for years and did not witness overt workplace bullying. However, I experienced petty workplace prejudice, malicious attitudes, injustices, and unfair treatments mostly by one woman of my own race who tried to get others to imitate her. It did not baffle me at all. My sad experiences with Sniffer were my initial personal encounter with office bullying toward me as a senior management professional in an organization. The idea that this could be a behavior that is rampant, widely tolerated, and kept under office carpets in several organizations was intriguing and frightening. I realized that each time I discussed Sniffer's bullying behavior and attitudes toward the hospital directors with my family, my daughters would exclaim words such as "No, she did not say that!" or "No, she did not do that! Oh, that is heartbreaking. What lady treats her director in such a demeaning manner? She must be power drunk" or "OMG, she is callous, but what goes around comes around. Karma will chase her down."

Looking at their young eyes and hearing their sweet little inexperienced and immature voices as each one of my daughters articulated comprehensibly frustrated remarks when I discussed Sniffer's bullying with my family, I began wondering how similar experiences could impact my girls when they become professional women and work in someone's organization. Besides, being a foreign-born and partially foreign-trained professional in America, I decided to investigate workplace bullying to grasp a more in-depth understanding of workplace cultures in America. I wondered if workplace bullying was a common phenomenon in our society. I wanted to gain an in-depth perspective to be able to share more with our daughters and prepare them for what may lie ahead of them in this respect. I had read several books on organizational culture and leadership. I had never read literature, witnessed, researched, or discussed workplace bullying.

As a healthcare professional and leader, I knew this was horrible managerial and leadership behavior. However, I too was silent about it because everyone around me was hush-hush about it at the two organizations where I witnessed leaders overtly bully followers. My silence was a result of multiple thoughts. At first, it was the idea that "these are pretty tough times. My family needs me working, and I need this job." Then it was, "No one is saying a thing about it. It must not be too bad here. Maybe I am just different. It is me. I am the new kid on the block here. Maybe it is me. I probably read too much into other individual's behaviors and attitudes." When I could no longer stomach what I was witnessing, I began praying at home and alone about a way out of what I heard and witnessed. As I prayed about it, I slowly began changing attitudes toward the environment. My thoughts then became, "I guess others are keeping their lips tight because we all need our jobs. But I can work elsewhere. I could be working elsewhere. I must move on. Many people detest change. Some are afraid of it; others are terrified by it. I often embrace it. I have lived in more than two continents, all culturally very different from one another. I am not afraid to change if need be. The values here no longer match mine. I will move on with the hope of finding my fit." With prayers and belief in my personal values, I moved on from the organizations where bullying was acceptable, tolerated, and even rewarded.

 At the time, I told Kay that when she becomes an adult and is introduced to work life in an organizational environment, she should be vigilant. She understood that a bullying boss is one that is verbally of physically aggressive with his or her staff member. I agreed with her but also told her, "Your boss does not have to be verbally or physically aggressive for you to know he/she is a bully. When she begins teasing, isolating, and encouraging others to isolate you, when she starts making you ask yourself if you are worth it, she has begun bullying you." I explained to her that "my experience with Sniffer was different from Danielle's. But it does not matter. It is called bullying. She sought to belittle me in front of other employees, isolate me, and encouraged others to do same through gossip. That is bullying behavior." I told my daughter that I could write another chapter on Sniffer the bully. However, she is used in this book to shed light on bullying that occurs behind professional walls; that is bullying bosses, bullying peers, and what workplace bullying characterizes. She is certainly not the only bullying boss in this nation or across the globe. Our daughters need to be able to recognize a bullying manager and be armed as they prepare to work as leaders, followers, or ladies in organizations in the near future.

We Are Not Alone

I realized that some incompetent leaders such as Sniffer hide behind a bully's mask. Sniffer was not just unprofessional; she was silly and devoid of serious or good leadership characteristics. I thought she lacked self-esteem, so she was out to ruin the self-esteem of some of her senior leadership team members. Bullies at workplaces, can ruin your self-esteem forever. Our daughters should be able to identify workplace bullying so that they do not quietly settle in when identifiable bullying behaviors surface at their workplaces. Concerned about Sniffer's troubling behavior at work and my desire to find answers to my questions regarding the degree of tolerance for this epidemic led me to stunning revelations about its presence in our society. Taking a deep sigh of sorrow, I muttered to myself, "Danielle, Charis and I are not alone? The employees at my former workplace were not alone?" Research supports the existence of the problem as a firmly planted one in some American workplaces.

According to Workplace Bullying Institute (WBI), workplace bullying is an abusive conduct that threatens, humiliates, intimidates, sabotages, and prevents one from getting their work done. The Institute compares the relationship between a bullying leader and his or her subordinates to that of an abusive spousal relationship where the abuser keeps his target very close and inflicts harm on them whenever he or she chooses. In a work environment, bullying mimics psychological harassment. It is repeatedly aggressive adult behavior that may also involve negative use of power over subordinates.

It may be characterized by name- calling, placing the blame for failure on a less powerful employee, therefore using them as a scapegoat. Bullying consequences for targets could include apprehension and stress, which usually impacts the commitment, motivation, and ultimately the performance of the bullied. After witnessing the effect that Sniffer's bullying had on Danielle, it is safe to say that bullying at work may also negatively affect an employee's mental health. Upon researching more on it, I realize that this is a widespread problem that should be considered serious. WBI indicates that this "remains an American Epidemic."

In 2007, WBI conducted its first survey on the issue. Three years later in 2010, it commissioned Zogby International to conduct two surveys with representative samples of all American adults. The one survey with multiple items had 4,210 respondents and the other with a single item had 2,092 respondents. The 2010 survey findings were fascinating:

35% of workers reportedly experienced bullying firsthand (an estimated 53.5 million Americans) 62% of bullies were men; 58% targets were women. Women bullies target women in 80% of cases. The majority (68%) of bullying is same-gender harassment. Bullying is 4X more prevalent than illegal harassment (2007).

Furthermore, results of a 2014 online survey of 1,000 adults in the United States conducted by Zogby Analytics for Workplace Bullying Institute reported key findings as follows:

27% of survey respondents have current or past direct experience with abusive conduct at work. 72% of the American public are aware of workplace bullying. Bosses are still the majority of bullies. 72% of employers deny, discount, encourage, rationalize or defend it, and 93% of the survey respondents support enactment of the Healthy Workplace Bill.

Where Are the Solution Starter Kits?

Bullying awareness is something that our daughters need to have, although I do not see a solution starter kit or toolbox anywhere. I believe they should be educated to do something to stop it whenever they identify it.

Bullying has endured for too long, and it is unimaginable that despite it being like the worse cancer ever to devour a large percentage of workplaces, school, sports teams, drill teams, etc., spreading very easily, affecting very young children as well as adults, and taking many young lives away from the surface of the earth, a cure for it has not been found. Bullying has no menu options for treatment of its consequences, making it quite a devastating ill.

How do our children fight the effects off at school and in their communities? What can adults do to clip its consequences on their personality, interactions, and even self-esteem at work when there appears to be no therapeutic options for treating its effects? Bullying is the one disease that researchers and the government have apparently caved in on, leaving individuals, communities, and parents to voluntarily combat it or give into it. Some of us have watched the chilling videos left behind on YouTube by young children who kill themselves because of the horrifying sequelae of the ailment. Sometimes we hear and see grueling images of it in the news. The evil persists around us and because some need to remain politically correct, we allow it to exist like a friendly thing among us. In 2007, the National Center for

Education Statistics conducted a study about bullying. It concluded that bullying was affecting several school children. It was saddening to learn that during the academic year 2006–2007, one out of three students in middle and high school reported experiencing bullying at school. One out of nine teenagers, or approximately 2.8 million high school students, said that during the academic year, they had been spat on, shoved, pushed, or tripped on at their school. What is worse is that 1.5 million high school students said they were threatened with physical harm, and 900,000 had experienced cyberbullying.

In their 2009 School Crime Supplement, the National Center for Education Statistics and Bureau of Justice Statistics reported that about 28 percent of students from 6th to 12th grade experienced bullying at school during the 2008–2009 academic year. The Centers for Disease Control and Prevention (the CDC), through its Youth Risk Behavior Surveillance System, indicated that in 2011 approximately 20 percent of US students in 9th through 12th-grade experience bullying at school.

It did not matter that ML was cyberbullied. The effect was the same as though it was done to her face-to-face. Whether it is done electronically or physically, both behaviors are similar in that they entail humiliating, victimizing, teasing, and harassing a target. Aggression is the underlying characteristic of the act.

Cyberbullying presents a challenge due to its potential anonymous presentation. So it is reserved for the cowards among the cowards who do not want to self-identify but hide behind the mask of their idiocy and hideousness while attacking anytime and as they please.

Kay gave herself the daunting task of finding ways to prevent the disease and its spread at her new high school. She was poised and calm when she joined me on the porch one balmy Tuesday afternoon during the preparation of her presentation for her summer school. "You know, Mom, I am thinking of my presentation, and I would like to share my outline with you. It is all right to discuss it with you now?" She appeared excited to join me. I ushered her into a seat next to me.

"Yes, child! Come on, let's chat. What do you have?"

She smiled "My plan is to identify the root cause of the problem. I have asked myself why some girls or students bully their peers. Why are they bullies? The reasons I can think of at the moment are that they may be bullies because they are envious, jealous, less intelligent, bigger, stronger, wicked, or mentally sick and naturally aggressive. Right, Mom?"

I agreed with her quickly. "Right, darling. Very right. They may also come from a dysfunctional family where relationships are chaotic, are suffering from undiagnosed mental issue, have low self-esteem, are on illegal drugs, or are naturally aggressive like you said and need an outlet, so they find a weak prey to torment. After you identify the root cause, then you can progress to isolating the appropriate solutions, I think. Also remember, prevention is key." I paused with an encouraging smile.

She went on, "If we could just find a solution to prevent this issue from happening that will be it. Right? Academic institutions must all develop strict policies that will truly impact the way children relate and communicate with each other at school, preventing bullying from happening among their students. And if it happens anyway, it should not matter if it happened on school campus, on the school bus, or off campus. The school must intervene using the policy. What do you think, Mom?" She appeared pensive. I understood this topic was very dear to her. She was passionate about strategizing to put up a good fight against this disease, but evidently, I had not thought about it as hard as she had. I was surprised she spoke about a policy against this.

I lost my tongue for a minute, then responded, "I think... Well, I think most schools have adopted anti-bullying policies from their specific state's legislature. I read that some states have enacted laws that provide guidelines for dealing with this at the school level. Local representatives or school boards would have that information for anyone who needs it. Surely good schools would have such a policy in place. In some states, teachers are required to take lessons on how to appropriately deal with it."

She appeared unresolved with my response. "Not all schools deal with bullying in an acceptable way. If they all did, then it won't be happening daily as it currently does. You know what I am talking about. Several parents in our nation will agree with me that some schools are not even doing a thing to prevent it from happening or protect the bullied. I also believe parents must be very involved in the fight against any kind of bullying involving their child. Whether their child is being bullied or is the bully."

She was focused on this topic wholeheartedly. Her passion for the topic was crystal clear. I completely understood the reasons for her stance against the ailment. I nodded to acknowledge her perspectives. "I agree with you, child, on all fronts. I believe that schools must create time to discuss bullying as an issue of utmost concern and hold frequent anti-bullying assemblies, have a policy to deal with it like you said, post class rules against bullying, present a no-tolerance attitude when reported as witnessed or suspected, and encourage every student to speak up against it. Principles such as these may not only dissuade bullies from committing further cruelty, they may even persuade students to stand up and intervene instead of being spectators and watching it happen. It may also likely prevent neutral students from crossing over to become bullies. I am so proud of you for working on this." I smiled.

"Additionally, whether their child is the perpetrator or the victim, parents need to play a critical role in identifying and resolving the issue. Parents must create sufficient time to listen keenly too, and speak with their children about love, respect, kindness and empathy for their peers. Sometimes everyone moves very fast because of our busy lives, but parents must find the time to spend just listening and talking with their kids about the issue. Understanding that this involves other children's feeling of safety at school or elsewhere, parents must not allow this to become a challenge for them. Parents whose daughters bully their peers should not condone with the negative attitude. They must be responsive and do everything in their power to alter their child's hostility toward her peers and her environment." I concluded to her nod.

Dance, Study, and Fight Together for Solutions

Kay then spoke about an extracurricular activity she participated in, and how some of the girls in her group of freshmen had been utter bullies, forming cliques, gossiping, excluding others, and nicknaming some. It is an esteemed activity. The group was founded with the best intent by a wonderfully thoughtful Christian lady. The founder and director of the team is dedicated to giving both the girls and communities all the best they possibly can. The team's director and some of the team parents acknowledge the bickering, name-calling, and bullying that takes place behind the scenes of the beautiful activity. It is a mildly competitive activity, but it is supposed to be a fun place for the young ladies who go there to dance and have enjoy themselves. The founder deals squarely with issues that are brought to her attention in a highly commendable manner. My questions that remain are as follows: Where is the focus of some the mothers of the young girls who call other children names and incite their peers to dislike or hate and isolate? Do they create time to talk with their children about the activities and relationships within the group? Are they aware of the group dynamics and all that behind-the-scenes drama among their daughters? Do they teach their daughters compassion, love, and respect for their peers? Have they suggested meeting with the director of the group to develop strict no exclusion and anti-bullying rules for the team? Have they discussed anti-bullying and no exclusion as a condition for participation?

Some of the ladies I personally met, spoke, and socialized with are naturally the nicest women you can ever want to meet. Their daughters' behaviors mirrored theirs. A few others were pretentious and disingenuous. On the last day of the group's meet, one of the nicest parents from the sophomore group came to bid us good-bye. "Kay is a very sweet girl. We will miss her. I hear that she is not returning to the group. It is a good decision. Quite a few girls from her group are not returning either. I heard that this freshman group is the worse they ever saw. You will not normally believe our young girls can be so vicious and ill-mannered. I wish you all the best Kay as you return to dance school instead." We thanked her and parted ways.

Despite knowing that the freshman group was struggling to eradicate some of the worse attitudes imaginable toward their peers, some of the mothers decided to behave just as poorly as their daughters.

"Parents need to understand the nature of the issues to shape their discussions with their daughters accordingly. It might be challenging for some parents to discuss bullying behaviors with their daughters, but it is such an important issue that requires the participation of all community members. The director alone, one team mom, or only a handful of team moms cannot effect the change that must happen within such a team and environment. Every parent must pitch in, and continually remind their daughters about how destructive bullying can be. So, parents and schools have a fundamental part

to play in the success of bully prevention or eradication," I found myself telling her.

Having a deep desire to **speak up against bullying** prior to this experience, Kay felt encouraged and responded promptly. "Hmm...well...Maybe parents who have been made aware that their daughter is a bully should start by reaching out to other parents in the same situation so they can form focus groups that strategize on prevention of the issue. It is also a question of morality. You see, Mom, the girls go back home and their mothers' moral values, as well as their perspectives on such issues, help mold their own attitudes as well. I think the community needs a firm focus on values to prevent what I witnessed on the team from happening on other sport teams, schools, dance groups, cheer and drill teams, camps, and other places. Girls can be cruel, but the adults in their lives have to help teach them that cruelty is unacceptable."

I couldn't agree more with her. *"Bullying should not be considered an individual's issue. It is a societal problem that warrants individuals coming together to deal with it. Cooperation between school, clubs, teams, and home is crucial to prevent or stop the issue."*

I pursued, "Consequences of this ailment are far too destructive and damning for parents to not get actively involved to prevent or stop it. A few months ago, I read a report that insisted that 'students who experience bullying are more likely to dodge school, suffer anxiety, and panic disorder and nurse suicidal thoughts. Many children have died as a consequence of bullying, so the agreement among us should be that everyone, including parents and school administrators, coaches, group and team leaders, mentors and tutors, must be responsible for preventing and arresting it."

I took a deep breath and continued after a sip of ice-cold water, "Girls and other students who are passionate like you are about ceasing this thorn should team up, join hands, and ignite the fight against it at the level of their school communities first. They should speak to their school counselors, teachers, principal, or the dean of students about their school's anti-bullying policy. Sport and drill teams should have and communicate the existence of such a policy within their teams. This is a topic that from my standpoint, students must discuss with their peers from across all educational background to understand what each school is doing to combat the issue. Schools and workplaces should have anti-bullying policies and follow them diligently after investigation confirms evidence of bullying among their students."

As I concluded my narrative, I looked at Kay, who was sitting there, listening with rapt attention. She was determined to fight the ill by every means possible, but she knew she did not have sufficient personal experience to discuss the matter. However, she would use research to write her discussion points and essay and then disseminate great information at her new high school. She asserted, "The research I have done has sufficient information to enlighten my peers and call attention to this issue at school."

Fighting It as a Village

It appears to me that oftentimes when our daughters are bullied, some of them do not confidently expose their experiences with the problem. I have wondered why this is so, and attempted to find answers to the question. Each bully victim would decide for herself if to expose her perpetrators and the degree of detail to share with their parents, friends, and well-wishers. My children always provide me details of their experiences, good or bad. Girls who have bullied their peers, and those with bullying tendencies need to come out of their shabby closets, confess, ask for forgiveness, and begin working toward healing those who have been impacted by the misfortune of bullying. However, those who have suffered the consequences of bullying are better placed to lead a team of girls fighting bullying and bullies because of their experience as victims of the ill.

As we now understand, bullying could be defined from a physical and psychological standpoint per the 2001 Journal of the American Medical Association. The definition of relational bullying, which is part of psychological bullying, is reiterated as being defined as bullying that occurs "when an individual is made to feel left out, ignoring or not talking to them and encouraging others to do same." I knew it was socially awkward to leave someone out or make them feel left out. It was eye opening and enlightening to understand that it was classified as relational bullying, including when "others are encouraged to do same." I realized I was not the only one who would learn this as I communicated with young ladies and other parents about some adolescents being or feeling left out among peer groups.

Discussing the topic in the recent summer months with a nice lady I am acquainted with, her response minimized the concern completely of feeling left out by a group of friends but instead she stated, "Oh, they will all be together again when school resumes," without second thought. Believing she is a sweet lady, I knew she was honestly ignorant of potential consequences of what was happening among a group of young ladies we interacted with, but she certainly did not mean harm. I thought to myself, she too does not understand, after her quick dismissive response to a young lady's expressed feeling of being left out. True friends need to fully comprehend these definitions and be armed with knowledge to make well-informed decisions, and to understand the power of collaboration which is symbolic of "its takes a village" to do something big such as to combat and eradicate a social ill such as bullying.

Fighting it as a village certainly has better a probability to succeed than going it alone or as an individual. I that bullying is like a multidrug-resistant microorganism, tough to eradicate due to its potential to resist several antibiotic therapies, but not impossible to eradicate with the right selection and dose of therapy. So too, bullying has for a long time resisted many good measures to combat it. Similarly to superbugs, bullying requires more powerful interventions, and that would be possible if schools, communities, teachers, coaches, parents of bullies or "mean girls," and parents of bullied victims work as a united front to fight off this enduring ill that has unfortunately claimed many young lives. Both the bullied and bullies need help from such a group fighting as a village against it.

Angel's mom shared with me how quite surprised she was when toward the last year of middle school and the summer leading up to that academic year, her daughter's supposedly friend group knowingly or unknowingly began ostracizing her from the group. She intended speaking with the women whose children were involved about what she was hearing from her daughter about the group, and she cried, "I postponed bringing them together to discuss it because I was either too busy or considered the woman whose daughter was the initial bully too fragile to discuss another heart-wrenching situation. It all happened fast, but I had a great strategy to execute. Angel openly communicated her fears with me on each occasion that she queried what she was noticing. Trusting of some of the girls' mothers, whom I had come to know to a certain extent, I responded with an emphatic, "No, you are thinking this too seriously. It cannot be." She confirmed that she was confident of the group's cohesiveness after one of the mothers insisted the girls' moms were trustworthy. What do you do in such a situation when you know a causal friend is traversing challenges? Don't you just give her a break? That is precisely what I did until things got out of hands and Angel was embarrassed and ostracized by the group of girls to the point she had to walk away from them."

Curious about my friend's regrets of not involving the village sooner to deal with the issue she was communicating, I inquired, "So what did the girls do? Did you involve all the right parties to strategize and resolve the issue?"

She stared at me. "It is a long story. You know Angel is observant and foresighted. Deala, one of the girls, began treating her with utter meanness. While at this young girl's house, all the girls served themselves cookies. Angel, being who she is, politely asked if she may have a cookie. Guess what Deala's response was?" I looked at her as if to say the response is like a slam dunk, then I said, "Yes, of course, help yourself to it just like everyone else is doing."

My friend Maria went, "Oh dear, that is too much. Deala told Angel, 'No. You do not get to take a cookie like everyone else. Don't touch the cookie!'"

Stupefied, I looked at her in complete disbelief and responded, "No, you are just kidding. Deala did not say that to Angel."

"You will sink in your chair when I tell you the several other disheartening things she did and said to Angel, including asking her to get out of a seat for another girl to sit down while at her house. She told Angel, 'You get out of that chair now. Get up for Awde to sit down—now." Maria then recounted the other humiliating incidents that Deala put Angel through and then looked straight at me and asked, "What do you do with that kind of information?"

I paused in complete shock. I shut me eyes very tightly and slowly shook my head from left to right as if I was trying to get something out of my eyes, then opened my eyes widely and asked Maria, "You mean Deala did and said all these things to Angel? Have you spoken to Deala's mother about these? What did she say, or how did she react? Did the other girls in the group witness these incidents? Why did she continue going to Deala's house after the first incident?" I was full of questions.

Maria looked at me and said, "These all took place on two occasions. In addition to my empathy for the challenges the family was experiencing at that time, Angel did not want me to speak with Deala's mother because she thought it would cause a group problem for her because once, she got me involved in a situation with another girl in the group; and although we never discussed the underlying issue between our daughters, the mom and I got them to unite and socialize, but things degenerated to being just cold between them after a while.

She stated to me that she wouldn't allow Deala's bullying tendencies to push her out of the group. But she was smelling a rat. At one point, the girls created a new chat group and excluded her from it. They all used it, but none of them wondered why Angel was not in it. And none requested that they add her to it as a group member. She said she wanted to stay with them, but she articulated serious concerns about the group dynamic and compatibility with her."

She smiled and added after a clearing her throat, "I told her she wouldn't go to Deala's house anymore until I spoke with the mother. And she's never been back there since. But Deala's bullying was ultimately too tasty for her when over lunch one day at school, Deala and Arrena began making fun of a certain ethnic group of people, their religion, and their choir, requesting that Angel imitate the choir members because she would do a great job at it and telling her to dress like those choir members for Halloween and lead a crew of sorts on Halloween night. That one got me into action. As patient and purposeful as always, I waited for the right place and time to speak with Deala's mother about the accrued concerns."

Maria paused for a few seconds and then pursued, "Understanding that the group of girls were witnesses to these incidents but failed to intervene in any way, or even identify it as bullying or discuss it with their parents, I knew talking with the parents about these issues had become critical. However, first I went to their school to discuss the ethnic and choir incident with the vice principal of the school."

My eyes were as big as an apple by this time as I listened to each of Maria's shocking account of Deala's bullying of a so-called friend at thirteen. I impatiently inquired, "What did the parents, Deala's mom, or the school say or do?"

Maria appeared sad as she spoke, but there was a tone of happiness in her voice that made me listen more attentively. She is a very sharp lady and very deliberate in her words and actions. "The vice principal was very attentive to Angel's concerns about the victimization and relational bullying. A dedicated Catholic, an artful administrator, and a great educator, she was prompt in handling the issue. She involved the school principal, and they both worked at making sure the girls understood they were all responsible and could do better when they witness bullying, intimidation, victimization, and extreme meanness. I highly commend the school's vice principal and principal in dealing with the concern."

I anxiously asked, "And Deala's mom and the other women, what did they say when you spoke with them?"

"This is a case where I had a strategy and anticipated we would team up as one voice to enlighten our daughters about bullying, peer victimization, intimidation and truly fight it as good Catholic women of the same school and church community whose daughters were friends. I anticipated we would discuss and collaborate to make sure our daughters know they can speak up, tell their parents if or when they witness sheer and utter meanness in the community even if they do not understand it is bullying and even when the meanness is committed by a close friend. It started off very well with Deala's mom.

Known at school for the wrong reasons, Deala created an early reputation for herself as a cyberbully. She was once mandated by the school to bring down her Instagram, so while her mom appeared stunned at what she learned, she was also honest with herself and expressed her deep regrets and offered apologies to me for her daughter's treatment of Angel. She wondered why I did not communicate with her sooner, and I explained my reasons. She worried that everybody was now aware of how bad her daughter is. I assured her I had only spoken with the vice principal and one of the other women whom I trust about the concerns. I told her that in such instances, we could elect to do one of two things with the information we have regarding our daughters: we deepen their rift further by fighting or arguing or we educate them, ask for forgiveness, make peace, and move on. I let her know my family and I belong on the side of peace, problem resolution, and forgiveness. She was amazed at how naturally peaceful I was about it, encouraging her to create more time to talk with Deala to understand why she so humiliated Angel. She confirmed that Deala had behaved like a very mean girl and outlined the consequences already in place because of reports by the school principal and vice principal regarding the bullying involving the ethnic group's choir. I let her know how each girl is continually isolating Angel whether intentionally or unintentionally, and that I had made the school administrators aware of the overt bullying of Angel by Deala and Arrera."

Maria sipped her sweet ice tea, took a deep breath, and then softly continued, "Later that night, she put Deala on the phone and had her apologize to Angel and then to me as well. The young girl sounded sincere on the phone and sobbed as she spoke with me. I highly commended Deala's mother for her initial handling of the issue. We planned to take the girls out to dine and chat. Then suddenly something went wrong. She ceased communicating with me the week after our discussion and plans.

Two other girls apologized as well after an investigation by the school principal and vice principal and discussions with the group of girls. Three girls in total apologized to Angel. The two women I expected would do the right thing did not fail me, and for that I commend them. But that is where it ended.

I would have liked for us to use these incidents to teach our daughters several lessons about the ill. It is lost opportunity to bond as a group and educate our daughters. Angel has forgiven Deala, Arrera, and the group, and we have moved on from there. Angel found solace with another group of girls, and she is enjoying her last year at the school with those peers. She is more in tune with some of the girls in this group. You know Angel is a more serious and less playful girl, an introvert until she knows you better, and very task- oriented, so she does not make friends like a talker or charmer would. She is poised, a little lady. We say she is thirteen going on fifty, very resilient and resolute. She is a very sweet girl. After the investigation and reports of the incidents, the vice principal said she is an amazing, wonderfully well-brought-up girl. And said I could be proud of how I raised her. The vice principal informed me after the school concluded its investigation that her peers all confirmed that the accusation of Deala was nothing but the truth."

I was bewildered and could only exclaim, "Wow! Wow! Okay, this is wild. So, this is where fighting it as a village would have been amazingly accomplished. It is in such situations that mothers, especially if they are friends, casual or close, bring their daughters to the place of understanding the ills of peer victimization, intimidation, and bullying in all its shades and definitions and help them join as a village to contribute their voices against it versus being admirers and tongueless spectators of the ill. You may not understand why Deala's mother suddenly changed course, but she sure listened to wrong advice, and that is her loss. Her daughter is a bully and could be a huge part in finding solutions to prevent this in her community, school, or another friend group in the future.

I commend you for being very cautious, resolute, and passionate about teaching our daughters to distinguish themselves in a world where some elect to entertain and encourage rat races, cat fights, gossips, Hunger Games–like situations and general moral malaise. Your patience in dealing with Deala, putting empathy for her mother before your own daughter's concerns, is hard to find. Your gentility in dealing with the situation, asking a trusted person for assistance on how to subtly speak with Deala's mom instead of storming her with annoyance on the entire situation, is admirable!"

Maria was quiet. She is a highly doting mother and loves Angel very much. The situation with the women bothered her because she had trusted some of them, including Deala's mom. She insisted, "I share this with you because Angel wants this shared as part of her journey. She wants this story to be indelible. Deala's mother wondered if other people knew how badly Deala had behaved toward Angel and appeared to worry about her daughter's reputation in the community. What do you think about that?"

Lots of thoughts crossed my mind during this conversation. Maria is a genuinely nice lady. I wanted her to understand some of the thoughts that ran through my head as we talked. I imparted an amazing sermon that was preached by a priest one Sunday, but I also shared the priest's story leading up to his sermon.

"Maria, honesty does not hide itself behind a golden mask. It faces its own truth and by so doing, empowers others. One Sunday after Easter, I attended mass at St. Francis of Assisi. I do not know the priests at this church because I attend mass there infrequently, but I enjoyed that particular service maximally. The priest told a story of a young school boy from a great home with a great life. The boy thought he could be over everyone and joined a bad group of students. The boy bullied others, and nothing was ever said of it. On one occasion, he bullied another boy, and that got to the school principal. His parents were called into the school and received the investigation results. Birthday celebrations were highly significant in this family, and the young man's birthday was approaching.

The parents decided to take away the single most important thing he was looking forward to as retribution for what he had done. His parents seriously reprimanded him and had him apologize to the boy he bullied and his family. His birthday party was cancelled. He ended the story by saying, 'This is my story. That boy was me. I was the bully. But I began changing that day and never bullied another child after that." He explained how he became part of the solution to stop bullying. He is a priest and tells his own story without worrying about what his congregation would think, if people will pass judgment on him. Why is this woman more interested in hiding the truth about her daughter's bullying than being honest about it, confronting her demons and being part of the solution? The priest told his own story to build and empower others. He talked of a fresh start, rebirth, forgiveness, and working together as a village to prevent the ills of society. I am giving an abbreviated version of his sermon and his story to the congregation that day, but his preaching was moving. Angel, who was undignified and felt the humiliation of being told to give up her seat to a peer, was refused a cookie, was denied access to petting a cat while others could right in front of her, and so on is willing to work with Deala, but I think the mother felt embarrassed of herself and cut communication with you. Or she was wrongly advised to do so and lacks the personality to independently do the right thing. She should not shy away from the truth. Instead, she should encourage reconciliation and peace. Her choices and decisions made during this period are serving as the sample for her parental guidance for Deala.

It is impossible to hide in one's shadow. Deala is a bully and could be instrumental in preventing peer victimization and bullying because she understands the forces behind the ill. She needs to understand the importance of collective power to fight bullying and stop worrying about people knowing how mean her daughter is and begin thinking of ways to help Deala be a better person like the priest. Hiding behind a golden mask does not help forever. The mask has already fallen off because Deala is known at her school for the wrong reasons and did cyberbullying before?" Maria smiled. "Your thoughts are beautiful. You learn from everything. That priest's story is very moving.

Angel has prayed for Deala and the group. She has forgiven all of them and has asked the Lord to forgive Deala's deeds and the rest of them."

"Often the bullied are too embarrassed to open up, and this is part of the reason some bullies get away with it. Fighting it together with past victims and even perpetrators would be the ideal. I wish girls on the drill team, and even the likes of Deala and Arrera, would join my endeavor. This is a fight I want to undertake for the victims, my friends, my peers, my sister, and the so many families who have lost children to bullies. Mom, this is serious. So when I present it to my class, it will open up a discussion, and maybe from there, we would begin building the village force to fight it. I will also like to speak with Angel about this." Kay who was part of our conversation stated with a firm tone of voice.

When Maria spoke with me about Angel's experiences with the group, I was certain this is not a fight you undertake without having experienced the malignancy of the cancer. Her expression and words assured me it would be amazing for her daughter to collaborate with other victims of this cruelty to establish a powerful campaign as a village to fight for the eradication of this evil. Fighting bullying and bullies will take a village of past victims to come forth and speak against it. Past victims do not necessarily need to reveal every detail of their experience if they do not want to, but they can be strong contributors and participants in a good cause to combat bullying.

"Academic institutions should have an anti-bullying policy. Our daughters, who attend schools without a policy in place, can also join forces to affect change by speaking to a trusted teacher, school administrative leader, or even the school board. Teachers have a professional responsibility to help shape the environment in which children learn and grow, so if you can, trust your teacher and ask her for help in creating a safe school environment devoid of bullying. There are often roadblocks when one tries to build a fortress against evil or when putting up a good fight against evil, but don't give up if you meet obstacles on your way. Instead, recruit more peers to join the fight and keep the discussion going until your school puts a policy in place. Think of potential solutions to the problem in an institution, such as an antibullying committee, a ban on hate speech, petition signing against campus bullying, peer mediation task force," I concluded.

She sighed deeply and sipped cold water. We both agreed that we had engaged each other in a very good conversation. She ignited a discussion that left me thinking to myself. *The world is replete with challenges. Our daughters encounter various types of challenges in their young lives daily. One of the biggest challenges they currently face is probably bullying.*

I turned to her and said, "You are admirable and a healthy girl. From what I have learned, healthy people cultivate a sense of resolve to conquer challenges, defend themselves, seek justice, and even defend the weak and defenseless. If or when you are confronted by the demon of bullying, refuse to stand by and watch it devour you or a peer. Instead, fight to conquer it by standing up to intervene and defend against it. Then, we discussed the following additional strategies to fight off and defeat bullies:

1. Go beyond the golden rule of treating people the way you would like to be treated and imbibe the platinum rule of "treating people the way they want you to treat them." In summation, instead of doing unto others as you would like them do unto you, begin treating others as they would like you to treat them. Most individuals appreciate love and respect from others, so that is what you give them. If you maintain self-respect and show love and respect for others, it is very likely that people will reciprocate by giving you back love and respect. The likelihood that you will be targeted for bullying will be less than minute, or at least minimized. But if you are targeted, do not bite your tongue about it. Speak up about and against it!
2. Know and trust your gut. When you identify an abnormal situation where you sense that you are being demeaned or that someone is purposefully embarrassing you in any way, shape, or form, you are being bullied. Do not think twice; react to it immediately by responding calmly, firmly, and appropriately. Tell the person you are not someone that is easily affected by poor attitudes, but you will not be spoken to or treated like that. Period. Do not condone it if you are sure this is it. Set a clear tone right there and then and ask that it not continue because it is unwelcomed. Always remember that you must not be called names or shoved, for it to be defined as bullying. Understand the complexities of what it is and respond to it in a timely manner.
3. Make your limits clear. Do not wave when you identify it. Call it as it is and call out the perpetrators on their act. By so doing, you set clear rules and guidelines for yourself and your peers. You are helping to identify bullies and calling them out to stop the ill.

4. Know that you do not keep this a secret once identified. Tell your mom and dad, your sister, or the closest relative, a trusted friend. This is not something to hide in a closet. Tell a neighbor whom you trust will help you fight it and do not be afraid to seek justice either for yourself or a peer. In a democratic society, such as the one we live in, it is only fair that justice be served for such a societal mal. Bullies are individuals who suffer a certain degree of low self-esteem and insecurity, yet they try to pride themselves as the wolf or the tiger, or maybe the fox, the fiery one whom others should not mess with. Do not be afraid. Let them know there is justice and that they cannot mess with that.

"Most people depend upon communities where individuals are dependable and trustworthy. Build your personal ability to demonstrate your dependability and trustworthiness to peers by doing the right thing to stand up against it. Theodore Roosevelt said, 'In a moment of decision, the best thing you can do is the right thing. The next best thing is the wrong thing and the worst thing you can do is nothing.'"

"You must not be a standby kid or individual who does nothing when something could have been done to either protect yourself or a peer. Make the decision to stand upright and fight for a good cause. It is not always easy to combat an ill. You may face challenges and obstacles for being the one who wants to stand up for the weak. Do not let any obstacles deter you when your gut tells you that you are doing the right thing. My mentor often told me when I was seriously challenged as a doctoral student that "to some, an obstacle is an excuse to quit. But to others it is an opportunity to grow stronger. Don't give up! Yes, don't give up!" Those brief words were powerful and inspirational. Don't give up and allow a bully to think of him or herself as a winner, the fox or fierce. Fight for what is right!"

"I admire you for selecting this topic and for discussing it so intensely with me, kid. You are a great girl, you have worked hard at it, and your presentation will be amazing. Lilly and others will be proud of you." She looked serious. "Thank you, Mommy. I just want to give a little contribution to the fight. Mine might be just a drop in the ocean, but I want to do something about it. This ill is too real. I appreciate your input. I will remember everything we discussed."

She looked up in the sky and exclaimed, "What a world, what a life, what a gorgeous day, Mom!" As she sat there looking at the lovely blue, sunny sky and sipping her water, I turned on her favorite playlist on my phone. She smiled and began humming a song and nodding her head to the rhythm of the music as she took my phone and danced her way back into the house. I just sat there and thought, what a great conversation we just had!

If you are a parent of a bullying daughter, encourage her to reflect upon the consequences of her behavior on other children, her peers, the community, her reputation, and your family's reputation and to assume responsibility for her actions. If you are a young girl in high school or university, answer these questions for yourself: Have you ever given or called a peer names to ridicule her? Made fun of her for whatever reason? Knowingly lied about her or encourage bad rumors about her? Shoved or push her? Encouraged others to isolate her? Why did you do these things, or why are you doing it? Whatever your reasons are for doing any of these, do you think they are worth it? Can you look at yourself in the mirror and be proud you did something great or simply nice? Shut your eyes and place yourself in her shoes for a second and imagine how you will feel if another peer treated you in the same way. Let this be a thing of the past for you. Tell yourself it is time to quit being a bully, the disrespectful, lousy, and miserable

Section 3: Bullying, Intimidation, and Peer Victimization

person that you have been to your peers. It is not too late to stop it today, right now, and become a nicer, more responsible, respectful, loving, considerate, and kinder peer.

Do it for yourself, your environment, community, family, and friends. There must be a relief to be a nicer peer than a monster individual who tries to scare or belittle others. If you are weak and unable to control yourself, your anger or your dislike, jealousy or hatred for your targeted peers, try uttering a simple prayer asking the good Lord to help cast away the spirit of bullying from you. Start talking to God about it and ask for his help to combat the mal. You can do so. Don't be afraid. Just open your heart and your mouth and there! Bam! You will see and hear yourself casting out loud the bad and unwanted spirit that controls bullying. You see, with God all things are possible. Go for it! I bet you the wish of your heart to discontinue bullying your peers will disappear completely if you just ask that God help cleanse you of it. Try it. Start now. As you seek God to pull you away from being a bully, I pray for the peace and love of God to abide with you.

As you read *Compass*, if you have experienced attacks by bullies, understand that the problem is not you. Bullies did not, have not, or are not attacking you because you have done something inappropriate or offensive. They are not targeting you because you are an unpleasant individual. My personal impression is that you do not have any issues that should make anyone treat you unfairly and differently from other students or colleagues in your institution. The issues lie within the bully herself. Her personal insufficiencies, unhappiness, and desire to obtain something she lacks or does not have is truly what infuses the heinous thoughts that drive her into the obscure behavior. If you are a leader who customarily bullies your subordinates and staff, I am asking you today to take some time, pause for a while, and seriously introspect. Dedicate some time to ask yourself pertinent questions about your personal and professional qualities and capabilities.

Additionally, take time to read about modern leadership concepts to determine the kind of organizational leadership styles you would like to practice or are already practicing. If you are unsure, read further and select the leadership patterns you want to practice and immerse yourself in learning how to lead a team or group without making them feel they know less than you or feel like they do not know enough of what they are employed to do. Seek therapy and renew your skills because you really need to. Most importantly, quit attacking your employees or colleagues because you are incompetent, childish, naturally unprofessional, unethical, or need more education. Instead, seek help for your personal enhancement, and learn to appreciate the people who work with you in a professional and collegial manner.

Sowing Seeds

As the parent and guide in my daughters' lives, I consider myself a front-liner in their moral education. Upright moral values are one of the most fundamental guiding principles in our lives as humans although we have all witnessed or experienced human weakness and moral failures in our families, communities, and even in our nation. Sometimes it feels to me like there is an overriding culture of immoral attitudes in contemporary society than there was in my parents' days. Besides, generational differences are making matters worse. Bearing these in my mind, I decided to present moral integrity as a principle for guiding teenage girls into adulthood. **Moral Integrity (MI)** is being consistently honest and truthful, and it entails having ethical core values and principles. It is the guide to making morally responsible decisions, and it is what assists us in behaving in a morally correct manner. As individuals, most humans aspire to be morally upright, but for whatever reasons, we sometimes fail to do the right thing. Examples of moral indiscretions and failures abound in our respective communities. As a Catholic, I wondered for several years with unanswered questions within me regarding child and sexual abuse in churches around the world by church leaders. This is an example of moral failure that I have not been able to imagine why it happened because of the milieu in which this moral lapse occurred. Nevertheless, this moral blunder is real and reminds all of us that "the flesh is weak although the spirit is willing," per biblical lessons. Because the level to which each mortal practices moral uprightness is different, it has become essential for mothers to not only discuss the importance of moral values with their daughters but to also lead objective moral lives, showing their girls that they can walk the walk and talk the talk. It is important for our teens to know that having moral integrity is a source of self-confidence because it elevates your self-esteem as someone who is being exactly who they are, with upright morals and an example to others.

Teaching our daughters to uphold good morals should begin at an early age and within the family because it is often within the family circle that early learning begins. However, some schools and some teachers, such as Kay's high school theology instructor, do a superb job with moral education. Listening to Kay explain the lessons she teaches the girls often brings me joy and appreciation to know that an amazing moral agent is preparing my adolescent daughter for her role as a moral steward in the society.

My parental obligation includes providing both of my girls not only quality academic education, but also the ability to have, and demonstrate acceptable moral values. I have held multiple conversations with both girls regarding their attitudes and behaviors with their peers, their friends, and their communities in general. Kay and I have had long conversations regarding values.

To maker her think critically , I asked her several questions regarding her core as an individual and the kind of moral lady she aspires to be considering her theology instructor's teachings, and her family values. We discussed moral values as a social construct from a host of perspectives. She had several excellent questions emanating from her theology lectures, so she was seeking my input and further depth on the discussions from school. For some of the questions, I asked her. "What was your response?" I x-rayed her perspectives, and we further discussed her questions and the responses in detail. I also gave her scenarios, and asked her what she would do if confronted with such situations.

Our discussion range from what to do if you find somebody's missing bag of money, postal package at Christmas, to witnessing or hearing about child abuse, how to dress as a reasonable and morally responsible young lady, how to treat, interact, and relate to other people, and how to effectively resolve a problem. We have all heard in the news about "lost but found missing" bags of money, and we sometimes receive a neighbor's postal package at our home. So, this discussion was a way for me to gauge her inner person's natural reaction in such situations.

At a very young age children's cognitive abilities provide them a good foundation on which to start sowing seeds for understanding and integrating moral values as part of their culture and fiber. I understand that some girls may grow up in unstable and troubled environments, and that environmental awareness may have an impact on moral attitudes. This does not mean that they cannot learn to have moral integrity. Everything is possible if one sets out to accomplish it with determination. A lovely lady who worked with us as our daughters' nanny told us many stories about her life. Our family liked her very much. As a matter of principle, we discuss moral values and use of language prior to hiring anyone who kept her daughters. A story she told us in response to questions related to moral values will forever be a magnificent and awesome example. She explained to us how dangerously and recklessly her mother habitually drove, even with her children in the car. She told us that for years, she drove her employers' children to and from their homes to a park or playground. She said she has never in her life of over forty years and more than twenty as a legal driver exceeded the prescribed speed limit of a zone. She explained to us that not only did her mother drive recklessly, she also often used profanities when she was not happy with the traffic situations on the roads. According to her, she frequently employed avoidable colorful language like d——, f——, or sh—— unnecessarily.

Life was not rosy for her family. They were two kids growing up with a single mother who worked as a babysitter and house help for a very nice and kind, highly responsible, and respectable family of four. It was the holiday period, and her mother was preparing the children for an evening occasion that the family was set to attend. The youngest child was ready but accidentally messed up herself while the babysitter was tending to one of the other children. When she realized the kid's mess, the woman cursed and cursed again, while she was tending to the little girl. The kid asked her if she was cross with her for messing up herself, but the sitter had entered her cursing mode and replied, "Sh——t, no, you have done nothing wrong. D—— it! Come on, I'll make you look clean and beautiful again."

The kid began crying and said to the sitter, "You just called me sh——t. You have just called me sh——t."

The kid was inconsolable because she liked the sitter and believed the sitter was cursing her. The oldest kid called their mother on the phone and reported the situation. The kids appraised their parents of the incident when they got home. The sitter accepted she was wrong to speak those words by the kids. Because this was the third report of the sitter's colorful use of language by their kids, she was disinvited from their home that night for her continuous lapse in judgment and loose tongue full of curse words by the kids. The children's nanny said her mother returned home and expelled all the curse words she had in her, cried, and promised to help herself resist using profanities. "I noticed my mom was making efforts to purify her tongue. She had lost her job and our lifeline because of her vile tongue. She loved that family, and they were very kind to her. The lesson was a harsh one because she was at home for some time before she found a family to work for. She began telling me and my brother to never curse because it could bring us down. She learned a lesson from that. After losing her job, we were hungry some days. It was harsh for us. I try not to use curse words, ma'am. I am a mature woman. I will not start now. I just keep my lips tight instead of cursing. If I have to curse, it will not be in front of your kids or even where they could hear me, I promise."

I looked her straight in the eyes and smiled. "That is a promise to keep. You just made a promise, and we are on the same side. You see, we sow seeds in very many ways, forms, and at very different times in our lives. I began sowing mine with these two girls the day each one of them was born. I want to keep the seeds healthy in every way, possible. We do not curse in our family. Thank you for the story and the promise." Her story was moving. She never broke her promise while working for us. Kay and Court remember her as the best nanny they had growing up. She did not sow any unwanted seeds in our family.

I share this because I have experienced situations and discussed with women who disregard the presence of their kids when they speak and act, especially in times of crisis. While exiting my work premises one evening in December 2004, I drove poorly. I wrongly calculated the distance of an approaching car, so I entered the road thinking it was very far away from me. The vehicle appeared behind me with a loud, unceasing sound of the horn. As soon as I realized my error, I waved and said sorry to the driver behind me. I looked in the mirror and saw the driver mouthing words angrily with hands in the air. A female with long brown hair was behind the wheel of the vehicle. The driver then quickly passed me and then stopped at the light ahead of us and exited her car. She approached me, screaming profanities at me. I placed my two hands together and said through my car window, "I am sorry, ma'am." She hit my window glass and returned to her vehicle still yelling. As soon as she locked the door of her car, two small heads raised themselves and looked at me through the rear window. The kids made faces at me and stuck their tongues out at me.

Several questions ran in my head as my mind revisited the scene at the stoplight. I changed my lane when I could and exited to the main supermarket. This was a tiny part of a small European city, and so I was not scared at all. The place and its inhabitants have always been very peaceful. Rather, I was appalled at the woman's attitude because even after I repeatedly said I was sorry, she continued ranting. While in the grocery store, a.k.a. supermarket there, who appeared beside me with two children— a little boy and a little girl? The woman from the traffic light incident. She looked at me and said, "You are the one who wanted to hit me by the school, right?" I responded, "Sorry, ma'am. Glad we did not have an accident." And I began to walk away. The boy who appeared to be six or seven years old said, "Stupid driver this one," and the sister, who appeared eight or nine years old, took over with, "B—— driver, crazy driver, crazy woman! Mommy, beat her up now! Beat her up, Mommy, now. You promised to beat the crazy, stupid woman!" It was evident to me that these kids already had some fast- growing sour seeds sowed in them. Evidently, their mother's values were being sowed as rotten seeds on very fertile and fresh soil – her children.

Ladies, our children are very smart and can learn quickly and very early in life from our words and actions. Although moral reasoning is one of those developmental abilities that come later, it starts developing as we discuss or exhibit personal or family values and as societal norms become inscribed in the brains of our kids. It is important to recognize it when you see evidence of emotional maturity in your daughters and begin inculcating acceptable moral values in what you do and say then. Notwithstanding, conversations with our children about appropriate behaviors, words, and actions can begin earlier by placing all the cards on the table regarding what to say, how to appropriately articulate it, and what to do in certain situations without cursing or beating up another person, a stranger or not, for whatever reason. Those healthy seeds, sowed early, can only be very beneficial to our children and our society. Education about what is good and what is bad behavior or what is socially acceptable and frowned upon behavior is often better to begin earlier rather than later in life. As a mom, I learned that what I do and say when my daughters are in the car, when I am on phone, when chatting with our friends, and what our kids hear us say influence their attitudes toward others and toward us. Curse, and they will also curse. Give the finger to a reckless driver or an unsafe user of the road, and they will believe that is the right thing to do. Swear, and you have told them it is okay to swear. Promise to beat up someone, and they will glorify that as the best action to take. As our daughters grow and evolve by us, we are the example for them. They will follow our footprints and emulate us because they will forever be influenced directly or indirectly by environmental and social factors in their young world.

We are in their immediate environment; therefore, the behaviors we exhibit has a powerful influence on them. Those are the seeds we are sowing not only for them, but for the larger society in general. Our dreams for a better world for our children may be smashed if our seeds are rotten even before we begin tilling the soil to sow them, and/or if we sow bad seeds.

In this section we discussed bullying with a plethora of examples ranging from school kids who consider each other as "friends," to older adult professionals in a board room. We discussed examples of bullying beginning the very tender age of four, and experienced an amazing mom who asserted that bullying was not acceptable in her family. In all of this, we highlighted anti-bullying principles such as (1) **speak up against bullying** when witnessed and (2) **social media utilization checks and balances** for teens to ensure their appropriate use and eliminate a potential miss of cyber-bullying events. Finally, we discussed sowing seeds underscoring the principle of (3) **moral integrity** as a foundation for guiding our teen girls into being the adults that we and the larger society would want to have in their time.

SECTION 4

FAITH JOURNEY

Faith

A typical Catholic, I grew up attending mass frequently. From Advent through Christmas, Lent, Easter, and other ordinary periods of the year during which Catholics essentially go to church, there was no shortage of reasons to attend mass daily. My best teacher at my Catholic elementary school was Sister Louisa, the nun who taught my class. She was fond of asking me questions about "our Way to God" even when class was over.

She smiled at every student, and on Fridays at the end of the school day, she'd remind each of her pupils, each one of us, to go to confession/reconciliation on Saturday and to attend mass on Sunday. Then there was our every-Sunday priest, Father Francis, a tall, slim, blond, and mid-aged priest. He wore glasses all the time. Even when we visited him at the Parish house, he always had those glasses on. I do not remember his sermons. However, at the time it appeared to me he always ended a sermon with "Let us pray." He was at mass every Sunday even when we had visiting priests. Father Polycarp, my uncle who is a priest, also celebrated mass. I remember the events leading to his ordination. My dad explained to me that his younger brother was going to take orders and become a man of God—a priest. I asked him what that meant, and he explained, "Your uncle has been chosen by God to be His disciple on earth and preach the Word to His people." My parents are staunch Catholics, church-going, Bible-reading, very prayerful people. Remember? They fervently observed the Sabbath, all things being equal, so I went to mass every Sunday and more. Our family was both Christian and prominent. Dad contributed huge sums of money to help build our city's church that holds over three hundred people, met Pope John Paul II, hosted by invitation-only faith dinners at our family house, dad built a Catholic school for his hometown, and the list of his philanthropy is endless.

Secretly, as a very young girl, I often asked myself, "What is all the fuss about prayers and church and God?" My early lessons about God is that he was everywhere, he was always watching and was always present, listening to the things I said and hearing the things I said, but I couldn't see Him. I thought of God as my Father in heaven, but I was curious. It was wondrous to me because I couldn't see Him, but I had to speak to Him several times a day: in the morning when I woke up, at lunch before my meal (grace before meals), at the end of the school day, and before bedtime at night. I thought within me, *'This is too much praying.'* I just said the grace before meals and sometimes after eating, I need to say a grace after meals? I can't see God. I am not sure what to do in order to see Him.

I heard Mom pray for her children, her sisters and brothers, our parish, the priests, the bishops, the pope, her marriage, for peace, the sick, her neighbors, family friends, and even the souls of the dead whom she said were the "faithful departed." When Grandma was ill, she would ask God to restore her health. It appeared God often answered Mom's prayers. At my young age, I did not fully understand who God was, what knowing God and leading a good Christian life really entailed. My mom and sister Louisa are the two women from whom I learned more about relationships with God and understanding Him better. Sister

Louisa, a nun, was an amazing woman of God whom I visited at the convent on some weekends. When I wondered about God to Sister Louisa, she would often say, *"Child, blessed are those who have not seen and yet have come to believe."* (John 20:29, NABRE). Then she would pray to the Lord Jesus to make me believe with all my strength and to obey His commands.

Back in my family, I heard my mother pray for everything, even the littlest things. Her voice was always tender no matter the situation, and even so, in prayers, Mom seemed to bring faith down from the sky into the daily situations for which faith and prayers were always needed. She was convincing in every word and deed. With her help, I memorized Luke 10:27 (NABRE) very early in life: *"You shall love the Lord your God with all your heart, and with all your being, and with all your strength, and with all your mind."* I came to realize that my mom led a true Christian life as a terrific woman of God and that she would rise from multiple trials unscathed. The best thing she did is that she brought me along with her to most of the daily masses at 5:30 a.m., to some of the church organizations, to Bible study sessions, and during Lent, I went with her to all the stations of the cross at the church and rosary sessions at home.

One evening, she prayed and said a lot of the words—faith and trust. After saying our bedtime prayers, I asked her, "What happens when God does not answer your prayers? What do you do? Do you get annoyed with Him and stop praying?" She smiled in response. "You believe in Him that He will answer when He knows the time is right. When it seems like He is not answering prayers, you still should tell Him, "Thank you, Father." Thank Him all the time. Have faith in Him. He knows best." I did not understand that type of explanation, but I wouldn't ask any further questions because I knew Mom was tired and needed to rest. And I trusted her very much. She looked at me tenderly, and we hugged good night.

In second grade, I was anxious and excited to receive the sacrament of Holy Communion. After going for confession on Saturday evening, I was excited to receive the Eucharist on Sunday at mass to further strengthen my resolve to do as God wanted me to. I knew He was always watching and listening, so I wanted to impress Him if I could, and I thought communion helped me to be a good disciple of God. After all, I had learned that the Eucharist was the ultimate Catholic standard for recognizing the followers of Christ. I would sing "I am the way the truth and the life..." often so I sincerely longed to see this almighty person who is everything as such.

At ten years, I mischievously but seriously began to ask God to make me see Him. I asked Mother why God wouldn't come so I could see Him. After all, my impression of Him as a loving, caring Father who answered my mother's prayers was unquestionable. Like every human, she had some uphill battles that I heard her pray about. In my teens, I heard her pray a lot about her marriage and her family. Occasionally, after our evening prayers, she would sit me down and tell me some things about her life with Dad before I was born. She would conclude, "You got to pray. Only God has the powers to destroy the enemies. He alone is capable of moving mountains. Have faith in Him, pray, believe in Him, and have faith your prayers will be answered by the grace of God."

I sincerely believed in God. However, I thought it was possible to see Him and if He wanted to be seen. By this time in my life, I had read several Bible stories that I loved so much. They all sounded like people had seen God. Whether it was God the Father, the Son, or the Holy Spirit, it did not matter as I knew it was one God and some people had seen Him. There are three in one God, so God had been seen. Bible stories such as Jesus walking on the sea, Noah's Ark, Adam and Eve and the Garden of Eden, the birth of Jesus and the Three Wise Men, the Good

Samaritan, Joseph and his brothers, David and Goliath were favorites at the time, and I had read, digested, and knew them well. I even cried reading about David and his brothers, and on very rainy days, I thought we were having another forty days and forty nights and may have to build our own ark like Noah. On such very rainy days, I would look out the window multiple times to determine if the rain was ceasing or not, and if the rainwater was rising to our rooftop. I imagined Jesus would come again and I would see Him. I never saw God anywhere. I learned to believe in Him wholeheartedly and maintain a very strong faith in Him since Mom and Sister Louisa had said so.

At about seventeen, I realized that sometimes God does not answer prayers immediately. I encountered a major setback that dealt a blow to my trust and faith in Him. The results for the most important exams that I sat for were not what I had prayed, worked hard for, and anticipated. Dad investigated the results at the headquarters of the ministry of education, and my test papers were pulled for him to see, and we realized I was missing three points on one paper and six points in another, to hit my target. It was a difficult period for me. Dad was very disappointed but, as always, highly supportive. I did not understand God's decision in that regard because I worked hard for that test. I was a very smart student who rarely dedicated much time to study. But for this test, I studied hard but missed my target. For some days, I was unable to pray after the results of my test. Mother and I talked at length about persistence and God's plan for each of His children. She taught me that ultimately "for those who love Him all things workout together unto their good." Mother said, "His time is best because He knows best. It is always in retrospect that we realize God's decisions for us are always the best for us. He loves you. Believe and give thanks to Him."

I nodded quietly, but my faith was shaken, and she could easily see that in my eyes. She demanded that I *"In all circumstances give thanks, for this is the will of God for you in Christ Jesus"* (1 Thessalonians 5:18, NABRE). Mom was very firm, but she was hardly convincing at the time. I thought I should believe her because she had witnessed amazing things done by Him, and she had seen prayers answered in the most amazing ways. I continued going to mass and praying till I left home for college. Our separation was painful for me. She smiled and patted my hair when it was time to separate.

"You have now become independent and will be spending your time as you please. Study hard. You will pass all your tests and exams, and you will be a successful lady. God will be with you throughout." She looked seriously at me and continued, "Trust in the Lord with all your heart and do not rely on yourself. Rely on Him." She continued, "There's always going to be battles and stumbles. To conquer them, you've got **prayers** and your **faith**. **Prayer** is the key. Prayer is the master key that opens every door. Okay, Susu?"

We knew that she so much wanted me to be a faithful and God-loving person. We hugged and said our good-byes after chatting for a long while. I promised her I'd do my best to remember all my lessons from home, and I assured her that faith in the Lord was at the top of my list. As I entered the new big world that college was, I held on to my faith. **Faith** was one of the last words I heard from my mom as I proceeded into the unknown world of college, so that word meant a lot to me. I thought to myself as I went on, I have faith. I will try to keep my faith. I must hold onto my faith in God, no matter what. That is what Mom said. I will pray and try to have true faith in God.

Graciously and Faithfully, Father

College was a big world for me. I slowly made friends in my dorm and at the faculty. I did not just continue praying while in college, I found myself praying even more than I did while in high school. I realized that within me, I was slowly regaining faith in God after my first trial. During my elementary school days, my adolescence, and as a young adult, I sang *"All to Jesus I surrender, all to Him I freely give..."* uncountable times. I was used to singing the song. I sang it in the shower and sometimes while in class, I realized that in my mind, that music was playing. In college, some days were very difficult for me because I missed Mom and home so much, I would sing and pray all the Catholic songs I knew, and then some. God was a constant friend to me at the university. I dedicated several evenings on campus to attending church with my mentor Dr. Okay and his kind family or with my good friend Edith and her loving family. I had prayed to meet good people and Christian friends at the university. I was very happy that I made friends who believed and prayed to God for everything, just like I had learned to do at home. I often prayed the "All to Jesus I Surrender" song, saying every word with my utmost emphasis.

"All to Jesus I surrender, all to him I freely give...I will ever love and trust him in his presence daily live. I surrender all, all to Thee my Blessed Savior I surrender all...make me Savior Wholly Thine. Let me feel the Holy Spirit, truly know that Thou art mine...Lord I give myself to Thee. Fill me with Thy love and power, let thy blessing fall on me. I surrender all."

If you know the song, you should pray or sing all the words as you please. It is a beautiful song, and the words are very powerful. You may be wondering, What about the song? And why do we have only partial lyrics here, or why do we even have some of the lyrics here? The lyrics highlighted here are precisely what left me shaking with joy and fright at a certain point in my life and have also provided me peace during very turbulent times on my faith journey.

I later understood that praying those words did something for me. Remember me wanting to see God and visit with Him during my elementary/primary school years? At the time, I was looking for answers to my many questions about Him. Later, I grew out of having questions and became close to being as good a Catholic as I could be with the help of my parents. Notwithstanding, I still secretly asked God to visit with me so I could know Him better. In high school, I spoke to Him often but not deeply enough as I discovered while in college. However, when I could, I sang my favorite song at the time "All to Jesus I Surrender."

Dr. Okay and I discussed religion, Christianity especially, and the Catholic faith during my freshman year at the University. My college campus had a big Catholic church that I attended. I made that known to him. He was glad and informed me that he and his family were a part of the congregation. Each time I went to his office with questions on academics, we ended up talking about Catholicism after my questions were answered. He invited me to his house and introduced me to his Canadian family. We became very close, and I always felt welcomed at their family home. He had three children: a son who was away in Canada for college and his two daughters who were attending my college. His spouse was frequently away in Canada. One evening, he asked me to accompany him and his family to the campus church, where he introduced me to some of the parishioners. He was a highly respected church leader. His children were fervent Catholics as well.

At my campus parish, I attended mass regularly on Sundays, Bible studies on either Tuesdays or Thursdays, followed by mass, or evening mass on Wednesday especially, and went for confession as needed. It was here that I actually began understanding God, His Words, their meanings, His unconditional abundant love for us, and the power of prayers even as a song. I prayed a whole lot during this period of my life. And it did not matter where I was, I prayed whenever I could, but I also prayed in my heart. Although I had read countless Bible stories from both the Old and the New Testaments and had done Bible studies with my mom and the Christian Family Movement (CFM) group, it was here at this church and in college that I could dedicate time to read the Bible of the New Testament from cover to cover and over again. It was here at my university that I began to truly lead a meaningful Christian life with Christ at the back of my mind. It felt like here is where I learned the true meaning of having a relationship with Christ. During this period, I heard the church leaders, while in prayer, call God names that I was unfamiliar with such as El Shaddai, the Alpha and Omega, the I AM, the Beginning and the End, the First and the Last, and Yahweh, which I had heard my mom and the CFM group say about God. By the age of six, I had attended so many masses that as our priest served mass, in my heart, I recited each step with him. I took great pleasure in saying the same words as our priest in my heart each time I attended mass.

However, it was at the university that I discovered myself as a Christian, explored God more deeply as a Catholic for better understanding, experienced my true love of and for Him, and enhanced my relationship with Him. Mom, Sister Louisa, and our Catholic community and the doctrines I learned during my Catholic school years had sowed seeds of Catholicism that were beginning to germinate and flourish while I was in college. At the university, my faith in the Lord remained an important feature, and I contemplated it as much as I prayed, in a principled manner.

During my second year in college, I had regained complete faith in God. At a certain point, I began experiencing what I considered at the time to be *"inexplicable and astonishing things."* The *"All to Jesus I Surrender"* song was my cuddly toy, my own very teddy bear. I loved it, so I continued to sing and pray it. God started revealing Himself to me in very small ways. My dreams would manifest near verbatim in the morning or during the day, or month, or I will be led during prayers to see things that will happen soon and say them before they occurred. With increased frequency of my dreams becoming realities during the day, week, or month, I shared with Dr. Okay, my friend Edith, and two other friends from church what I was experiencing. At first, I would cry because I was scared when something I dreamed of manifested. I thought it was ridiculous for me to experience such things.

Dr. Okay helped me understand what was happening to me after I explained to him that I stopped shutting my eyes during prayers because sometimes when I shut my eyes, I see incomprehensible and almost inexplicable things. He said I was ridiculous and had a lot to learn about God. I agreed I had more to learn about the Almighty. He referred me and the group to Genesis 37:5, Matthew 1:18–25, and Daniel 4:5. There were verses regarding God's use to dreams to communicate, lead, and direct His servants. I wondered why Mom did not tell me that. I guess she could not have told me everything I needed to know about God. I wrote to her frequently and explained my new experiences as they occurred.

I woke up one morning and wrote out several questions that I saw in my dream on a notepad. Then I took the notepad of questions to my faculty professor whose course it was about. I explained to him that I saw the questions in my dream, and they are supposed to appear on our final exam according to the dream. I told him I wanted to know if my questions were close to what he was thinking about, if my dream was true on this occasion, and if so, if he could change the questions. He took the questions from me, kept them, and asked me if I dreamed things that happened often. I asserted what I was experiencing with some of my dreams coming true word for word, and I insisted that some of my peers and even the associate faculty dean who was my mentor, also known as Dr. Okay, is aware that some of my dreams often become reality. This happened approximately four weeks prior to our finals. I left him with the notepad, per his request.

A few days after my meeting with the professor, a departmental meeting was scheduled, and I was summoned to answer questions from a panel of all my professors about the questions I gave to the professor. The professor alleged that those were all like his final exam questions and that the questions had either been leaked to me, or I had sneaked myself into his office and copied the questions. I asserted to the panel that I wrote them out from seeing them in my dream. I informed the panel that I could not have imagined how I could have entered a faculty office to look for and find the questions for my final exam or how those questions would have been leaked to me if the professor himself did not give them to me, thus leaking his own exam questions. And he certainly could not have given them to me. I insisted to the panel that the case was absurd, I had never done such an act and would never in my wildest imagination even think of doing such a thing as breaking into a university professor's office for whatever reason. I insisted the idea was unfathomable and emphasized I was the department's best student for my year of studies and had won the dean's scholarship the year prior.

I was studious, intelligent, and was highly admired and liked by my peers, several departmental upperclassmen, and most, if not all, of our professors. I concluded by saying to the panel, "You respectable professors do not honestly think I would do such a thing, do you? I study hard and earn each of my grades from hard work, and you all know that, or not? I am on scholarship here by merit. Thank you, sir."

Very many sympathizers flocked to my side in support of me and the action I took after seeing the questions in my dream. Some said I was foolish to have taken the questions to him. Others thought it was naïveté that made me share them with him. I said if I thought for a second that sharing with him would cause doubts in his mind or cause me hassles, I would not have given him my notepad of questions. However, I thought it was the right thing to do. After my testimony and witness testimonies from several peers and few friends to whom I had spoken about my dreams, I was informed by the dean that the case had been closed and dismissed as unfounded after a week of investigation and scrutiny.

Dr. Okay, who was part of the panel, had remained very supportive during the process. I prayed a lot and cried over the professor's initial accusation. I was thrilled when the case was dismissed and exams moved forward as planned. Dr. Okay had warned me during the process to "say the truth at all times and the truth shall set you free." He insisted, "I know and believe you because you have dreamed of unbelievable things that have happened, including my daughter's emergency surgery and others. I told the panel that I am a witness for you. Only the truth matters. I know you are honest, and all the professors believe you are honest. It will end well with the truth."

Although it had ended very well, I was scared that having dreams may lead me into some serious trouble. One evening in church, we were asked to pray before Bible studies. When it was my turn, I began seeing and saying scriptures that I had neither prepared nor thought about prior to the group meet for Bible studies. On this occasion, I felt overwhelmed by the presence of the Holy Spirit during my prayer. I felt the hand of the Lord over me as I prayed. I began praying what I could not interpret and did not know why that was happening, but I could not stop myself even though I wanted to. Here I was in a Catholic church, praying in a strange language that I could not explain where it was coming from. I never heard Mom, Sister Louisa, our priests, nor anyone in the Catholic church pray in a different language. The only foreign language that had been used at our Church is Latin. And I did not speak Latin. I never heard even my uncle Father Polycarp pray in a language other than in English. When I was done praying in the foreign language, I could hardly raise my head. I was ashamed of myself, unsure of what just happened to me, and felt very embarrassed. I was still, numb and confused. The pastor walked away from the group to begin evening mass. On this night, the scriptures I mentioned would be the ones that the priest would share with us, and his prayers would stay in line with my prayers in English during our group time before evening mass. Dr. Okay was with the group. Like Mother, he is a good Christian, Catholic follower of Christ. After mass, he and other church elders encouraged me to not be afraid. "Instead of being afraid," he said, "rejoice because God has bestowed gifts upon you."

I responded, "I am confused because I do not understand what happened to me, and I don't know what I was saying, but I felt happy saying the things I said in prayer. I wanted to stop, but it was just impossible for me." Dr. Okay's fatherly voice immediately interjected, "You should pray as the Spirit leads you. That is what Jesus said. Don't fret. You have the gift of the Holy Spirit. You just prayed in tongues. It is nothing strange. It is the prayer of the Holy Spirit. It means you have a spiritual gift. We will explain it to you using the Bible. When Paul went to Ephesus, there he laid his hands on the people who received the Holy Spirit, and they prayed in tongues. You will find this in the Acts of the Apostles." I remained perplexed, indeed very perplexed and astonished. Dr. Okay insisted, "There are verses you should read before our next meeting to assure you that you are not insane." His family and some of us were invited into the back office, where we sat and discussed the Bible again before parting for the evening.

As I walked back to my dorm, a secret cloud of fear of the church enveloped me. I was afraid for the first time since I left home for college. Several alarming thoughts ran through my head, and my heart began to pound with fright. I wondered if I had unknowingly joined a secret society and must find a way out of it. How would I begin to try to find my way out of it since it was made up of mostly very powerful university staff and their students? Maybe I could call my sister in London to explain or just run back home? I opened my Bible to Acts 19:6 and read it as soon as I entered my room before arranging my books, purse, or changing into my PJ's. I wanted answers and more reassurance, and that was the first Bible reference we received that evening at the back office. I read it over three times and thought of Dr. Okay's words to me in church. The church elders had a rich repertoire of Bible verses to help us understand when any one of us expressed doubts or had queries. That night, I wrote a letter to Mom explaining all the strange and new things I was experiencing in the university campus Catholic church. I included the verses that the church deacons had shared with us to help us understand a few aspects of speaking in tongues.

After reading Mark 16:15–18; 1 Corinthians 14:2 and 14–15, the envelope of fear began dissipating, slowly making way for confidence and faith in the Word of God as testified in the Bible verses I had just read. I went to bed reassured that our campus Catholic church was truly a house of God and not a bizarre society where I had been infected by a weird virus that could make me speak a strange and incomprehensible language as prayers to our Holy Father.

I did continue praying, per my mentor's advice. I learned about fasting as we studied the Bible further. When I encountered difficulties, I fasted and prayed both in the spirit and in English. Dreaming, knowing, and saying some things before they happen continued. Sometimes I had scary dreams that made me cry and woke up crying real tears. Some of my scariest dreams included a devastating fire engulfing my family home, my father's numerous properties, and making us very sad. The fire happened. It impacted my mom, my family in general, and made me cry a whole lot. I began wondering, Why me, Father? Why do I have to see all these scary things before they occur?

My whys were many. I had no immediate responses. It took a little while before began getting answers by having flashes of the words of the song "All to Jesus I Surrender" appear to me in bits. When I wondered, I saw the words "Make me Savior Wholly Thine. Let me feel the Holy Spirit, truly know that Thou art mine." At other intervals, I heard the words "Lord I give myself to thee. Fill me with thy love and power, let thy blessing fall on me. I surrender all." It dawned on me that for a long time, I not only asked to see God, I also asked Him to let His blessing fall on me, that He should let me feel the Holy Spirit and truly know that He is mine. I was reminded by the Spirit that this had been requested by me repeatedly in prayer and while I sang the song. The result was staring at me right in the face: God had answered my requests in the beautiful lyrics that I cuddled and lifted to Him on countless occasions. It took a while for me to realize it, nevertheless, I finally did with the help of the Holy Spirit. The lesson I gleaned? There is a God. Believe in Him. Have faith in Him when you pray or sing to Him from your heart. He is omniscient, omnipotent, and omnipresent, and He answers prayers in all formats possible. Know what you truly are asking of Him. Be certain that it is your heart's desire because He is a faithful Father who answers prayers and delivers our requests in His own time according to our needs. All things are possible with Him. He is much more than I can write in these few pages of *Compass*. He had answered me by filling me with the Holy Spirit who made me pray in tongues and opened my eyes to see things in dreams. He had sent His amazing spiritual package to me per my requests in that song and He had signed it "Graciously and Faithfully, Father."

The Journey—with Twists and Turns

Continuing the journey with Him as part and parcel of my life, I experienced His mercy, grace, love, peace, and the beauty of His presence in my life as my Shepherd in countless different ways. But it has not been an easy journey, a straight route without bumps or a journey where I sang my favorite hymnals all along. It has been a beautiful journey, however, with highs and lows, laughter and tears, joys and sorrow, questions and answers, dreary and very sunny days. This trajectory has been one of honesty, openness, and hard lessons learned. Due to my weak human flesh, I would fail Him along the way many times, I would fumble in front of Him on certain occasions and acknowledge my mess before Him. I would go to Him for reconciliation and do my penance, and as merciful and loving as He is, He would wash me clean each time and set me on a golden new path for the honor and glory of His Holy name. And I would mess up again, and He would forgive me again, over seventy times seven, per His own words, because He is the One and only Father that is capable of such unconditional love and enduring mercy for me, a fleshly child.

The eye-opening situations that God made me go through during the journey would be very humbling and become part pillars of my growth and experience in a rough and tough world that I took for granted having grown up privileged. The amazing trajectory continues, however, as a journey of love, trials, faith, promise, and hope.

I was twenty-one when I started praying for the man I'd like to marry. One afternoon, I retired into the guest room of Edith's aunt's home and knelt before our Lord to pray. An incident in the family home prompted my prayers. On that occasion, I prayed for the struggling British couple we were visiting, their family unit, and I also prayed for myself. It was in that room and during that prayer session that I finally enumerated the qualities I was looking for in a man and confessed to God about the type of man I wouldn't want to befriend or even marry. I did not have a boyfriend and was finishing my junior year at the University. I had turned down all amorous advances from the handsome young men on campus who tried to woo me. I did reject their advances because I was sure they were not right for me. Edith and I had our focus away from the guys, but we had several good friends among the boys in our department. I continued praying to meet a guy that was created just for me. It will take a few years more for that to materialize. I was in no haste.

Many plausible suitors were available to me, but I did not get the right feel for any of them. A blonde German suitor travelled from Frankfurt to our home in England to ask me out after our encounter on a flight. He was persistent and flew to Africa to visit my extended family, but I would not give in because I did not feel he was the one. On a nippy Saturday evening in February of 1995, I saw a guy at a friend's party and immediately thought, "Oh wow! I don't know this guy, but he looks like the one I would marry. He is very good-looking. I hope he has a great heart and soul." I had not looked at a man and thought of marriage prior to that occasion, so I gathered my thoughts quickly, and imagined friendship with this beautiful stranger. There were people at the party that I had never met before, but this one person caught my attention. I had fun at the party, but we did not speak to each other although he wandered around me a few times while I was in conversation with friends. He looked like the man I would like to befriend and get to know. But was he Christian? Was he Catholic? Mom had told me to be sure to marry a Catholic man for various reasons that she shared. I could not answer my own questions, so I left the party that night and returned to my usual busy life and quickly forgot of the pretty face I saw there.

A month later, he felt he had done enough investigation, had sufficient information about me, and wanted to know me better, so he asked a mutual friend to call me and introduce him to me. We all lived in different cities. Esther, our mutual friend, would call for the introduction and to obtain my permission to share my telephone number with him. When she told me his name is Emmanuel, I felt that was a great sign. She had my permission to share my number with him. Another month passed before I could create time to meet with him to dine and chat. We would become best friends forever and forge a union that I believe was ordained by God. With all my character and personality flaws, he accepts me daily for just who I am. We pray together, laugh, and cry together, but he has never betrayed me.

The most important things I asked God for in a man that I marry are found in Emmanuel aka Manny. When I am weak, tired, and unable to pray, he prays for me and helps lift me up. When sometimes with tears in my eyes I say to him, "I cannot even find words to send up to Jesus today. I am so weak and do not know what to say or where to even begin," he simply takes my hands and begins to pray for me. Then he finds my favorite playlist and blast all the encouraging songs on it and let me digest the words that ultimately help purge my soul of its sorrow. Some call it soulmate, yeah? I found mine. I call him one of the greatest blessings I received from God through prayers.

Manny joined me on my faith journey without asking many questions because he is a baptized Christian and child of God, not born Catholic but would become one because he married me. As a young couple, Manny and I discussed our unborn children and planned for our daughters' arrival. We both prayed to have girls. For me, it was easy because of my presumption that I wouldn't know how to work with a son during his adolescence and I may let my child down. Besides, I wanted to be able to dress my daughters up beautifully, but I also wanted to have girls because I knew I'd relate to them from a feminine perspective better than if I had boys or a boy—personal preference. Manny just wanted healthy children. It did not matter to him, but if he had his way, he said he'd love to have daughters. When our first daughter was born, we thanked God for blessing us with a healthy baby girl. I had promised God that if He gave me a girl, I would commit her into His mighty hands so that He could bless her and use her to glorify His name. When she was less than two weeks old, sitting on our bed holding and lifting her up toward the ceiling in our bedroom, I offered Kat up to God in thanksgiving and prayers. I blessed Him for answering our prayers for a healthy girl, committed her into His mighty hands, and asked Him to touch her and do His will for her, bless her abundantly, protect her, and make her a woman of God. Although Court was not lifted in the same way as Kay was, similarly, we offered Him our blessings and prayers on the day she was born.

Both girls have grown to believe in God and join me on the journey. They also speak to Him in prayer multiple times a day. They are learning and seeing that it is crucial for young ladies to know, believe, and honor God. They have learned that God wants the best for them and is inviting them to lead a magnificent life in Him.

My family and I have experienced situations of hardship and inconveniences on this faith journey. There have been occasions when I asked, "Father, where are you today?" or "Why is this so, Father?" or "What do you want me to do? What are you telling me by doing this to me? Why, Father, why me? This is too hard for me. Help, Lord. You said so and so, but see what's happening." Through the years, I learned that he is the best listener we will ever have. When he says no to me, it is usually for an excellent reason, and it has been to protect me or whirl me to a direction he knows will be more beneficial for me. I always understand only in retrospect that he says no to a request because he has a yes for the best option for me. Even after questioning and asking all the whys, I have seen Him trade defeat for victory and turn seeming loss into something beneficial in my life and the lives of several people I know. Kay and Court are witnessing these as well on the faith trip with me. They understand that when we pray, we can expect miracles to happen, but we must also understand that God sometimes takes time to deliver our requests if he decides they are good for us. No matter what our trials may be, they know that we must keep praying, hoping, and believing in our hearts that our Father in heaven will answer us. Some mornings when I am driving them to school, we share the word in the car. Each girl reads a verse from the Bible, and we each say a prayer. We start out our day with prayer, and we end it with prayer. We pray to give thanks, to worship His name, to honor Him, and to ask Him for guidance and all sorts of favors and blessings. It is a tough journey but not at all a lonely journey.

My family has had serious trials and tribulations for which we have had to rely substantially on our faith in God to survive, continuing daily with prayers, singing songs of praise to Him in the morning and in the evening. In Hebrews 12:7–11 (NABRE), we are told to *"endure your trials as discipline; God treats you as sons."*

One cold Saturday morning in the fall of 2012, I was low, very low indeed. I could hardly pray or sing. My doctoral program was tough and very frustrating. My husband was thousands of miles away working in another continent. I was mad inside. "What good can there be if a family is living apart because the man can only find work in a foreign country?" I asked God. "Why would You no longer create a place here for him, Father? What is the matter? What do You want from him? Father, why then did You bless our transatlantic transfer if only to find this heavy rock blocking his progress now? Father, why would we move to a place where You would allow our family to live separately like this? When he interviewed for work here in the state where we reside, some employers told him nonsense such as, 'You are overqualified for this job' or 'You should interview for the VP position instead. This job is not for you. I am the director of the department, and you know more than me,' etc. Decidedly, for him, for our family, interview and employment tales of that nature would last for an unbearable length of time. We agreed he needed to accept international job offers that were pouring in for him. After prayers, we decided on one. He flew off to Europe for work. It was very, very hard for me alone with our two daughters. Without him, it felt like our tight family unit had been fractured. It was not the same without him. Although we all Skyped and talked very frequently and at very odd hours given our time zones and their disparities, I was sad and mad about the situation. Court, very close to her father, did not make this part of our life easy for me. It did not matter how often she Skyped with her father, she asked when he would return and cried frequently from missing him daily.

That morning, Kay came into my room, looked at me, and said, "Mom, this will come to an end very soon. You look sad, Mom. I know you are sad. This will soon come to an end."

I did not respond because I wanted to hold back my tears of anger from the child who often says to me, "You are a very pious lady. You love and believe so much in God, Mom." I did not want to speak because I was near screaming out my lungs, just crying. She jumped onto my bed and murmured, "You know how you always say God will make a way even where and when it appears very bleak and there seems to be no outlet? Hope, Mom. Hope is what I heard you tell Dad. God will make that way for us. You know how much he loves us. He will answer our prayers. You pray a lot, Mom. There is no way he will not answer you."

I gazed at her again, speechless but encouraged to think positively as she reminded me that God has our backs and is a miraculous working father who does things to our favor in a way that man cannot see. These words from my own daughter were like food to my spirit and soul. In a split second, I thought, she believes, has faith and hope, and is propounding and pouring out my very own philosophy to me. Gee, I better sit up for her, or for our family. Her beautiful words lifted me up and reminded me of the amazing things that God does for us daily: he makes a way for us through each trial that befalls us. She had just reminded me that there is no issue bigger than our Lord can handle, that I needed to lay my worries at His feet and believe in Him to help me out as I prayed. I acknowledged her by smiling and kissing her forehead.

Then tears began running down my cheeks. I quickly wiped them off. It was tough. I had been up for a while, just thinking. I was overwhelmed and did not even know what to say to God. I could not find words to pray to Him. My spirit felt washed. I was just silent. My educational pursuit was tough, very challenging, and almost defeating me; my children needed me, and my spouse was away in Europe for work. I was like a single mom with two little girls to raise. I had neither anticipated nor planned for a period like this. Kay took my hands and said, "Remember when you told Dad to cry when he feels he has reached that place? You often say to Dad that Jesus wept for a reason. If our own gracious Lord could cry, then who is man to not feel sorrowful to the point of crying? You have said it is okay to cry. You too can cry, Mom. Jesus also cried. He wept. He suffered and died for us. I guess you are suffering something too now. But like you say to Dad, it will come together if we just trust in the Lord. Cry, Mom, but trust in Him like you ask us to. He makes a way for us. That's what you say, Mom."

I ceased sobbing in disbelief and looked at her straight in the eyes. In my mind, I wondered, was the Lord talking to me through her? Why did she come in here now when I am in this shapeless shape? Father, is it you?

I shut my eyes for a second and garnered a small amount of strength, opened my eyes, and said, "Thank you, darling! Thank you, sweet girl. Your words are encouraging. I'll be fine. We will be fine. Thank you."

Her words were a lesson to me when I desperately needed encouragement. She took my phone and turned on my playlist to my favorite songs of praise and blasted the volume. Then she began smiling at me, "Come on, Mom! Come on! This is your song. Come on sing, Mom, sing."

Her words of encouragement and the music kicked me out of my sorrowful mode, and I felt my heart faintly and slowly begin thanking God for this kid, for our kids, His grace, love, mercy, our lives, our health, the situation, His presence in our lives, and our countless blessings. Kay made me understand right there and then that she knows that the only way to obtain some of the good things in life including but not limited to inner peace, patience, hope, understanding, wisdom, grace, joy, empathy, etc., is through God's grace. For my return to inner peace that day, she was very instrumental and persistent. She reminded me to have hope and faith in the Lord as I prayed. I was somewhat fully revived from my pitiful state of sorrow when the phone rang. It was Manny. He wanted to Skype.

During our conversation, he thanked her for speaking to me. He confessed that he continued to have a hard time falling asleep on his big cold bed in a big well-furnished company house on the other side of the big pond without his family. He was also feeling the emptiness of life in Europe without us. He said he was sad. We all Skyped for hours that day and as usual did not want to stop. It was very hard for us as a family.

It is important to remember God in our daily lives no matter the circumstance. As I continue my journey of faith in Him, my reliance is solely on Him daily. I invite Him to journey with me every day. He is indispensable to me and my family. My experience is that some days I have had to bear a cross for which I turned to Him and asked for His help to either lift the cross or discard it, take it away from me. On other occasions, I know that my tears have flown and will certainly still flow from sorrow or fright as long as I am alive. I am not sure that as humans, any of us can escape sorrow or tears, whether it is for ourselves, our family, or a close friend. At all times, my hope is that I continue to humble myself in front of Him, seek His face, and ask Him to graciously wipe my tears. At times, I only sing praises to Him and just say, "Thank You, Father. You are magnificent to me, to us. Thank You for today. Thank You for your unconditional love and your endless blessings. Thank you so much, Lord, for everything. You are my light, my strength, my refuge. I love you, Lord."

I write this not because he asked us to "give thanks for all things" but because I believe that we have more to be thankful for than to worry and cry about. One of my mentors said to me in one of our numerous conversations, "When we cry and worry, we are complaining about God. We are saying that He does not know what He is doing, so give thanks no matter the situation. I understand that it is a difficult thing to do sometimes but consider this situation a blessing in disguise. Trust Him, something great will come from this." He usually follows this with biblical stories and references that always, always help me.

On this journey, my daughters and I pray as the Spirit leads us. As Catholics, we also have favorite scripted prayers that we love to pray. There are countless of them. We use them according to the season, theme, occasion, habit, and as the Spirit leads us. We also love to sing songs of praise. We have countless favorites. Depending on the occasion, my daughters could be singing "Our God Is an Awesome God," "This Is the Day That the Lord Had Made," "How Great Thou Art," "Amazing Grace," "Because He

Lives I Can Face Tomorrow," or "What a Friend We Have in Jesus." It all depends on what is happening at the time.

Psalms 100:1–3 (NABRE) asks us to "*Shout joyfully to the Lord, all you lands; serve the Lord with gladness; come before him with joyful song. Know that the Lord is God. He made us, we belong to him, we are his people, the flock he shepherds.*"

During the twists and turns of this journey, I contemplated these words a lot. Understanding their full meaning has been very beneficial. What cannot be missed from my experiences with the difficult times we experienced on my faith journey is my thought that during those trying periods, I was struggling and fighting battles from multiple fronts. Battles lost and won are all necessary growth ingredients in our lives. They have helped me in varied ways. They help us understand our strengths and weaknesses, teach us grace and how to be still. Struggles help us understand the world a little bit better and become wiser as individuals. At least this is what it is for me on this trajectory.

Although I have read the Bible and the New Testament from cover to cover several times, when I am attacked by an adverse force at work or elsewhere in our larger community, or when my family is confronted by challenges, I use several Bible verses in prayer, repeating His promises to us. But I meditatively run only to a few: Psalms 23, 34, 43, and 121. They have proven to be powerful ammunitions to me. For worship, verses that praise God abound in Psalms. Notwithstanding, as a family, we read different Bible verses depending on the season (Lent, Pentecost, etc.), occasion, or day of the week. We often read or study chapters or verses from the different testaments so that we can learn lessons from the various books of the Bible.

Sometime ago I was challenged by adverse spirits at work. My very good friend and colleague, Hugo, gave me a great prayer book titled *Prayers That Rout Demons and Break Curses* by John Eckhardt. The several prayers in that book, which fortunately reference the Bible throughout, are excellent resources. I have Catholic prayer books that help guide my prayers. The principal of Overbrook School in Nashville, Tennessee, gave me a great one titled *Every Day Is a Gift* introduced by Reverend Frederick Schroeder. I ran to it daily for a few years. I still do, especially on the weekend. My mom has an abundance of prayer books for me, and I like all of them. In addition to praying as our Lord leads us, my family also prays intentionally, and we often pray the rosary together. I pray it alone too, most often.

During the very early stages of this faith journey as a young adult in college, and with fervent participation in my campus ministry, I came to understand that the Bible is replete with verses for every kind of occasion or situation that everyone may need. There are verses for bereavement or mourning, hopelessness, trust and faith, love, courage, depression, baptism, marriage, sickness, fear, joy etc. You name it or need it? The Bible has it for you. Whether you have also read the Bible from cover to cover or not, God loves all of us His children, and His Holy Book is an amazing weapon that is available to all.

What I ask our daughters to not do as children of God, and which I try to avoid at all cost on my faith journey, is to go about a day without dedicating our activities and committing our lives and that of our family and friends in the Holy and mighty hands of God. Sometimes, I begin by asking, "God, guide and guard us throughout the day. Be ever present in me so that the words that I speak, my actions, and the thoughts of my heart may be acceptable to You, Father. Give us strength and grace to deal with any temptations that come our way on the road as we drive, at work, and wherever we go today. Let our light shine through our good deeds today all for the glory of your name. I pray for our daughters' protection throughout the day. Please, Father, shield them from accidents and physical pain."

We try to make prayer time sacred to us no matter where we are at the time. Whatever the prayer, the circumstance or place where I find myself in prayers, throughout the journey, I try to focus on the revered nature of the activity and situation. When praying in church, I know I am standing on Holy ground. When praying at home, in a car, ship, on a plane or boat, in a bathroom or shower, I tell myself I am praying in a blessed place. I tune out everything else and just focus on my activity. During my faith journey, I have prayed in airplanes on countless occasions, especially as I traveled across state lines very frequently for work. What mattered to me on such occasions is not where I was but who I was communicating with and how I was doing it. The prayer time was sacred to me and remains sacred whenever I do it. As a family and as an individual on this journey, praying in the car is part of my life. The same principle applies as praying on a plane. I just pray in there and speak with our Heavenly Father in the most devotional way I possibly can in the given space.

I tried to maintain my own little ritual during my faith journey. My mindset is what it ended up being after these years of traveling with Him in the most fundamental love relationship I have. It is an honest relation, and so I prefer being myself with Him. After all, He knows me inside out. I like to end my day with thanksgiving, after asking God to pour down His fountain of purity and cleanse me of any sins that I consciously or unconsciously committed during my day. Maybe I sinned through my thoughts, words, actions, or omissions. I believe as a sinner, I require cleansing or atonement by our Father before I begin talking with Him. And He has the fountain of purity ready to pour on us and wash us clean, forgive us each time we ask for His pardon.

However, I pray as the Spirit leads, I love to end my talk with Him by giving thanks to Him for a blessed day, and all we received from Him that day—travel safety or journey mercy, improved knowledge of His Word, and multiple other blessings that we cannot see, feel, or touch. In Psalms 107:1 (NABRE), we learn that we should *"give thanks to the Lord for he is good."* Additionally, we are told in 1 Thessalonians 5:18 (NABRE) that *"in all circumstances give thanks, for this is the will of God for you in Christ Jesus."* So then, I believe it is a great thing to give Him thanks every day, and unfailingly at the close of the day.

There are nights when I feel ultra-fatigued and sleep off while trying to help one of my daughters understand or memorize a lesson in science or social studies or religion. When I suddenly wake up on such occasions, I just say a brief declaration of love and thanks to Him and hop on my bed like a bunny.

On this journey, I would thank Him even when the best employer and company I have worked for so far, with one of the best leaders I have met in health care, would cut my corporate position including others due to voluntary workforce reduction for cost containment. Instead of shedding tears and lamenting due to the huge loss, I gathered my family, and we gave Him thanks and rejoiced in Him because he said "to give thanks in everything" not in some things but "in everything." Although Kay, almost an adult at this point, would cry and question God, and ask me why I am so trusting and faithful to Him, and although Court was very saddened by the news, I reminded both girls that he has excellent reasons for letting things happen the way they do. "So, give thanks for that is the will of God in Christ Jesus for us," I insisted to them. "No tears, only Thanksgiving. He knows best and will always do. Give thanks, sweet girls." And so, we all gathered together in the evening time and thanked Him for one of the biggest losses my family has experienced on this faith journey.

No matter the circumstance or place, I consider that nightly Thanksgiving crucial. If I wake up in the morning, then great and the glory be to my Father. I will continue praising and thanking Him. However, if I do not wake up in the morning because my

Father called me in (and I pray often that I will wake up the next morning for the glory of His name), then I had time to love on Him the best I could and thanked Him before I met Him in glory.

My daughters have been a part of this trajectory, but I wanted to immortalize our experiences together, my faith journey as an individual, and also share with our friends and your daughters. In part, I want both of our daughters to remember our journey together, hold on to our memories, and refer to, or use part of this faith journey to benefit their relationship with God. And also, I want our daughters to remember our journey, and not fail to always rejoice in our Father's magnificent love with faith, trust, and hope in Him. Hence, in this short paragraph, I decided to share with you ladies the simple but powerful words of Philippians 4:6 (NABRE), *"Have no anxiety at all, but in everything, by prayer and petition, with thanksgiving, make your requests known to God."* Life can be tough sometimes. Friends may fail you, and you may wonder what in the world happened to your only love, your best friends, and sweet neighbors? Whatever the troubling situation you may encounter, don't let dark thoughts drown or paralyze you. When life deals you a heavy hand, do not fret and allow discouraged thoughts to sink your spirit. I have experienced acutely dreary days and inexplicable difficult times. But through prayers, faith, and hope, I came out of the tunnel laughing and praising His Holy name and making my requests continually known to Him.

Remember that Jesus never fails, and turn to Him for anything you need. Pray without ceasing according to His word, and, yes, take all your worries, burden, and troubles to Jesus in prayers. I sincerely believe that it is an honor and a great privilege to know God and experience a love relationship with Him. It is an honor to be able to trustingly tell Him everything in prayers. He listens and answers us accordingly. He is the most faithful and will remain my and your refuge when all else fails. He will not fail to turn your dreary days into the sunniest seasons you experience.

Personally, I cannot imagine what life would be like for me without knowing God, believing and trusting Him profoundly. He is my all, my everything, and I would be very lost without Him in my daily life. Remember that, okay ladies? Look up to Him daily for everything, with confidence and hope. Do not forget that *"You who dwell in the shelter of the Most High, who abide in the Shade of the Almighty"* may say that He is your fortress and your refuge and you trust Him. (Psalm 91:1, NABRE). And always remember, *"In green pastures he makes me lie down; to still waters he leads me. He restores my soul."* (Psalm 23:2–3, NABRE).

Look to Him, my daughters, like you have witnessed me do on this journey, and remember He is always there for you, with wide-open arms.

The Bible and the words of God are very powerful ammunitions at our disposal. During my faith journey, I have learned a lot from this precious and most important book I have. I am still learning His words, understanding them, and using them as appropriate in prayer. When I pray, I speak directly to my needs, joys, gratitude, fears, and troubles as well as my hopes. Sister Louisa once told me to "own your prayers to God and believe in His power with faith in Him to answer you." I remember her words from my elementary Catholic school days and during my visits to the convent. Mother said multiple times over to have faith in the Lord, but I struggled with it, as shared earlier.

As a young adult in college understanding my religious affiliation and relationship with God better, I would learn the significance of faith from His words in the Bible. As I walk daily with our Lord, when I pray, especially when I am afraid, worried, have doubts and questions, I use His words as ammunition to support my prayer. In the Gospel, according to Matthew, when Jesus healed the boy of his demon and His disciples wondered why they were unable to do same, His words are clear, *"If you have faith the size of a mustard seed, you can say to this mountain: 'move from here*

Section 4: Faith Journey

to there,' and it will move. Nothing will be impossible for you." (Matthew 17:20, NABRE).

As my faith in Him established during this ride, I have come to rely solely on His words and power to do the things He has promised to do for us, such as answer me when I call, and have faith in Him that He will be there for me no matter the circumstance, if I just have faith the size of a mustard seed. St. Jerome Emiliani said that God provides those who have a deep faith and hope, the fullness of His love, and does great things for them. Rev. Frederick Schroeder provided the excellent reflection for strengthening our faith following the words of St. Jerome in Every Day Is a Gift: "God of power and might, let me place all my trust in You. Strengthen my faith and deepen my hope that You may be able to bring about the wonderful things You want to do for me."

During the initial stages of the journey, long before I understood my role in my faith, my relationship with our Lord and my responsibilities as a follower of Christ, I had a nightmare. I was a young girl of approximately ten. I woke up crying and went straight to my favorite older sister. She lived and schooled in London at the time, and was home during a school break. Half crying and half speaking, I told her what the dream was. She looked at me and interpreted the dream in her own way. It was a very bad dream about my family. At the time, I discredited her interpretation of the dream and asked her, "But how can that happen?" I said to her, "That is not possible. That can never happen." Recently my mom and I discussed that dream again. My family is living that nightmare after decades of me having the dream. The solution was provided in the dream, but it is not easy to begin piecing together the puzzle pieces that are the foundation for resolving the nightmare as seen in the dream. Never in my wildest imagination would I have thought as a young girl growing up privileged, in wealth and luxury that our beautiful, loving, caring, kind, very popular, and well-connected family would someday experience the overwhelming darkness that was present in that dream. Seeing things in dreams as part of my faith journey continues.

I have silently been afraid of this gift because I have seen the good, the bad, and the ugly in my dreams. I have shared my worries with Manny. But the cup is still in my hand as I have been woken up by my spouse from a sound night's sleep, screaming, "Praise and all glory be yours, Jesus" or simply responding, "Yes, Lord, I will" or crying, "Jesus, Jesus…yes, Father!" or "Thank you, Jesus" and laughing or rejoicing hard in my sleep. Some nights I must wake up from a crazy dream and begin praying against what I saw, heard, or was told. It has been a journey where I do not ignore any dream I remember or take any of my dreams for granted. It is a journey that has shaped my life and carved my spirituality. After fasting and prayers, I have been able to find great solutions to work-related issues, family concerns, educational pursuits, and in our everyday lives as a family and members of an extended community of people. It is a continuous trip for which I am wholeheartedly grateful and thankful to God.

Amazingly, when we are expecting a decision or an answer to something critical to us, Kay, Court, and their dad ask me if I know the results or if I have been told the answer. Sometimes I laugh hard at their questions. Sometimes I frown and ask them to leave me alone. No matter how I react or respond to their questions, I continue to be used by Him, so sometimes I do have the clue, sometimes I don't. It is a blessing to be able to hear from the Almighty in such a way, but it can sometimes be scary to know that a mighty power tells you, "This is it. This is what might happen" or "you go do this for me no matter how much you do not want to do it" or "Now is the time for you to do this or that" or "Take this route, and you will get this result."

Uncountable experiences have made my husband and children to ask me if I can find answers when they have questions. When someone has high-stakes concerns or decision to make in our family, our daughters often joke by saying, "Just ask Mom to answer your question because she has a direct dial to Jesus."

I respond to this by telling our daughters that on this journey, my only direct dial to Him is through my prayers, faith, and hope. I believe wholeheartedly in Him, I have raised my daughters to believe in Him, and I am urging them to entrust themselves to Him even in my absence or when they leave home, and they will be amazed at what magnificent things He will do in their lives. He is really an awesome God, and I am honored to believe in Him.

Love and a Grateful Heart on the Enduring Journey

As I continue to walk with Him daily, I am experiencing the beauty of his love and power in countless different ways. Manny, my best friend and spouse, knows how to best help me when it appears like the craziness of the world around us is taking its toll on me. He knows the importance of the Word of our Lord to me, so he resigns to it as our most important resource when he notices that I am weary and teary. For us, His Words are more than uplifting. They feed our spirit and open our eyes to the reality of who He really is: an amazing Father who has deep, enduring, and unconditional love for us, the one who has loving thoughts and plans for us that we don't know. He is the ultimate comforter we can call on at any time, and He will be there for us. All we should do is know, trust, believe, and have hope in Him; pray, honor Him, and try to do His will on earth the best our human selves can possibly do and love, love Him. During my lifelong journey,

I understand clearly from Paul's first letter to the I Corinthians 13 how He wants us to use all the magnificent gifts He has bestowed on us and how He is asking me to prioritize as I continue my faith ride with Him.

"If I speak in human and angelic tongues but do not have love, I am a resounding gong or a clashing cymbal…Love never fails…So faith, hope, love remain, these three; but the greatest of these is love." (I Corinthians 13, NABRE).

St. Ignatius of Antioch helped us to understand that "faith is the beginning and love is the end-and God is the two of them brought into unity." He said, "Then comes everything else that makes up a Christian." I reflect on His words during my ongoing journey and pray that the "Almighty Father would let my beginning faith end in true love for Him," as Reverend Frederick Schroeder advised. But 1 John. 3:18 (NABRE) says, *"Children, let us love not in word or speech but in deed and truth. Confidence Before God."*

The bottom line here is that our love should be true and honest love. I have prayed to God and continue to ask Him on this trip to help me with true love in the words that I speak, my actions, and even my omissions. That I may be honest in my love for Him, as well as my love for my friends and neighbors.

This is a tough world and a complicated life, so as I proceed on this journey, sometimes I wish I could obey Him all the time, but He is right: I have *"sinned and fallen short of his kingdom,"* so all I want to do is know Him more and better, lift my voice in praise and worship to Him daily, ask for His mercy and forgiveness for my sins, keep His commands the best I can as long as I live, maintain a very strong faith in Him, rejoice in Him with gratitude and say, "Thank You from my grateful heart, Father, for this very lovely journey and my numerous blessings," and "I love You so much, Father."

(1) Prayer and (2) faith are the principles shared in this section!

SECTION 5

FRIENDSHIP

The Concept of Friendship

I do not know any legal definition for the concept of friendship as I know there exists one for marriage and other relationships. Friendships appear to be at the core of many people's daily lives. I hear colleagues talk about their best friends; acquaintances and friends talk about their friends and best friends, young adolescents discuss who their true friends are, and my own daughters call other girls their friends and best friends. Besides, some of my good friends and I have discussed the concept of friendships and our daughters' specific friendship experiences at school, especially in high school.

Although my daughters have had slumber parties, playdates, and varied types of outings numerous times with their bffs, they recently expressed more curiosity about friendships, asking me countless questions regarding the subject. Both of our girls had a few great friends at Overbrook school. After relocating to Texas, Kay quickly made several new friends since she is characteristically sociable. Courtney, who is more cautious and critical with regard to friendships and usually takes time to know a girl prior to formulating a trusting relationship with her, is now asking me countless questions as well. Court remained mildly introverted until recently. I have had to work with her personally to get her to be a more social young lady. She still has a little way to go in that regard.

After spending a couple of years in her new school, court forged relationships with a group of girls she called friends. They played frequently together and enjoyed each other's company. However, the group of five girls faced a continuous partnering challenge, which she narrated to me when it started and as it endured. We examined the group's dynamics, discussed possible reasons for the challenges, and agreed on what actions she had to take to mitigate the situation. Although she was very attached to the group, I was amazed at how well she received my counsel and adhered to our plan of action. She happily followed my advice and began enjoying herself better at school using our action plan.

While in high school, Kay also had to spend a significant amount of time discussing friendships during our intimate one-on-one weekend open-door conversation time as we call it. I have had to use my personal experiences and observations through life situations when discussing the subject of friendships with them. She wanted me to share my anecdotal insight here in Compass as it might be relevant for their future children as well. As this book embodies several of our discussion topics as a family and a very small piece of what I would like our daughters to remember me for, I agreed to incorporate the friendship conversations we had in this section of *"Compass."*

Friendships are important to each one of us. They can significantly contribute to children's social and emotional growth. As both of my girls' relationships with their elementary school friends blossomed through the years, I noted remarkable emotional and social growth that took place. With the challenges court's group of friends encountered in elementary (fourth grade) school and again in middle school, she continues to enhance her perspectives on friendships, interpersonal skills, appropriate social interactions with the diverse population of peers at school, as well as emotional control.

At the beginning of fifth grade, she had to check her class list to see which of her friends were in the same class as her. "I hope I am in the same class as my friends, mom. I am freaking out, mom. Please tell me something before I check the list," she said anxiously, holding me around the waist.

I smiled at her little anxious person and responded, "go check it out. I am sure you have several girls whom you related well with that will be in the same class with you. It does not matter now who is in the same class as you. The list is up."

She finally pulled herself together and checked the list. She was happy with the list, which she called "refreshing," although she was not placed in the class or homeroom of the teacher she would have liked to have. She noted, "mom, it is interesting that the school has placed me with the girl with whom I had issues last year, but they separated her from the other two girls with whom she had issues as well. Basically, the two of us have been left alone together to sort it out while the other two girls in the group who also had issues with her have been placed together. One girl who is her good friend is now alone in another class. They could have placed them together at least. She needs her friend too. Mom, this arrangement is interesting. Is it possible to request that your child and her friends be placed in the same class? Mom, is it possible that the school did this on purpose?" She asked, gazing at me. "This is what I am talking about..." she explained her thoughts again.

I asked her to focus on her class placement instead of guessing on her former group of pals. She continued, "I think someone asked for that. I think there was group fixing there." She sighed and then continued, "yippee...I have some nice girls in my class this year, and they are my friends. They are in volleyball too." She appeared satisfied with the class arrangement. She happily bounced up and down the hallways, texted some of her peers, and then returned to me "I will have an excellent year. May I please have a playdate with so and so? May I, may I please, mom?" I supported and encouraged her, "I am very happy for you darling. You have all these lovely girls in your class! Amazing!"

Kay and I watched her as she happily danced around the house to celebrate the good news of being in the same class as her friends. My conclusion from this experience was simple: no matter whom you are—a little girl, an adolescent or an adult lady, celebrity, blue blood or commoner, rich or poor—friendships certainly occupy some of our thoughts and time, and very good friendships matter to all of us.

As parents, we understand that friendships are important to the extent that they serve as social identifiers for our children, providing them a feeling of belonging, thereby boosting their self-esteem. Some serious friendships are born during adolescence when our daughters socially identify with peers of their liking, whom they understand and respect as friend. Others establish during the young adult years, and yet some friendships begin at a later stage in life. No matter when a tight or strong friendship establishes, I understand it is a big deal to have true, good friends. Best friends or bffs, according to my daughters, are also of importance.

In fifth grade, court pinpointed her close friends. They were in the same class, and sat close to each other in class. They played together during recess and ate lunch together daily. Further, she and some of her friends visited, texted each other, or skyped on the weekend. Some of the names of her previous group of friends were conspicuously missing from her new list of friends. During our group conversation one weekend, she discussed her entire week at school and named the girls she mostly interacted and played with and explained why. Her sister was intrigued at the number of missing names on her list, so she asked her: "have you forgotten to mention some names?" Missy smiled. "No. Well, I have new friends with whom I play, talk, and eat lunch." Kay was not surprised. As a high school girl at the time, she was also learning how friendships can evolve and what true friendship was beginning to look and feel like. She said to her sister, "I totally understand what you are saying because I am seeing that some girls who were best friends from preschool to eighth grade no longer talk to each other now that they are in high school. Your group of friends might change in middle school and even in high school."

Court quickly responded, "I hope to keep these friends next year when we get to middle school. I hope we remain friends in high school and beyond." She insisted, "you and MB Hasty, Rachel T and others are still friends, same as with others…. You have been friends for…hmm, how many years now? It's been at least four years. I hope I keep these friends I have now."

I admired her pureness of heart, spirit, and her genuine desire to keep her present friends for a long time, but Kay and I understood she has enormous room to grow and learn more realities about true friendships.

Reciprocity

The successes or failures in a department of friendship depend totally on the individuals involved in the departmental activities.

In response to their numerous questions, I shared with my daughters that there are several characteristics of enduring, genuine friendships that explain why some of the relationships are the way they are. Kay is a golden heart, sweet soul who used to call acquaintances friends. We clearly defined it, agreed on the distinctions between the two, and have since been clear how to define friendships and true friends. To underscore the significance of a true friend, I told them that personally, sometimes I think of my true friends as sisters. And they likewise see me as more than a friend. We share like loving sisters would. And our relationships are founded based on the two-way street principle. True friendship should never be one-sided in any way. It usually has resounding reciprocity between the parties involved. Several years ago in England, I received a nice gift from a good friend with the engraved words "friends are the family we chose for ourselves." This has remained with me and I shared it with both girls.

My friends and I have confidence in each other and our relationship. We are dedicated players on a team, and are devoted to the success of our team goals and friendship department, but we are very genuine women who cherish, respect, and understand each other well. We continuously reciprocate our thoughtfulness, care, love, loyalty, patience, kindness, support and respect for each other.

Time Factors into its Growth

It takes time to cultivate and nurture friendships into best friends. This is my reason for telling Kay that as she evolved in high school and learned who her true friends from that environment are, she should not take a relationship she considers very good for granted because it is not easy to find a genuine and very good friendship that may evolve into best friendship. And it could take a long time to get to that stage of friendship. Sometimes, it could all truly begin in high school when everyone is a bit more mature and then grow stronger with time and faithfulness to the journey as friends. True friendships do not happen overnight; it takes time for friends to nurture a very good rapport into a great one through shared experiences, genuine love, kindness, understanding, trust, and commitment.

Qualitative versus Quantitative

What should truly matter in a friendship are the qualitative aspects of the relationship that exists between individuals. Quantitative relationships may matter to some, but in the world of my two cents, it is more fulfilling to have a small intimate group of very good or great friends who are genuine, respectful, honest, trustworthy, understanding, and reliable than to have a village of women you call friends but with whom you do not have much in common; they often dominate you in conversation, talk over you, consider themselves superior to you, believe you should look up to them, critique everything you do or say, misunderstand you, laugh with you when you are up, and distance themselves from you when your days are dreary and you are down.

True friends are those who stand by you when you need them the most, especially when you are in fear, in doubt, need someone to talk to, have questions, need advice, and are going through rough patches and bumpy routes. Those who stand by you during good as well as bad times are the ones you should consider the significant friends in your life. If you have a handful of such people in your life, then you are blessed. You count them as part of your blessings. They are the qualitative makeup of your friendship department.

The quantity of friends may not necessarily reflect the quality of friendships you want. Think quality not quantity, and you will be better satisfied with your group of close friends at the end of the day.

After Kay explained how apparently some long-standing relationships between several girls in high school were evolving, I realized she had become highly interested in what my experiences were with friends during my school years. In response to her questions, I shared my recipe for sweet friendships at her age.

"Foremost, your relationships should have compatibility, and you should each have a good feeling of emotional connectedness and intimacy. If the relationships are spiced with mutual respect, honesty, trust and understanding, support for each other's goals and aspirations, and an openness and willingness to share your values and profound beliefs on any topic, and you are loyal to the friendship and each other, you have a solid foundational rapport. That is where you start," I concluded.

"Well, since I disagreed with my friend Amme recently when we attended the football game, she appears to be mad at me. She has avoided me at school this entire month, and she no longer speaks to me at all. I don't know if we have the emotional connection you just mentioned. I have tried to understand the reasons behind her sudden change of attitude, but I don't get it. What do you think I should do?" She inquired. She had explained the events that occurred between her and her friend at the football game. I did not think she was wrong to refuse to go across the street from the campus football field with a group of boys she had never met, although one of her friends invited her to join them on the walk to the other side of the street, off campus.

"Do you ladies at least say hi to each other? I thought you sat together in some classes?" I was perplexed. I did not know this issue continued to be alive and had caused a rift between she and the other girl. She did not mention the topic during our open door the previous weeks. She smiled. "I say hello each time, and she responds. She does not greet me first." I continued, "well, well, well then! You say hello to her next time, and gauge her reaction. When she says nothing and you equally say nothing, that makes the two of you. But you should not be the one to greet her first all the time. I believe you did nothing wrong to deserve her silence. Even good friends have rebuttals. But they can respectfully disagree on any subject and remain good friends if it was meant to be that way. They would demonstrate adequate willingness to dialogue, resolve any issues, and move on, rather than retract themselves after such an incident as the one you reported. Your good friend should not pressure you in any way to do things against your will. You were right to say no to her pressures and to stay where you considered safest for you that night." She listened attentively and then said, "I want to be sure it is not me and that I did nothing you would have considered wrongful to a friend. I just wasn't comfortable with that whole situation at the football game, like I told you before."

I nodded and firmly stated, holding her right hand between my hands while rubbing the back of her hand. "This is your food for thought: remain very vigilant with the type of friends that you surround yourself with. Peer pressure begins with the very group of peers one calls friends. Evaluating relationships is critical for making sound decisions regarding very good friendships. There are myriad questions you must ask yourself about the company of friends you keep. Some people experience friendships of different sorts: they have friends with whom they hang out and attend happy hours for the fun of it, or if they are students, they eat lunch at the school cafeteria together because that is where they all sit to eat lunch and discuss theology, algebra, or computer science class. But they also have friends with whom they feel very close or intimate and discuss more personal and serious matters with. Happy-hour conversations are casual, general knowledge discussions such as our kids because they attend the same school and are in the same class, or we discuss church matters etc. She listened keenly.

"Each group or type of friend is important in varying degrees, and you should have fun and enjoy yourself with them. One should still be compatible with their happy-hour friends. You should allocate Amme's place in your relationships among the friendships you are cultivating. When she is ready to talk, she will find you. If she doesn't, then she is not whom you think she is.

You leave it at that and leave her alone so you can dedicate energy to friends you deem precious. Friendship forms naturally, voluntarily, and mutually. And good friendships are like fresh flowers. They require nourishment. If you do not water and feed them, they wither away and die. One person is trying to nourish this relationship, and one person says hello as it stands right now. I am searching for the mutuality in the relationship as we speak. It is not apparent to me. I would advise that you relegate this rapport because it is seemingly challenging, though in its infancy, and nurture your better relationships that are standing on pillars of mutual respect."

Kay sighed. "I wanted to share with you and see what you think about such a friend. We are just so different right now, and i am seeing more that I did not see before."

"Your friendships might continue shifting until your junior year. Don't lose sleep over this one, will you?" I smiled.

She quickly responded, "absolutely not, mom. To be honest, I do not care much. I did not like the persuasion or pressure. I think it was ridiculous how she fussed about it and said I am no fun for refusing to go with a group of stranger boys off the Jesuit campus where the football game was taking place. Right now, she is so boy crazy. We are very different, and I am cool with her silence toward me. I am learning fast. I have seen one of my supposedly good friends from middle school tilt away from me recently. I have known Amme for one year, so this is not something that will cause me heartburn."

I admired her resolve and confirmed, "oh yeah, kid! She is the newest kid on your friendship block but not the first to show you the yellow card. I love what you just said. We are on the same page, child."

She continued, "some of my good friends left for different schools this year. Do you think we can still be good friends despite of the distance between us? We've been texting and talking. Sarah

Hodson, for example, is an amazing girl. We are so compatible. I really miss her. What do you think, mom?" She asked not sure if she had enough time and energy to dedicate to good friends whose schools were not proximally located to hers. I knew she had a good friend who was not returning to her school. They are kindred spirits, very compatible and respectful young ladies. Kay had spoken very highly of Sarah, and knowing my daughter's personal values, I was immediately certain that Sarah Hodson was a genuine young lady with great values. I had met her a few times and loved her when we first met.

I responded, "there might be physical distance between you and your good friend Sarah, whose parents transferred out of state. If you were true friends, the relationship will endure without a doubt. Situations such as relocation help people see who their true friends really are. That is when you determine and realize how deep or shallow your friendship was. Did you share experiences and memories that may keep your relationship binding and worth it? Did you each feel a deep connection with each other that is worth preserving from a distance? You know how many very good friends I have out of town. Recently your godmother visited us from out of town. Debs and I have not ceased our relationship either because we moved here. Same as Mrs. Theresa Byrne, Court's Godmother and others. Hence, you and your friend Sarah should determine how to preserve your friendship if that is what you want. Despite the distance between us, my friends and I e-mail, text, and talk on the phone whenever we feel the need to. There is also skype and video phone to use to connect with friends. Do you get it?" She lit up. She is generation t, and so explaining to her how technology can help her preserve relationships with her good friends was slam dunk for her. "Oh, mom, we are already keeping in touch, pretty much through texting and brief phone calls. You know Sarah and i call each other, right? I did not know if you would approve of me furthering our conversations, so I wanted to be sure. I know you really like her."

I smiled at her anxiety to hear my perspective. "Sarah is a very sweet girl. You both are compatible and fun together. She is respectful and responsible. The relationship is yours to build and nurture. It is not my place to pour cold water on it when there is no reason to. Distance is not a reason to clip a very good relationship such as that."

"I appreciate you sharing your point of view." She smiled. "That viewpoint is only relevant when everything is well between the friends involved in the relationship and they are willing to maintain it despite the distance separating them. Distance has the potential to dampen or even murder relationships. When friends separate due to relocation or migration, one of two things might happen. One, either they keep in touch and maintain their union, or, two, they let the friendship fizzle and die from lack of effective communication. You know people say 'out of sight is out of mind'? Yeah, when that happens, the distance between friends might grow bigger and bigger until it pops due to the void. When it pops, that is it. It no longer exists. Nevertheless, it can casually exist after it pops, which returns us to the fundamental questions of distant relationships with good or close friends. Is it worth preserving despite its challenge of the distance? Are you ready to spend time and energy preserving it? The response to these questions could be yes or no depending on both parties' desires and views of the friendship. No matter which way the response leans, new friendships will form in Sarah's new environment, and each one of you will move on with fond memories of the other if it does not work out. However, your friendship might flourish despite the distance separating the both of you. Don't we have several examples of such situations?" I paused.

"All right, momma! We all have examples we can share on that. Yeah, we do, momma! This conversation is freaking me out because my dear friend moved to California this summer. Uggh! Sarah dear, we will conquer the distance!" She sighed, looking anxious.

"What are the expectations you have of girls you want to call good friends?" I tried to probe her perspective in the department of friendship. "Well, I will say genuineness, if that's even a word. Is it, mom? Okay. A genuine girl who knows how to be herself, true to herself, and honest always no matter the circumstance. I need a good listener and a friend who sees our friendship as one that is unconditional, not like if you come across the street with me and this group, then you are my friend. If you don't come, I'll stop talking to you.

My friends should not be threatening or pressuring me in any way implicit or explicit at all. Additionally, I like all the attributes of a good friend you already listed. I would like to be able to count on my good friends and vice versa. A good example is when a friend asks that I accompany her somewhere because she wants her best friend there? When I ask her of such a favor, I expect she can return it easily. Is that being reciprocal?" She pursued, "you sometimes say, 'birds of the same feathers flock together,' kind of like, "show me your friends, and I will tell you who you are or 'you are the company you keep".

I want to flock with gracious, levelheaded girls who can have fun without being unnecessarily loud, obnoxious, and kind of attracting attention to themselves. I want company that can be trusted as an ally, with whom I can be silly, funny, and serious when necessary. I want someone fun with whom I can hang out, go see a movie, or eat a bite from wherever, go to a concert and just have fun like girls of my age do, and they must share my values. No drugs or alcohol, self-respect, responsible... What else, mom? No gossiping behind my back like you know who did. Just a plain honest, loyal, good, and genuine friend. Like Sarah."

I looked at her and smiled. I wanted her to tell me what she looked for in friends since she wanted to discuss this. "Mom, you have some marvelous friends who truly love you, and always go out for you when you need them. Most of your friends are from here, well except the ones in England. I know you were very popular at school, and dad says you have always been a popular person like that. When you were my age, did you have good friends? What were the characteristics you sought after?" She asked curiously.

I was surprised at her question. Since I made some good friends at my adult age and my daughters know all my very good and very close friends, I have mostly focused on relationship discussions that involve my girls rather than me. With my schedule and crazy busy life, I focused on other pressing priorities than wanting to forge close friendships, though I am still meeting very sweet women. I smiled. "I had several friends at your age, but none of them were good friends. I guess I had classmates, and we all just mingled with each other. I managed to keep a few good friends between elementary and high school. Most of my middle school years were spent in a boarding school. I had fun there and have several lovely friends from there but I am pretty close to only a few of them. Some of the girls were hypocrites. One girl was very polarizing and often tried to place a wedge between me and any good relationship I was having. The great thing about me and my middle school friends is that whenever we talk, we have a lot to share and talk about. Although we communicate sporadically, we are never short of what to discuss and we are better friends now than then. My high school was a blast. It was close to home. A few of the girls were jealous and harsh. Some of the girls as I remember high school were disloyal and cynical. Some were gossips and could not be trusted. There was something about my high school peers. The girls either liked you, were genuine about it, or they made up a reason to dislike you. I saved some good friends from high school. University was a blast throughout. I enjoyed true sorority there. I saved five or six very good friends from my university. I met some excellent girls at uni.

"As you know, I also have a handful of amazing friends whom I met while in my thirties. They are a blessing in my life. I have a respectful, honest, and trustworthy relationship with the ladies I call close friends today. We have a lot to discuss each time we are together, e-mail, text or chat on the phone. They are very reliable and can count on me anytime same as I can count on them. We are genuine and open with each other. These are the friends whom when they miss a call from you, they call back to make sure you are alright, or want to answer any questions you may have, or that you get what you needed from them, period. They wouldn't make excuses or pretend they did not see my call or text message. This must be mutual or reciprocal. You see, friendship has a give- and-take concept. It should be genuine like you said, with a foundation of trust. Good friends should be able to communicate openly even if or when the topic is serious and uncomfortable but quite necessary, required and worth having. They are the people who do not shy away from theirs and your reality."

I laughed at her pensive gaze and continued, "I thought it was inconceivable for me to create room in my life for genuine solid friendships because of my current priorities. However, I am surprised at how many very good women I meet as I continue to do life. You know it when you meet a genuine lady. You feel it. Your connection is natural and reciprocal. You talk with ease and enjoy your conversations. Well! This is not about me. My friendship department is busy, although my prime focus shifted from friendship formation a long time ago, although I am still meeting very good, trustworthy ladies. I pray and hope God blesses you and Court with the most gracious, loving, kind, understanding, and genuine ladies you can call great friends. May God give both of you enduring friendships! You are great young ladies and deserve nothing but the best of girls as your friends." I took a breather. "Mom, you are the best. I hardly can image what I will do without you," she said, reaching out for a hug. "I am right here, lady. Not going anywhere!" I laughed. She gushed, "yay, I believe that!" We both laughed and hugged like old friends.

At the time, I held less intense friendship conversations with Court. She was in elementary school and was having utmost fun with the girls whom she called friends. She previously experienced a group dysfunction, as mentioned earlier, and learned from the experience. She is experiencing the friendship shift and therefore naturally has questions. I respond simply and honestly to her questions and encourage her to have pure, simple, and good fun with the girls who are respectful, courteous, and want to play with her or be friendly with her.

"Be nice to your peers and friends. Learn to forgive immediately after your peer or friend hurts you, realizes it, and apologizes for it. Do not shun any kid who wants to play a safe game with you. Be respectful of yourself and your peers always and avoid those whom you consider mean-spirited. I remember a nun once told me that "some little girls are very mean." I agree. Those are the ones you avoid so you do not get into trouble at school. Just enjoy yourself and your time with girls with whom you share a reciprocal appreciation for each other's company.

She attentively agrees, "yes, mom." Then she beamed. "My friends are really nice, and I hope they don't change like you said. These are really nice girls, mom. They are well behaved, and we all play volleyball, although they are on the other team. I really want this group to stay together. I will pray for it."

She sounded rather pure hearted than naive. It was just great to see that kiddy pure-heartedness in her. I reminded her that she and her good friends might end up in different homerooms in middle school, causing a potential change in friendship dynamics.

They may also end up in different high schools. Hence, her young and pure mind should be open to changes that may occur.

"Oh yes, that's true. I hear Kay say some of the girls who were friends with each other while in middle school have changed so much in high school that they no longer speak to their former bffs. That's sad," she exclaimed.

I wasted no time in concurring. "Right! You see? Most humans are often unpredictable. Just be open to changes, enjoy this time, and pray to God for the type of friends you would like to have. He answers prayers, you know," I maintained.

She insisted without hesitance, "yes, mommy, I pray to him for everything. I will pray to him to keep my good friends."

The importance of the concept of true friends and good friendships cannot be minimized given how often I have to discuss the topic with my daughters. Friendships are central to, and hold a prime place in the lives of my daughters and, I believe, very many young girls and women around the world. A few days ago, as Kay and I discussed the level of influence their friends have on each other's life, she affirmed, "one has to know their good friends intimately. Good friendships should not be taken for granted, and we must bless God for placing special friends on our path because it is not easy to find good and genuine friends. That is a gift—the gift of good friends. You know my current bff and I have been each other's support during trying times with other girls and situations that we encountered. Of course, we speak to our moms about situations, yes, and we also discuss and support each other through young girl issues we encounter. Friends can either make or break you. I thank God for my friends so far."

I agreed with her, then added, "I have to be completely honest with you and tell you that some girls are phony and incapable of protecting good friendships. It is an absolutely terrific thing for anyone to have known some of their friends from preschool, elementary school, or even middle school or high school and college, but there is no guarantee to this, given the hypercritical nature of some girls. Things might change. I don't want to dampen your current glee. I just want to be pragmatic and prepare you for the unforeseen. Life has some of those, even in friendships, as you are already witnessing at school. Whatever happens, don't allow anyone to break you in the name of friendship. If you ever feel that a friend can break you, they are not one of your true friends. But I know what you mean, so enjoy your sweet friends and remember it gets complicated with us women at times. Sometimes, where we should be united, caring, and supportive of each other, we fight senselessly. The most surprising thing is, it can begin at any age and can happen anywhere in the world."

She smiled. "Yes. Unfortunately, some girls do have a special knack for that. I think others try to be good girls to their friends, and need support from their parents to foster appropriate friendships according to their values. It was a good experience to see girls apologizing to their peers and friends at our recent school retreat after we listened to the Christian teachings of the day. It was amazing to see that girls can be impacted by the word of God and lessons from the teachings about the life god wants us to lead, to the extent of desiring to change their squabbling and bitchy ways to become more reasonable, responsible and simply nice to their friends. Maybe some parents really just need to spend time sharing true Christian values and intimate theological lessons with their girls to help them become better ladies and better friends to their very own pals. During our recent class retreat, I received an apology from a remorseful girl. I was shocked but glad to know she had gained something from our retreat enough for her to think seriously of what she did and do the right thing to say she was sorry. High school is showing me so much, mom. High school is very different from middle school. I am experiencing so much more now about girls and friendships. This is the awesome thing about attending an all-girls catholic high school such as UA. Going on such retreats and taking time to delve back into why our parents send us to such a wonderful school in the first place, our lives as young Christians or Catholics, as true followers of Christ, and just reflect a bit on our ways as true friends. Girls realized at that retreat after reflections, adoration, and prayers that Christian women should be better friends."

I just listened, happy that she brought back so much from the retreat she mentioned. "I am very happy for you, my little, big darling—all grown-up young lady. It sounds like your retreat was very beneficial. See what an excellent catholic school can provide? Awesome!" I laughed.

The Best Friend

Although I am their mother and have established boundaries with my girls, as a matter of principle, I pride myself as my daughters' **respectful best friend**, and they know that. The countless changes that are continuously taking place in the world present several dangers for our daughters in the department of friendship. Therefore, as a respectful best friend, I have positioned myself at a central point with a broad view of their relationships so that danger zones can be easily identified, and avoided early enough. As the best friend, I assist them in making good choices by understanding that their lives are replete with daily pressures that do not exclude friendships pressures as I have learned.

For this principle, the respectful best friend mom is the one who remains engaged and well-informed of her daughter's daily activities. Per the principle, she establishes a respectful, trusting, and responsible rapport with her daughters so that at any given time, she would know where her daughter is going, why she is going there, who she is going with, at what time she will return home, and her means of returning home to you. As it becomes more difficult sometimes to deal with kids as they mature into their teenage, it is critical to presented ourselves as the best friend with the most genuine interest at heart for them. With my daughters, I am the best friend who is respectful of them always, and I often tell them that so they understand that no matter what shortfalls they have or present to their best friend-mom, I will be respectful of them.

Here is what I let my girls know is my personal definition of a *Respectful* best friend and what the principle means:

R – Rapport. I have established a rapport of trust between us. I let my daughters know I want them to feel completely free to come to, and tell me whatever it is they need to verbalize. My belief is that they are more liable to be open with me and tell me everything that is happening in their lives if they know our rapport has an indisputable and unconditional foundation of trust, love, openness, and respect. Our girls want to know we respect them even when we disagree with their perspectives.

E – Explicate. Transparency and understanding are crucial to every relationship therefore, I make sure that all my intents and actions in their regard are explicit to them. Friendships are crucial to our children, and they sometimes think their friends are everything to them; hence, they may be blind to the ills and pressures accompanying certain friendships. This explains why I fully and completely explain what I am doing for them when we discuss certain friendships, and why I am doing it. Our girls want to know that their moms or parents have their best interest at heart and are there for them always. I let them understand this is why moms ask questions about their friends and friendships, where they are going, with whom and why. Do not hesitate to fully explain the reasons you may raise questions regarding the type of friends and company they keep.

S – Support. Be supportive of your daughter's choice of friends when the friendship makes moral sense and mirrors your family values. Support their decision to build healthy relationships with friends, and to make wise friend choices considering peer pressures and all that comes and goes along with friendships. I remain the best friend who knows the friends and their parents. I remain their pillar of the strongest support system they can rely on at any given time, and for all their requests that make moral, ethical, and legal sense.

P – Protection. I have asked my girls this question several times, "have you heard of the saying "prevention is better than cure?" Mom is the best friend who wants to know more about your friends so that if she detects any potential issues with the relationship, she can advise you better to protect you from running into problems due to poor choice of friends. Let your daughters know you are the friend who is there to prevent their relationship missteps. Their teenage years are a time when they could be introduced to vaping, smoking, underage drinking, premature sexual encounters, pornography etc. By knowing the company your daughters keep, you are better armed to respectfully counsel and protect them from hanging out with the wrong crowd. By protecting them from getting involved in some of the ills that are destroying several of our youth, you prevent your girls from bad habits that might take years to fight off once gained.

E – Encourage. Parental encouragement in the moral, bold and good decisions made by our teenage girls is critical for their self-esteem. For example, I encourage mine to be good friends to the girls that they identify as their good friends. We have identified and discussed some characteristics of good friendships so that they know what is expected of them as good friends, and vice versa. Considering my daughter, Kay's words, "friends can make or break you," I do not see why. So, I encourage them to analyze their friendships and friends' attitudes at the most important times in their relationship to better understand the friend: for example, I told her that you can assess your friends when you accompany her or she accompanies you to an important event, at celebrations, parties, etc. Assess if your friend is an honest young lady. Does she easily lie to her parents? I encourage them to look beneath the surface of a seemingly sweet girl in order to make a well-informed decision or choice of friendship. Each time that I have told Kay that a certain friendship does not look good to me for reasons that I always make sure to put forward to her, it ends up that I was darn right. By being encouraging in this and many other ways, I help them avoid the "make or break" that she mentioned to me because it shouldn't be that way and is not necessarily true. Friends should not make or break anyone or anything if the friendship is genuine and mutually respectful. So, I further encourage them to let go when it is clear that the friendship has a questionable or potential negative influence on their espoused values.

C – Connect, care, and communicate. I try to connect with my daughters at both a superior and ordinary level. At a superior level by praying with them as frequently as possible, and at ordinary levels, I connect with them by keeping the lines of communication between us open always, for dreary and sunny days; by laughing with them, and by sharing in the multiple challenges they confront. Tell and show them you care and make communication between you all honest, respectful, and positive, even when you disagree with them. When they know they have a best friend who is willing to listen to them without being judgmental, a friend with whom they can talk about anything and everything, one who can connect with them at any level, they will run first to you with their heart's deepest fears, questions, issues, and joys. And caringly, you can easily guide them when need be, through the smooth, tough, and rough phases of life.

T – Trust. By creating time to bond enough with your daughters, you get to understand each other very well, and also establish a never-failing trust between you. Once you make a promise to them, be sure to keep it under all circumstances, and she will trust you deeply. When she gives you her confidence, remain respectful enough to not betray it, and you will have a trusted-friend for life in her. Once your rapport is rooted in trust, you are sure to hear her tell you often, "mom, I have some things to discuss with you when you get a chance." She may or may not add, "this one is urgent, mom, please." Or if not urgent, she may say "mom I am so looking forward to our open-door this weekend, so much to discuss!"

Mom to two teenage girls, I can assure you trust is one of the biggest elements of a great mother-daughter relationship. When a very trusting rapport exists between you and your girls, it is easier for them to adhere to family rules, and follow your guidance without the teenage fuss, fighting with you or putting up barricades and resistance that often lead them to the wrong routes and decisions. Let them know you trust them, and they will tell you everything truthfully, respect your set curfew or call to ask for an extension of the curfew, comply with family rules and make sure to live up to them because they believe you trust they will.

F – Foresight and forgiveness. As a mom of two girls living in a beautiful but dangerous world, I have learned to develop a sixth sense. It serves as my intuition and foresight in matters that involve my children. Be aware of ways to protect them from harm when you can. Harm may come to our daughters in the form of bullying, peer pressure of any kind, peer intimidation, meanness, failing grades, truancy, serial partying, underage drinking, vaping, pornography etc. Keep a clear view of their relationships and activities so that you can see things on your radar fast enough to be able to protect them from such ills.

Be the best friend that readily forgives them when they make a mistake, and count on you for forgiveness and support. Remember that perfection does not exist on earth, so be the best friend that is ready to catch them with two strong and forgiving arms when they come short and fall like we all do. I do not try to make mine perfect, but we discuss excellence and their best as good enough for me, and most of all for them.

U – Unbiased. Be not the friend who is biased and discriminates between her daughters' friends. That is not a good example you want your girls to emulate. Respect diversity and encourage your daughters' friendships based on moral values and compatibility factors. Kay especially has a diverse group of friends—all of them well-mannered and responsible teenage girls. I met the parents of all her friends and know where each one of them resides. When you inject bias in the minds of your girls, you are teaching them to be partial, intolerant, pretentious, disingenuous, and unfair. To build a better world for our children and grandchildren, we should be unbiased toward the diverse types of friends that they may have if the friendship is nonthreatening to their safety and moral values.

L – Listen attentively. Like my dad would say, "we have two ears so we can listen more. But we don't. We all like to hear our voices and want to talk more than we listen." I continuously try to be a loving and attentive listener to my daughters when we intentionally communicate at open-doors. Sometimes it is hard because they can keep going till your ears can listen no more, because your head is spinning. That is when they do not know where or when to stop. Right? Well, having **dialogue, open and honest communication** as a principle to guide them, I sought to enhance my communication skills, to effectively communicate with them. To achieve our collective goal of effective communication, I listen to them attentively to learn what is happening in their lives, understand their feelings and perspectives, and what mitigating role I can play as a mom or parent as the need may be.

When communicating with or listening to your daughter, show genuine interest in what she is saying by maintaining eye contact with her while using a caring and understanding tone of voice instead of a nagging or blaming voice. Also, try not to interrupt them with questions because she or her body language will let you know when to respond. Your primary reaction to her words is to just listen attentively. I learned this from my own daughters as Courtney seriously dislikes interrupting questions while she is still narrating. Both of my girls can talk my ears off during open-doors, but each time, I remember to listen well even when my head hurts as a result of the discussions.

Through the years I have learned that when I have to attentively listen to my girls, it is important for us that I tune off all environmental distractions such as television, music, cell phones, and even other family members who are not part of the discussion. Often, we use a quiet locale for our talks, and I intently focus on them and listen attentively to them. Several people I have spoken with in and out of boardrooms say they find attentive listeners very endearing and attractive because of the focus and attention they grab from them. Imagine that your teenage daughter considers you endearing and attractive! Is that even realistic or feasible? But how awesome will that be if it materializes for you?

I encourage you to be the best friend who shares a respectful relationship with her daughters. What your respectful rapport does is that it provides your girl the best tools and ammunition to use in arming herself against friendship pressures and stressors. That respectful liaison as defined by my personal experience helps her construct a firm foundation for a resolute personality that is resilient to friendship bumps. Friendship bumps could result from her resistance to one or several peer pressures or anywhere for that matter. Do not minimize the potential for friends to coerce your daughter into dangerous dieting so she can look like a "tiny barber" because that is what the media portrays as the "best look." Other pressures may include perennial partying, the use of drugs and ecstasy pills, etc. A girl with a resolute personality wears a natural raincoat built and gained from the respectful interactions with her best friend—the mom. The raincoat helps her to be ready during the dreariest friendship days. Wearing the powerful raincoat from her respectful friend, she can shake off even cube-like raindrops more easily than a girl who is less resilient and ill prepared for the rainstorms that sometimes accompany even the supposedly best friendships.

Notes Following This Discussion

I was writing the manuscript for this book as my daughters were maturing. They are both amazing young ladies now with fabulous friends with excellent values. Kay saved some amazing friends from high school. She and Sarah Hodson, her friend who transferred to California as mentioned in the friendship section, have maintained an excellent long-distance friendship like never before seen. She has been to California several times to visit Sarah and her family, and spent holidays them. Despite Sarah's family's move to Cali, the girls took a senior trip together with Sarah's family. Sarah has also visited and vacationed with us. Both girls are amazing, genuine, honest, responsible, respectful, loving, loyal, kind, sweet young ladies to each other. They are best friends, and like a sister to each other. Their friendship survived the long distance and is thriving even as they reside in different states. This beautiful and terrific relationship is an example of what true, honest friendships should be for our daughters. Kay left high school with a few very good friends.

Court has not done badly either though she struggled more through no fault of her own. Although she was left out by a group of girls on a few occasions and experienced verbal intimidation and peer victimization from two of the girls in the group, she immediately and seamlessly moved on with her initial group of friends and with the girls whose values and behaviors aligned more with hers.

The sad thing about the girls who victimized her is that they did not even realize what they were doing was very wrong, until she walked away from them. She then returned to her initial group of friends and was received with open arms by most of the girls.

Happily, things in this department are going well for her, and her dream of long-lasting friendship with her initial group of friends has been very good. She has remained tight friends with her original good friends from elementary school and has saved best friends from among them.

This is what I told both girls during their adolescence: "At your ages, friendships can change any time. Some adolescent girls can be very mean as you know. Indeed, girls can be -itches. Be vigilant and resilient about what does not sit well with you in a friendship. Adulthood is when more serious, trustworthy, honest friendships may form for some people. But you may meet your best friends for life at any age. Whatever the time or situation may be that you meet, watch out for opportunistic and fair-weather friends as you continue to do life, especially during your adult years."

Kay said, "friends could make or break you."

Her sister, Court is a very resilient girl who luckily refused to be broken by the bullies that she has unfortunately encountered in her very young life. She decided to extricate herself from a group of girls whose values did not match hers, and moved on, warning me she will not adhere to the advice I gave her pending discussion with the girls' parents. She would take matters into her own hands, refused me from discussing with the girls' mothers, understanding deeply the type of adolescents she was dealing with and believing in her intrinsic values as a well-raised young lady. I will forever admire her strength as an adolescent young lady who identified and defied bullies on her own terms even before I could get involved in the situation.

She said to me at the end of it: "you know, mom, you have always asked us to look deeper and do a drill down of situations and things for which we have questions. I questioned that any young girl in her true senses would treat a true friend the way those girls treated me, and you agreed with me but said that I should walk away from them only after discussing the issues. They did not deserve my discussion and what would discussing it have done? I received their apologies and their tears but my mind was already made up. I know it when I interact with a true friend. It feels natural, honest, loving, and just nice. Those girls were off, I will say. They did not understand me. And I did not like their behaviors and attitudes. We were incompatible. I have learned some invaluable lessons this year, and it has helped me grow, like you would say, 'in the friendship department.' I am at peace with myself now after leaving them and their apologies behind me. Since we pray for true, good friends in our lives, I have faith and hope that I will meet and make friends that share my values, are compatible with me, and are ready to journey with me as true friends. I am ready. High school, here I come."

The focus in this section is one of the most serious and important topics for both of my daughters and all the adolescents I spoke with about the topic. There is something beautiful about genuine friendships and in search for that, both of our girls came to me with multiple questions that challenged me to device my best strategy to help guide them in the matter. I discerned ten principles to help me, help them in the department of friendship like we say in our family, and I grouped the principles into one namely (1) Respectful. By being the respectful best friend mom to them, I used the afore-explained principles to help guide them. Hopefully they in turn become their daughters' respectful best friends some day! Besides, in the section, we further discussed the significance of the letter L in "respectful" which is listening and its importance in (2) effective communication since open, honest communication is a principle discussed in section one.

SECTION 6

A FEW IMPORTANT TOPICS

Diversity and Inclusion

As most of us in the United States of America have already noticed, the demographics of this terrific and exceptional nation is fast changing. I imagine that the hallways of academic institutions and the classrooms behind the high walls of several universities and colleges today include students from varied cultural backgrounds and family lifestyles. Some of these students most probably also come from a wide range of geographic regions, ethnic and racial backgrounds, and they must be of different genders. Some of them certainly grew up in different environments, express themselves differently in the same language and live in families with different structures, incomes, and lifestyles. As I understand from traveling, schooling, research results, the news, and working in different industrialized nations, the American society and most Western nations are becoming more racially diverse, meaning that the race that was previously considered dominant and majority is fast fading. From traveling in Western countries, I am confident to write that today there is hardly a homogenous face of several Western countries. Right here in the USA, as I watched over the videos of President Barack Obama's first and second election nights, I was amazed at how diverse the people in the videos were. The demographic makeup of the footages was supremely colorful. It was a true rainbow. The diverse nature of the population gathered during the election night events for President Obama was a far cry from the type of population I saw when I watched our beloved President George Walker Bush's election night events or President Bill Clinton's. Besides, during a seven-month period, I conducted an observational study of diversity in interactions between leaders and managers in a busy medium- sized health-care organization. Personal experiences and our girls' experiences and numerous questions and statements about discrimination prompted me to conduct further research into diversity to understand how parents can appropriately guide adolescents in the matter. Conclusions drawn from the election night videos, the observational study, and results from further research helped me develop the principle of **diversity and inclusion** in guiding teenage girls into adulthood.

Diversity is a social phenomenon echoed across the world in several industrialized countries. Certainly, you have heard of diversity and sensitivity, or diversity and inclusion or both. To some, simply put, diversity means that people belong to distinct social identity groups. To others, it further speaks to the demographic differences between individuals. So, one may wonder what really diversity is. Diversity in the context of *Compass* is the awareness, understanding, and respect of other peoples' race, ethnicity, national origin, gender, age, sexual orientation and preferences, religious affiliation, socioeconomic level, height, and weight.

Inclusion in the context of *Compass* is the practice of giving everyone in a diverse group of people equal access to activities, processes, opportunities, etc. fairly and respectfully. Inclusion means not discriminating against or disfavoring, not marginalizing or excluding people considered disadvantaged, disenfranchised, or minorities.

Diversity and inclusion are different phenomena that are inextricably linked in the context of *Compass*. Diversity and inclusion are interrelated and go glove-in-hand for diversity to be meaningful. To say that one understands or respects diversity but fails to recognize or honor inclusion is meaningless thus it is essential for some parents themselves to understand both concepts to help guide their teen girls as they morph into adulthood at a time when the American population is fasting changing.

The Facts of the Matter

Often, the understanding is that diversity is belonging to historically excluded demographic groups. Wondering about the growth or stagnation of such demographic groups, I turned to the boss of demographics in the United States. The US Census Bureau, which releases national census every decade. In the latest census report of 2010, where it provided a snapshot of the 2010 census showing the diversity of America's population, over half of the growth in the total US population between 2000 and 2010 is the result of the hike in the Hispanic population. The report indicates that "between 2000 and 2010, the Hispanic population grew by 43 percent," increasing from 35.3 million in 2000 to 50.5 million in 2010. The increase in the Hispanic population represented over half of the 27.3 million rise in the total US population. By 2010, Hispanics made up 16 percent of the total US population of 308.7 million. Reports from the Census Bureau indicate that in 2010, 299.7 million or 97 percent of the total US population reported only one race. Among these, 223.6 million or 72 percent of the population indicated they were white. African-American or black population totaled 38.9 million and represented 13 percent of the total population. Asians represented approximately 14.7 million people—that is, 5 percent of respondents—and 2.6 million people indicated they were American Indian and Alaska Native. In addition to releasing national census every decade, the office also releases national population projections periodically. Based on the 2010 census, national population projections were released in 2012. The projections covered the period from 2012 to 2060. The Bureau uses a cohort-component methodology to make projections and bases its assumptions on future birth, deaths, and net international migration. According to projections, the population in this country will be "considerably older and more racially diverse by 2060." According to reports, Americans should expect to see the current trend of increased multiculturalism continue.

The nation is headed toward a more culturally and ethnic diverse demographics. Projections indicate that the non-Hispanic white population will peak in 2024, at 199.6 million, an increase from 197.8 million in 2012. Yet its population will gradually decline and reduce by roughly 20.6 million. The Hispanic population will increase from 53.3 million in 2012 to 128.8 million. The African American or black population is forecasted to jump from 41.2 million to 61.8 million. The anticipation for the Asian population is that it will hike from 15.9 million in 2012 to 34.4 million. American Indians and Alaska Natives are projected to move from 3.9 million to 6.3 million. The population of Pacific Islanders and people who identify themselves as multiracial will increase.

Conclusively, we learn that by 2043, the United States will be a plurality nation with no majority group. Nevertheless, the non-Hispanic white population will remain the biggest single group. Minority groups make up all but the single-race non-Hispanic white population. Armed with this information, I believe we have a responsibility or duty to prepare our daughters to live in a more diverse nation.

Note Worthy

Diversity and multiculturalism are a social phenomenon valued in many industries, such as health, education, media, government, and certainly others that I have not mentioned. Given the current bourgeoning demographics and the projected growth, it is important for families, especially the adult women of the family, to begin introducing their young daughters to the realities of the times regarding diversity and inclusion. As citizens in a highly multicultural nation, we understand that some educational institutions have planned and implemented learning environments that are reflective of our children's life experiences and responsive to their educational needs. I know this because Kay's high school has these in place. She recently studied and socialized at school with children from different countries of the world who were visiting her high school and living with families that have children in the school. The school has gone beyond fostering diversity; it is fostering inclusion and education in a more globalized manner.

As the United States and the Western world become more diverse, my perspective is that families and communities should begin encouraging their daughters to be more open and receptive to peers from other cultural, social, and ethnic backgrounds. This may not what some people want to hear, and no one will force anyone's hands on something that is not in their heart to do. But as a mother raising two sweet young ladies, I promise you this is important. As mothers, we should encourage our daughters to engage in, and not shy away from interactions with students of various races. It is more beneficial than not to encourage our daughters to observe a decided openness and inclusive attitude toward their peers who look and sound different than them. Educational institutions may encourage and foster learning environments that are responsive to the needs of all our children, but when the children return home, what type of comments do they hear from their parents about groups of people who do not look or sound like them?

Stereotypical comments? Comments that sow seeds of divisiveness, supremacy, and exclusion? Or comments of openness, inquisitiveness, encouragement, and inclusion? Mine and my girls' experiences and those of other minority girls are astonishing.

Impactful Words and Actions

I shared with Hugo, my good friend and former colleague, what Court told us one afternoon when she returned from school. She and her friend had planned a get-together either at our house or at her friend's house. The friends had carved out their plan for that playdate. She wanted to know what Saturday I'll be available to take her and her friend to the movies and later to the park and then go eat pizza and cupcakes for dessert. They had it all planned, per Court's outline of the activities, and it appeared she just needed a free day on my schedule. I gave a date, which she shared with her friend. We agreed I'll call her friend's mom and discuss the plans with her. Court was excited and looking forward to the date. She returned to school and shared with her friend that I will be calling her mom to concretize the plans. I had neither met nor spoken to her friend's mom prior. We were fairly new to the state and school, and I had not taken out time to get involved at the school like I did in Tennessee, so I had not known many people in the school community.

When I picked Court up from school the following day after I promised to call, she appeared forlorn. "How was my student's day at school today" I queried, using our usual open-ended question to allow her to vent about what was causing her mood.

"My day was fine. I played with so and so, and I had lunch with...I got a caught being good slip..." She shared with me the highlights of her happy moments at her school that day.

"It sounds like you had an awesome day then," I perused. She took her bag of snacks and started eating. Then she took a deep sigh. "So, you remember all the plans we have made for that Saturday for a playdate with my friend Aline?"

I responded rather quickly, "Yes, darling. I will call and discuss it with her mom this weekend. I am sure it will be fun if you girls can get together." She sounded disappointed. "Well, that's the point. We will not have fun. Aline says her mom has refused her from having any play dates with me. She says her mom wants her to be friends only with the other children because she does not have time for another friend. She said her mom does not want her to have a playdate with me."

I turned and looked at her. "Awww, darling! Did she really say that to you? Did she say her mom said so? Did she explain why her mom said so?"

Her little eyes looked sad. "No, Mom, she did not explain. She just said although her mom does not want us to be friends, she still wants to be my friend, but we can only play at school."

It sounded simple, yet I knew that did not sound right, and I did not know what to tell her. She was giving me information that came directly from her friend. She and her friend initiated the playdate plans. Now she was telling me her friend has pulled back. "Oh well, my little one, I will call her mom and just see what she says. Do you think that might help?" I asked, looking at her via the rearview mirror.

She shrugged. "Aline said her mom said not to play with a kid like my skin color." I was not shocked but very surprised, given the type of school environment our kids were spending their weekdays in learning. "Oh dear! Did she really say that?" She responded promptly, "Yes, Mom. Those were her words. Well, her mom's words."

I smiled. "Don't worry about it, baby. You have several friends to plan playdates with, several. This is a new friend and her mom I have not met. I am not sure her mom means what she said. You girls play at school and have fun then. Okay, baby?"

I thought to myself, well, I will not call her mom. There's no use. She is one of the very ignorant bunches. Court understood. Hugo was not surprised by what I just recounted to him. He said it was sad to hear from kids that some of their parents tell them who to play with and what skin color to not be friends with. He said he was not surprised by what I just shared with him. He commended her for understanding. I assured him that she did completely understand.

We have had several conversations regarding diversity, inclusion and the different treatment she and Court may receive because of one or several of the demographics they belong to. In my quest to have an insight of this family without asking my daughter questions about her friend, and not wanting her to wonder why I would ask her such questions, I called Aline's mom and spoke with her regarding the kids' plans. She told me their weekends were booked two months out and that she would call us when they had openings. I told her life is equally very busy for us, but for the children's happiness, I'd create time whenever she called back with a convenient weekend time for her to allow the girls to have their planned play date. Aline's mom never called back as promised. Missy made sure Aline was invited to her tenth birthday party. Aline insisted her mom did not receive the electronic invitation or e-vite. When she learned from the other girls at school that they had received the invite and would attend the party, she asked her mom to revisit her e-mail and be sure her e-vite was not missing. Aline confirmed that her mom did see the e-vite eventually and that she will be attending the party. Her mom RSVP'd, affirming the kid will attend. We expected to see her the day of the party, but she never showed up. Aline later told Court at school that her mom said she had other things to do so Aline wouldn't attend the party.

Court had become friends with some peers who all played on the school's volleyball club. She wanted to join the school volleyball club and insisted on it. I got information from the school that a parent was the head coach for the volleyball team and got her telephone number. I was informed that the team was incomplete so my daughter could still join if she wanted to. She had spoken with the coach's daughter, Jeejee whom she said was her friend, and indeed, she spoke often of Jeejee and her other close friends. I called the coach and spoke with her about Court potentially joining the team pending availability of space. She informed me that she would look at how many girls are already on the team and call me back within the week with a response. When I did not hear from her, I called her at the close of the week. I finally left her two voice messages to which she never responded. Court spoke with Jeejee at school about my calls to her mom, and Jeejee informed her that her mom just did not want to respond, and that her mom says she needed to stop that friendship with Court who insisted on inviting her to her birthday. As a kid, she is entitled to invite friends she likes to her birthday celebration, and so I made sure to send Jeejee an e-vite. Her friend confirmed that her mom received the e-vite and she RSVP'd. Like Aline, Jeejee's mom ignored decency and courtesy and did not inform Court that her daughter would not attend the party. At school, Jeejee informed Court that she was not allowed to attend her party, and although she reminded her mom about it the day of the party, her mom told her that she was busy cleaning her closet, and Jeejee needed to clean her room instead of attending the party.

These are two of several similar experiences Court has shared with us about parents denying their children the possibility of being friends with a child from another race. Some of her friends at school innocently let her know their parents have refused to invite her but would rather have them invite other friends. On one occasion, a friend told Court that her mom said because Court had a different skin color, her kid should not take her home for a playdate nor visit to play with her. This led Court to ask me one day after school why there were different skin colors, and who made the skin colors different?

Sally is from South Africa, and Jenna is from Ethiopia. They have been in the United States for almost two years. They both explain a near similar situation they encountered at different time periods, as sophomores in different high schools. Recently in her high school, Sally had a team project to complete. Like each student in the class, she had been placed on a team by the teacher. The team had taken turns going to each of the five team members' home to discuss and plan the project, share responsibilities, and start the introduction. Sally is the only foreign-born student on the team. Each time her team meets to discuss the project, she returns home feeling less than a team member. Whenever she speaks, none of the other four students listens or acknowledges her perspectives. She bluntly tells me and her mother, "They don't even make eye contact with me. Sometimes they just keep talking over me. When I raise a good point, no one acknowledges it, but later when the same point is repeated by another team member, they all agree it is a great point and add it to the plan. I once said, 'But that's what I said earlier.' I got no response. Two of the girls have asked me during our planning sessions to be quiet. One of them said, 'Shushhh, Sally.' This week we will meet at my house, but they have all said their parents would not bring them there so we should meet at another student's house. They don't look at my face, even when I am contributing important points that we end up using for the project."

Jenna attends a dance group and was asked by the instructor to lead the group during a dance practice session because she had the best understanding of the specific dance routines they were practicing. The other girls all decided if she had to lead, they would not follow because they do not think she knows the routines better than they do. She initially danced the entire routine alone, then attempted to lead, requesting the group to copy her moves. Some of the girls questioned if she was really doing it correctly. From behind the room, the dance instructor told them she was spot-on with the routines and asked the group to learn from her routines and grace the dance floor. The group grudgingly followed. She intimated to me that the girls in the group never speak to her nor look in her face. Yet they speak to each other in the group. Jenna says she will not leave the dance school because of them. She stated to me and her mom that she loves her instructor. She has been dancing since she was three years old and will not let a group of girls who do not want to accept that she is equally as talented as they are push her out of the dance sessions. She reported to the instructor that one of the girls walked up to her and said, "You can never dance better than me. My mom even confirmed it last week when I explained to her what happened during the lesson. She said, 'How can a kid from some tiny and unknown place come here and dance better than all of us on the team?' You don't know how to dance."

Jenna appeared astonished at what occurred in the dressing room section of the studio.

After listening to these stories which include my own daughter's experiences, I thought to myself, other students may have similar stories about peer disrespect and marginalization of their minority counterparts. It could be innate, or it could be emanating from some form of parental disregard for diversity and inclusion such as my daughter experienced. And such parents are possibly ignorant of just how their negative attitudes impact their daughters and their peers. While some educational institutions are encouraging diversity and inclusion, we all, as parents, must do our parts at home to compliment the invaluable enlightenment our children are acquiring from such schools instead of sowing seeds of bias and division in our children.

The Bottom Line

As parents, some of us still need to enlighten ourselves and understand generational differences, and the cultural shift from some of the ideals of conservatism to progressive ideals, and modern liberalism. It is legitimate to worry about the kind of friends and company our daughters keep. Behold, I believe it is impossible to not ponder on, or want to know who our daughters are friends with, what their family background is, what their parents' public or private reputation is, what their values are, etc. However, it may be shallow and ignorant to think or believe that because someone is from a culture different than yours, if they look or sound different from you, they are less likely to understand and respect you and the community or simply be decent people. It is legitimate to try to influence our children's decisions about relationships that pose potential hazards or dangers with peers that negatively influence them or exert negative pressures on them. Nonetheless, if what preoccupies us in the friendships our daughters want to nourish is the rejection of cultural, racial, socio-economic, diversity, then we should attempt to understand what our daughters or children appreciate in the relationship, and analyze what makes them happy in the friendship.

As I continue to hold conversations with my daughters on varied topics including diversity and inclusion, and as I analyzed the sad experiences of the young ladies I spoke with regarding this subject, I realized that we need to primarily understand the implications for the generational shifts that are already taking place in our communities. Sometimes I was prompted to ask our daughters diversity-related questions, to which they both responded saying:

"Mom, you see, my friends do not think like that. That happened during your middle school, which is a very long time ago. These things are not what preoccupy us children" or "today belongs to twenty-first-century kids. My group of friends think differently from people of your age."

The conclusion of my thorough analysis of several situations where aspects of diversity and inclusion were at stake helped me understand better, and determined to share in *Compass* that as parents, we must make the effort to not inject personal, petty grievances and false opinions in our children's young, unadulterated minds because we consciously want to help strangle the relationships that they may want to cultivate with a girl who looks or sounds different from them. Knowledge and conscience should compel us to arm our daughters with the truth—that no particular group of people is bad, whereas the other is good. We should endow their hearts with love rather than with bias and uncertainty, and refrain from shielding them with quilts of mistrust for those with a certain skin color, ethnic background, religious affiliation, sexual orientation, weight, height, or general looks. It is our responsibility to strive to reject the myopic supremacist view that a certain type of people is better than another one, or the idea that because an individual has migrated from a different part of the world to the United States, he or she necessarily knows to dance less well or knows certain dance routines less well than a child born in the nation. We should educate them to start appreciating the differences that each one of our children brings to the table no matter how different they look, think, or speak from each other.

As "children of the twenty-first century," like my daughters put it, ours and their generations think and act differently. A typical and excellent example of the generational difference in the acknowledgment of the other and inclusion with disregard to evident differences is the bourgeoning generation that elected President Barack Obama twice as the United States President. That generation, also known as the millennial generation or the generation Y, appears to understand diversity and inclusion better. They have become the shifting power in America, electing its first African American president not once, but twice, to the most powerful office of the world. An office that was said to belong traditionally and historically only to white males. Some of the millennials we know said they casted their votes for Mr. Obama in complete disregard of his skin color but in acknowledgment of his capabilities and intelligence, and several other factors that are considered to elect someone to such a post. Some said they disobeyed their parents in that election, and some lost friends and even family members because of their vote. Their decisions were theirs, and they appeared to own their choice proudly in spite of family dictates and other pressures on them to vote differently.

I do not want to overemphasize the importance of diversity and inclusion in our society and communities; however, I would like for us to begin seeing that most of our daughters are rising above the divides that occurred over a century ago for despicable reasons, and that have left a stain on America's reputation on race relations. A bottom line is that the ideological shifts between us and our daughters regarding skin pigmentation, religious affiliation, racial origin, disability, etc., and the value of an individual are already occurring in our society. Negative undertones and underlinings because of diversity considerations, as outlined in *Compass* may be fading but more work has to be consciously done by very many in our various communities to continue pushing for diversity and inclusion in our larger society. Our daughters need to move forward, not backward in their acceptance of the other, and be inclusive in these modern societies and times. It is parental responsibility to not shut that door to inclusiveness but rather to have a parental principle of diversity and inclusion as they guide their teenagers into adulthood.

The importance and benefits of understanding diversity is more than some parents might be willing to acknowledge. However, it is smart for parents to understand that the demographic shift in the nation is well beyond the halls, classrooms, and playgrounds of our children's schools. School children and students who acknowledge, befriend, understand, and respect peers from a different background will be better prepared as professional adults and leaders when they enter the workforce and the extended society. My personal experiences from hospital wards to professional forums, executive boardrooms, and a doctoral scholarship journey that included residencies with a diverse group of intellectually sound minds provide me the leverage to write this. Parents who are yet to comprehend or accept the concept of respect for diversity and inclusion should be aware that as the demographics shift in America, businesses are increasingly acquiring diverse groups of talent from national and international talent pools for their organizational effectiveness.

Several modern institutions understand that there is immense value when diverse pools of talent work together, that regardless of students or employees' similarities or dissimilarities to their institution's culture and norms, each member has a voice and opportunity to participate and fully engage in the institution's values, vision and goals. I am part of the international talent pool in this country, and I have worked with a host of healthcare professionals, including physicians of varied specialties, administrators, frontline staff, and executive leaders from all over the globe. I have a thorough understanding of this concept and could dedicate another book to discussing it in all its shades, shapes, and forms. The benefits of diversity and inclusion cannot be overstated in here.

As the world slowly globalizes, I realize that some educational institutions, such as Kay's high school, are providing their students diversity instruction to enable them to fully participate in a multicultural society. America is already a highly diverse nation compared to many Western nations. So, as we continue to move from a homogeneous to a heterogeneous society, I would like to invite mothers, grandmothers, and aunties to discuss the importance of diversity and inclusion with their daughters, granddaughters, and nieces or sisters. Maybe we should begin by encouraging our daughters to say hello to the new kid at school whom they have never spoken to because they look so different from each other, and don't appear to have something in common. That is where it all starts—in those hallways and playgrounds—but it will never end there as long as our children grow, develop, and move on, into the modern workforce and the larger societies of our world, making this an imperative principle for guiding adolescent girls into adulthood.

The general understanding in my adult and professional environments currently is that several industries and employers are doing their utmost to mold their business brands to resonate with diverse population groups that are targets for employment. As our daughters prepare to lead our nation in their time, I believe it is critical for us to guide and prepare them with all the tools necessary for them to function as effective leaders and team players in a multicultural and diverse nation. As we hold deep conversations on varied topics, I explained to both of our girls that they need to understand that diversity and respect for all is one of the fundamental tools for successful leadership not just in

America but globally. One of the reasons I discuss this very important matter with them is that when our daughters enter the professional world as leaders, they might or will work with a multitude of folks that they probably never imagined meeting in their lifetime, possibly from all four corners of the world. My perspective is that the coming together of such a diverse team of professionals to brainstorm on a project could look like a million fireworks falling from the sky on a peaceful winter night. The fruit of such a team can be nothing short of strength, enlightenment, knowledge, experience, growth, and admiration for diverse talent or knowledge from all over our small world.

Among the few bottom-line highlights of this discussion, I insisted to our daughters, "For you, the most important bottom line is, no matter your ethnicity, race, gender, religious preference, age, sexual orientation, weight, or height, have a high enough opinion of yourself, and do not let disparaging words from a peer or derogatory innuendo from their parents draw you down. Understand that you and your peers are all different from each other, and that it is absolutely acceptable and okay to be different from other individuals. As people of this earth, or even of one nation, we each differ from one another, and that makes diversity the unique characteristic we all share as humans because we are all different from one another. Even the man I am married to is different from me in a thousand ways. We acknowledge, recognize, and appreciate our diverse nature. Most of all, we respect and celebrate our different qualities, and we enhance and fortify our knowledge base, and enrich our spirits by drawing from our differences and our diversity. Diversity has a uniqueness to it that makes it beautiful and admirable. Each and every human can identify with it. The abundant uniqueness in diversity is what makes it brightly colorful, inviting, brilliant, beautiful, and worthy of our acknowledgment. The fear of it currently is like fearing death. It is inevitable. Hence, it is critical for you to understand it, and understand sensitivity so that your base is broad enough to enable them comfortably accommodate others, and feel accommodated in the professional world of their time. Forge on as confident girls that are different from others, and let not questioning eyes make you doubt yourself."

Killers on the Roads

Kay was evidently perplexed when she realized through social media that some girls at her high school were reportedly hosting parties where they drank alcohol. Incriminating photographs of some notorious "party babes" circulated on Facebook and Instagram, sending shock waves throughout the academy. She had me watch the video posts on social media. As some parents and their daughters became aware of the scandal, they openly articulated their disappointment regarding the situation. We all agreed it was disappointing to know that some of the girls at this amazing institution drank alcohol as early as in their sophomore year. Understandably, it is not entirely the institution's responsibility to educate its students about underage drinking, misbehaving outside of school, and then showing it off on social media. Although consequences from the school administration follow such undignified behaviors of its students, the institution can only do so much for the girls. Parental and personal responsibility is the true culprit here. In spite of having easy access to it, Kay had never drunk an alcoholic beverage prior to our conversation due to our principle of **absolute no underage drinking**, and her adherence to our family principles. She became curious about alcohol consumption and had a multitude of questions for me during our "open door." I answered her questions the best I could. She recognized that underage drinking and abusing alcohol was not acceptable in our family, was an ill and since she was vexed by the conduct of some of her schoolmates, I explored the opportunity to examine her questions and to further educate her on the potential consequences of alcohol consumption.

Her father said to me, "She will soon be on her way to college. You could consider this part of our preparation for her leaving home." I agreed the time was appropriate to let her understand that she could well stumble on peers who drink, and should be able to tell when a peer is under the influence of alcohol and take the appropriate action.

I have met female high school and university students who were victims of motor vehicle accidents (MVA) due to alcohol use. In college, I suffered the loss of a dear friend to MVA and have spoken to parents who shared their loss or anger due to their child's involvement in alcohol-related MVAs. It is concerning that people drink and get themselves drunk, but it is even more troubling to me to understand that teenagers drink enough to get drunk. Kay's reaction and questions regarding the situation involving her peers, coupled with my experiences, helped me think about not only alcohol but also about vaping, drugs and other ills that our children may be exposed to or confronted with, as adolescents and young adults. Incumbent on parents to develop principles to guide their adolescents to responsible adults in the adulting process, I decided to discuss alcohol and drugs as true killers on our highways in *Compass,* to encourage parents to institute the principle of absolute no underage drinking in guiding their teen daughters into adulthood.

In the Know

We have all heard on multiple occasions that alcohol and drugs are responsible for countless preventable motor vehicle accidents

(MVAs) and deaths. Some of the reported accidents have involved college students while others have been said to involve young high school students still in their adolescence. This puts drunk driving on the radar and makes it undeniably one of the pressing issues facing the youth of this nation. According to records on public health and safety, alcohol-and-drug-related MVA have reduced since the year 2000, but the issue remains a notorious and leading danger to public health and safety. The records reveal that approximately twenty-five thousand Americans die each year while seven hundred thousand are injured in alcohol and drug related MVAs. I was astonished to learn that "over 50 percent or more than half of lethal crashes involve an alcohol-impaired driver and 65 percent of lethal single car crashes are similarly alcohol-related." Reports from the records indicate that law enforcement efforts to reduce such accidents are being heightened continuously but that some users of the roads and children are not heeding. Seeing this information reassured me that it has been in the know that alcohol intoxication and drugs influences are true killers on our highways and roads and that our children needed reminders about the dangers of these killers.

    I met adolescents and adults whose lives have forever changed because of poor judgments on the roads while driving after alcohol intoxication and/or drug usage. My children hear me comment daily on the absence of guarantees on road safety. I am not sure who has not noticed that some of our roads are wildly dangerous. The unsafe and predictably threatening nature of our roads are that way because some drivers are oblivious of the importance of their own lives and the lives of other users of the road. Some of such careless road users get behind their wheels and drive when they are intoxicated with alcohol, others drive after taking illicit drugs, while others drive in a 100 percent state of lucidity, but dangerously, just because they are wildly foolish, careless, stupid, idiotic, egoistic, think they are invincible, or are simply chronically irresponsible.

On Health Day in 2012, Health Days News reported from results of a study that alcohol and drug use is common among American teenagers, noting that over 15 percent of teens in the nation could be categorized as substance abusers per the study. Adolescence is a trying period in most children's lives. It was reported that adolescence is the age when kids experiment using alcoholic beverages and drugs. Such invaluable but scary information makes me to believe it is indispensable and a must for parents to help our adolescent daughters, soon-to-be young adults, to understand details surrounding the use of alcohol and drugs in our society. It is not a secret that many youth resort to using alcohol and drugs for varied reasons. Some children are naturally predisposed to using and even abusing alcohol because it runs in the family, while others have easy access to the substance. Some go to it as a temporary pain relief for their personal issues, academic difficulties, or psychiatric ailment.

It is imperative for parents to actively prevent their teenage and young adult daughters from alcohol, vaping and drug use. As an adolescent, I thought of the male gender as being the sole culprit with regards to excessive drinking but over time, I realized that it was an error on my part to think like that. Easy access sometimes causes the real problem for adolescents, no matter the gender. Some of our teenage daughters in their sophomore year in high school, as we now know, have already experimented drinking alcohol, are serving alcoholic beverages at their hosted parties, and so parental vigilance is required, especially for families who have wine cellars, home bars, or simply stock their homes with bottles of wine, beers, liquor, or alcoholic drinks of other nature.

Knowing May Be Half the Battle

I was astonished to learn from the National Institute on Alcohol Abuse and Alcoholism (NIAAA), that "1 in 4 children grow up in a home where someone drinks too much." That statistical information can be translated to indicate a real potential risk for underage drinking for children growing up in the environment with that someone. *I want to say adults need to be careful and fearful of copycat behavior from their children when they knowingly drink too much.* I understand from the NIAA that underage drinking is real and that it appeals to several adolescents and teens. Knowing the law on alcohol in the nation, I am certain that as guardians or parents, we and our adolescent children understand that underage drinking is when an individual begins consuming alcohol before he or she reaches the legal minimum drinking age of twenty-one years.

As I dug deeper into the killers of the road, it saddened me to realize that aside from being illegal, underage drinking is a widespread public health problem. As a public health worker or a health-care professional, I know frequent and excessive alcohol consumption poses many health-related and other risks. Well then, to start at underage must also pose different kinds of severe risks. Considering it significant for me and my daughters to know, I thought it may be critical for other parents to also know the risks involved in underage drinking, can recognize the signs and symptoms, and know preventive and resolution strategies.

Discussing with some parents about our daughters' imminent adulthood and transiting to college, it hit me hard when one parent bluntly emphasized her true worry about her daughter's going to college is due to the rampant use of drugs, alcohol, and the lack of willpower for abstinence on college campuses in America. We agreed that college drinking problems are exceptionally widespread, especially as a DFW University was in the news due to alcohol- and drug-related death of some of its students. Analyzing the concern critically, it is evident that the real issue with alcohol use lies with the negative effects resulting from excessive drinking rather than the act of drinking itself. Yeah! Excessive intake of alcohol is certainly destructive, and our daughters' young bodies and systems may not be equipped for the high volume or percentage of alcohol that may be ingested.

When high school and college students experiment with drinking alcohol, they probably are not aware of the ramifications of alcohol on their lives, their families and friends, and their communities. Did you know that according to the National Institute of Health (NIH), approximately four in five college students consume alcohol and that whether an alcohol consumer or not, almost all college students experience the repercussions of college drinking? The NIH reports that every year, drinking alcohol affects college students, their loved ones, and their communities in the following manner:

1) 1,825 college students between 18 and 24 years old die from unintentional alcohol-related injuries.
2) Over 692,000 students of ages 18 to 24 years are assaulted by another student who has been consuming alcohol.
3) More than 97,000 students of age 18 to 24 years' experience alcohol-related sexual assault or date rape.
4) Approximately 25 percent of college students underperform academically because their drinking alcohol.
5) Over 150,000 students develop an alcohol-related health crisis, and 1.2 to 1.5 percent of students report attempting to commit suicide because of alcohol and drug use.
6) 599,000 students ages 18 to 24 sustain unintentional injuries while under the influence of booze.

Considering the scary statistics on the killers of the road, I felt armed to add this topic in *Compass*, because it better prepared me to discuss the rationale for the principle with our daughters, alcohol consumption, and excessive drinking among some high school and college kids. Additionally, since knowledge and information sharing are fundamental, "Knowing may be half the battle" for parents and kids because Knowledge is ammunition. It is very empowering to know. It is only possible to proffer solutions to problems when we know what the issues or potential issues are or may be. Knowledge may be half the battle on this issue because the more parents are aware of some of the realities of these hazardous issues, the more likely they may be to hold honest and open discussions in that regard with their high school or college bound children; they may be less likely to be afraid to confront the existing realities of the issues, or feel alone if they face challenges with such issues, and less likely to harbor false notions of any kind in relation to this subject matter.

B and G

Betty, one of my close friends in college, was from a great family. She had it all going for her. She was young, kindhearted, sweet, beautiful, and intelligent. Her family was well-off. But she had a dark side that only her very close friends such as I knew. She was suffering inside because her father had an extramarital affair with their housekeeper who had just given her dad a baby from the affair. Consequently, her parents were going through a very bitter divorce. Despite her father's persistently pleading for pardon from the family, her mother had declared that she wouldn't stay married to a man who stooped low enough to bed her housemaid. Betty told us her mom said she felt dirty and insulted by her father and the maid and was unable to see her father because of the strong negative emotions she was feeling toward him at the time. Her mom had ejected their dad from the family home they shared for over eighteen years. He was still living in the same city but miles away from the family home. Betty had selected her escape route from all her worries. It was alcohol. Initially she indulged in binge drinking for comfort, drinking discreetly in her university apartment. Then she started drinking like she hated alcohol and wanted to eliminate it from the surface of the earth. We spoke to Betty several times about the ills of her exaggerated alcohol consumption.

After the annual school awards, Betty and Getty her best friend decide to attend a party hosted by another good friend. She had also worn a faculty award, and so we were all celebrating that Saturday night. The atmosphere was festive. There was the sound of light rock in the air. Some of us remained on campus and celebrated with a group of friends while others went to parties off campus, to the city. Betty and Gertrude (popularly called Getty by friends) drove together in Betty's car to attend a grand party hosted by a rich kid who lived on the outskirts of the city. I declined attendance to that party because I received best student award for my year and faculty, so my family friend, Dr. Okay, was celebrating my success at their family home.

I was alerted late on Sunday afternoon that Betty's car had traveled off its normal path and run into an electric pole as the girls drove back from the party and that both girls in the car had been rushed to the hospital emergency department early Sunday morning. A group of friends drove to the hospital to see them immediately news reached us. A crowd of students gathered very quickly at the university teaching hospital that afternoon. The families of both girls were notified. They arrived separately at their respective daughter's bedside that same day. We learned that both girls were unconscious when found on the scene of the accident. They had been urgently transported to the hospital. In spite of spending a significant amount of time at the hospital that day, we were not allowed to see either of the girls due to their condition. And hospital personnel caring for them only told us "they are unstable at this time." While visiting both students at the hospital, we learned more about their condition from each of their parents.

On Monday night, news got to us on campus that Getty had succumbed to her multiple injuries sustained from the single car crash. Betty was still in the intensive care unit fighting for her life. The atmosphere on some sections of the campus was suddenly very quiet and somber. The news had traveled ultra-quickly. All of us gathered in one campus apartment were evidently numbed by the sad news. Betty's mom told us that her daughter's blood alcohol level at the time of the crash was twice higher than the legal level. She sobbed, "Indeed, Betty was very drunk behind the wheels. She was drunk and incapable of driving her car. I didn't know she drank alcohol!" She was looking very desperate as she spoke. She had been crying from the day she arrived at the hospital and saw her daughter. Upon our arrival at the hospital, she asked us to pray for the girls to survive the crash. We were informed that at the announcement of Getty's death, she sank into a seat and screamed, "No, no, no, no, this is not true. No, no!" She cried like a baby right there at the hospital. Her daughter's best friend, whom she knew very well, had just died from a car crash. Her daughter was the driver of the car, and she was still in critical condition, unconscious. "Tell me it's not true. Oh no, no, Lord, no!" She cried inconsolably in the arms of her son, who was three years Betty's senior. We were all shocked by this very sad news. The atmosphere was one of profound sadness and we were all enveloped by it.

Four hours later, bad news continued to travel and consumed the campus. Betty had just passed away too. Two inseparable friends, young, passionate about life, intelligent, genuinely kind and loving young girls had just given in to multiple organ lacerations and physical injuries sustained from a preventable car crash. Their families were devastated and confused. Our university campus felt like a graveyard, deserted and somber. All the sounds of music that filled the air less than forty-eight hours prior seemed to have never existed. A frightening silence had taken over the place. Some friends were crying and exclaiming while others sobbed silently. Some mourned openly, and some revolted and blamed it on the parties and carelessness. The host of the party cried, "I should have stopped them from leaving. Betty was not evidently drunk, but she had a drink in her hand when they left. Getty said she'd drive, but Betty argued that she could drive and ended up driving. This is unbelievable. I don't understand…"

For months, we mourned the gorgeous duo by wearing pink or gold heart pins made especially for their remembrance. Some of the pins we wore were plain; others were engraved with words such as "B&G Gone too soon," "B&G in loving memory," or "B&G in our hearts forever." The university president and the administration supported anti-alcohol campaigns campus-wide, and anti-alcohol solidarity movements that started thriving on campus initiated by the student body that worked to keep the memories of our friends alive. We also marched for "awareness to the dangers of alcohol" quarterly after their death. In fact, we all worked hard on campus to not forget both girls and to raise awareness against alcohol intoxication. We did all we could to not forget them. They died too young, were gone too soon, and alcohol is to blame for the cause of their untimely death.

N and V

Twin sisters Nicky and Vicky were smart young women who attended a Saturday-night birthday party at a club in December of

2004. Their good friend was turning twenty-one and had decided to celebrate the milestone by throwing a big bash at her uncle's club. It was the most festive season of the year. Everyone was happy to be home for the holidays, and friends wanted to reconnect as usual after being apart for college. The young ladies were excited and happy to join in celebrating their friend's birthday during their first long break as upperclassmen in college.

Nicky, the older of the twins, had agreed to drive her sister and two other friends to and from the birthday party. They set out to attend the party in a group of four bubbly young ladies. It was said that when they got to the party, they met some of their usual boy pals and chatted for long periods with them. They also danced with the boys and shared their time together as friends. They were all university students full of Christmas period cheer and festive spirit. The party was a success, and the students enjoyed reconnecting, eating, and dancing together again.

As the four girls drove back home after the party, they did not imagine the fatal fate that awaited them on their way through the sleepy town and shiny lights. They had enjoyed themselves. Nicky had too much to drink, but it was not evident, and no one stopped her from driving the crew back to their various houses. As she sped through the twinkling Christmas lights, a fourth girl screamed from the back of the car for her to slow down or stop the car for another driver to take over, but the alcohol had taken the best of her. Nicky sped onto the country road after passing through the city and drove on somewhat blindly and under the influence. It was also reported that one of the girls was sleeping at the back of the car when Nicky lost control of her car that freezing early morning in December and smashed it into the trees of the slope. She bashed the car off the road and down a slope of large trees and bush. Some of their friends were in another car that was driving behind them at a slower pace. Those friends called the ambulance after noticing the car crash minutes later. They were the first people to arrive at the crash scene to help the girls out of the vehicle. They were unable to because the doors of the car were all locked and the girls appeared unconscious and unresponsive.

All four girls were rushed to the nearest hospital as soon as the ambulance arrived on the scene. Nicky and her sister were killed in the car crash. They were pronounced dead two hours after arriving at the emergency room. Nicky had a blood alcohol level just over the legal limit. Her sister's was almost twice the legal level. The other two girls suffered serious injuries but survived the accident. The third girl who lost a limb in the accident had twice the legal limit of alcohol in her blood. She reportedly slept upon entering the back of the car. The fourth girl had no alcohol in her blood. She fractured her pelvis and both knees in the accident. She underwent surgeries to replace both of her kneecaps and was said to have sustained pelvic bone fracture that would affect her ability to carry a pregnancy to nine-month term. She had to learn to walk again through acute rehabilitation for several months. An only child, the fourth girl was known in the community as a good Christian lady. Her involvement in an alcohol-related car crash shook her parents.

The police and media reports confirmed that she did not drink alcohol that night as evidenced in her lab results. She asserted that she did not know how much alcohol the twin sisters consumed or she would either have helped as the driver that night or would have called a parent to come help lift them back home. Her parents reportedly said to the press that they had warned her to never drink alcohol or enter the car of a drunk individual who was going to be in control of the wheels. Her parents were quoted as saying, "You drive the drunk person back to their house and make sure they are safe. But don't let them drive you."

"They just had life in them and were having fun," a friend recounted the events that happened at the party while discussing the defunct twin siblings. "They drank some alcoholic beverages at the bar, for sure, but I didn't know how much. I never thought anything of it because I didn't think girls drank much alcohol. Now it is clear some do. Those girls were probably just drinking without counting or being self-conscious and cautious. Sometimes you imagine that university students, and girls for that matter, would think twice before drinking alcohol, but they sure just drank excitedly. This is sad, this is very sad. What a waste of life," one of the girls' friends muttered after the incident.

Nicky and Vicky were two fascinating young ladies. The community was shattered by the news of their death. Alcohol-related deaths are often sudden, unexpected, and highly traumatic for families left behind. The parents of Nicky and Vicky set up a foundation for their only children and are a strong voice across the nation against college drinking. They have visited countless college campuses preaching against students' use and abuse of alcohol. Besides, they have shared their daughters' stories with thousands of students across the globe. Their mom often begins her speeches at events by saying, "Alcohol stole my only children from me. They were about to turn twenty-one when they died from a car crash after heavy drinking of alcoholic beverages at a party. I am happy to see all of you young men and women here. Let's get started."

Alcohol-related car crashes are not unique to college students. High school students and teenagers are also often involved in fatal car crashes that are alcohol-related. In fact, alcohol and drug use among American youths are correlated to increased car crashes on weekends according to some reports. Alcohol use and abuse is a big-time public health concern in this nation, per stats. What I have shared with Kay and Court is that abuse of these substances increases the risk for several issues. Driving while drunk and causing a car crash involving the death of passengers could lead to charges of homicide by motor vehicle while under the influence. These are some of the discussions we have had and which mothers should not hesitate having with their daughters because we never know, and "knowing may be half the battle."

CY

Cy lived with her parents, who are both lawyers in their hometown. They have a home bar and confirm they drink a bottle of wine daily at dinner. Cy has alcohol in front of her daily. She has never been told by her parents to not try it. However, her mom told her she expects Cy will drink only modestly when she becomes of legal drinking age. She is an only child and is very lonely. She has young male friends among the family's group of close friends with whom she plays and hangs out after school. Cy reported to her PCP that she started drinking at the age of thirteen. She said at that tender age, she could have any type of alcoholic beverage she wanted since she had ready access to whatever type she wanted, desired, or liked.

Her parents went to France often and brought back home countless bottles of alcoholic beverages. She had access to vintage, nonvintage bottles of wine, and champagne blanc, rosé, and brut. She said at thirteen, she drank true Sauvignon and other true French champagne such as Moet, Dom Pérignon, Veuve Clicquot, Bollinger, Perrier Jouët, and Krug. She reported that Bailey's Irish Cream was her favorite alcoholic drink. She would add ice to it and fill her cup with the creamy and sweet beverage, and said Bailey's was to her what milk is to Court because milk is her best beverage. If she is not ready for bed, give her a glass of milk, and she will relax almost immediately, and be ready to sleep. That was Baileys for Cy. She openly asserts that she drank heavily from the age of fifteen till she left for college. While in college, she felt something was missing, and she was unable to focus on her classes, campus life and activities without alcohol. She missed the drinks so much she decided to return home one day during the week to take some bottles of alcohol with her while her parents were gone to their various law offices.

Cy had drunk so much during her teenage years that she was beginning to experience some of the effects of alcohol in her life. In college, she got drunk often, especially at night and the weekend. She was known to have a very nice personality, although she was reportedly rude when she was under the influence. She remained abusive to alcohol until she was nineteen. She had several friends because she could pay their way to museums, trips, etc. But she was a young alcoholic, and her friends knew that. Her parents had been informed of their daughter's relationship with alcohol and the consequences being witnessed on campus. They tried helping her and blamed themselves for what had happened to their only daughter.

She was expected home on the weekend of Easter 2011. She and her best friend left campus and drove to her friend's home, where she dropped off her friend. Then she drove off, heading to her family house. She decided to drink some alcohol on her way home. Evidently, Cy drank herself to a dangerous proportion. The alcohol in her system altered her mental and reflexive abilities. She became reckless and drove her car so fast that she crashed onto a concrete wall on the road. Her car then somersaulted and landed on its roof while the tires suspended in the air. Traffic was immediately stopped on the long and busy interstate by witness who called emergency services. She was airlifted to the hospital by a paramedic helicopter. Her parents were notified promptly since her car was matriculated in her parents' name. They left for the hospital as soon as they were notified and arrived at the hospital to be by their only daughter's bedside.

Seventy-two hours after her accident, she was still unconscious but alive. She was in a state of medically induced coma and would remain in that state for over a month. She suffered multiple traumas but survived the crash. She spent several months in hospital and received excellent care. The accident impacted her life badly. Cy suffered traumatic brain injury, also known as TBI, and could not recognize her parents during her first five months of hospitalization. She suffered severe cognitive impairment secondary to the TBI. She was in cognitive and speech rehabilitation for six months in a European hospital. Cy's recovery was slow and painful for her parents, family, and friends. She underwent multiple surgeries secondary to injuries sustained from the accident. She remained disoriented to time, place, person, and situation for almost half a year. She remained hospitalized in an acute rehabilitation center where she received intense physical therapy and learned to walk again. She had to learn to use her hands, improve the general functionality of her upper extremities, and perform her personal hygiene after countless sessions and several months of both physical and occupational therapies. Her parents watched their adult daughter behave like a kid, relearn basic skills such as reading and eating again because of the severe impacts of the single car crash.

The accident affected her for life. Due to the TBI, she remains irrational, impulsive, irritable, and very nervous. She is incapable of keeping a good job, and all her friends do not always understand her new personality. She no longer drinks alcohol, but daily she and her parents suffer the sequelae from her alcohol-related crash. During a fund-raiser for kids who'd been victims of alcohol, drugs, and addiction, her father spoke tearfully. His Words to the crowd gathered at the occasion could hardly be forgotten:

Thank you all for being here today…I assure you ladies and gentlemen that drunk-driving can kill anyone faster and more easily than a heart attack… You should avoid alcohol at all cost. It is a drug and can be very addictive. Once upon a time I imagined life differently than I do today. I have an only child…My daughter.

… She is the apple of my eyes…It is exactly three years today since her preventable accident on a highway as she made her way home from Uni. She had consumed alcohol and felt high. She drove her car like someone who did not like herself. She drove like she did not like her life. But I can assure you she did love herself and her life because she has fought to preserve both. She needed help in making the right choices and the right decision…that is to avoid alcoholic drinks, especially when you are a lady and you are a driver…" He narrated the circumstances that surrounded his daughter's accident and explained her life before and after the accident. Several people in the audience teared up while listening to his moving narrative.

"When you drink and drive, you not only endanger your life, you put the safety of other users of the roads at risk. Alcohol has a terribly negative effect on behavior and performance. When a drunk driver is high, the road becomes a senseless marketplace where she can no longer focus attentively. When a person is drunk, she is more likely to be euphoric, aggressive, less risk-averse, and less cautious. You see folks, alcohol is like a sleeping pill, it is a drug that puts people to sleep. So what does this mean to drivers who have consumed too much alcohol? Like my only daughter, they are at risk of falling asleep while trying to steer the wheels of a motor vehicle. While driving, my daughter was drowsy and could not perceive the danger she was in because she was drunk. She was not vigilant and was therefore unable to react in a timely fashion when her car swiveled out of control on the interstate. You see, she was alone in the car but from the reports we all got, she missed killing many people on the road that day because of aggressive and irrational driving…I am not here to ask you to completely avoid drinking alcohol. As adolescents and young adults, it is acceptable and welcomed for you to refuse alcoholic beverages. Young ladies especially should refrain from consuming this drug we call alcohol. However, consuming a small amount of alcohol does not usually have the detrimental effects that accompany moderate to heavy drinking. I am here to share the story of how alcohol destroyed my daughter's bright future and altered her life forever. The decision is yours to make to *say No to alcohol*...whether it is mild, moderate or heavy drinking, today is the day you begin to tell yourself I do not want that alcoholic drink. I see no need for it in my system. I want to always remain responsible. We do not need any more drunk drivers killing themselves and others on our roads. If you are the parent of adolescents and young adults, if you are an adolescent, male or female, it does not matter. Today is the day you want to understand the ills of alcohol on your emotion, focus, perception, judgment, attention and your entire thought process and behavior… Life is a precious thing. Value it by refraining from operating a motor vehicle while drunk or under the influence of alcohol…Value it by saying goodbye or *No* to alcohol today once and for all…"

Answering Our Daughter's Questions

After discussing the indiscretions of the so-called party girls at her high school, Kay asked, "So can parents easily discern it if their child has consumed an alcoholic drink?"

Manny, walking through the door, felt free to chime in, "Yes, ma'am! Her breath is the first thing that might tell she has consumed alcohol. Also, certain behaviors betray someone who has drank even just a normal amount of alcohol. You see, parents usually know their children very well that the slightest change in behavior could be telling of something. Alcohol does impact social behaviors. For example, if I have an introverted or often calm child who suddenly returns home and is outgoing, impulsive, is mildly euphoric, if that child begins talking louder than usual or appears unable to hold a sensible conversation with me and appears to be high, I will want to check her out to see if she has consumed some wine, beer, or liquor, whether she is predisposed to drink or not. If my daughter returns home and cannot walk straight or stand upright or walks into furniture and appears to be half asleep while walking in—Oh, if her speech is slurred or she can't make a sensible sentence, then evidently she is drunk."

Kay opened her eyes widely and responded, "Wow. Okay, that is wild. Why then do the parents of the party girls not see these things?" I was fast in responding. "Who knows? We don't know. Maybe they did. We will never know what the right response to your question is. What you should know, however, is that alcohol induces behavioral changes that are easily detectable by parents, law enforcement agents, friends, teachers, peers, neighbors, and whomever."

"In addition to what your dad said, other consequences of alcohol intoxication may include a decrease in alertness, impaired motor skills, altered judgment which may lead to slower or heightened reaction time. These consequences often contribute to road accidents. People who drive after drinking intolerable amounts of alcohol are less cautious because of the alcohol intoxication or their blood alcohol content, also known as BAC. These are the guys that are said to have been driving under the influence when caught by law enforcement after a crash, unlawful speeding, or reckless driving. Driving under the influence is also known as DUI."

She insisted, "These girls don't drive drunk, Mom. They just get wasted and probably have the less drunk person in their group drive them home. Or I don't know. Whatever they are doing, it is sad to see it posted on social media like they want the world to see that they are proud of being wasted or drunk."

I continued, "So being wasted or drunk is the same, right? It is better, though, to not try to drive drunk but instead have the sober one in the group be the dedicated chauffeur then. I am not saying being wasted is acceptable but if identified, better do something about not driving while drunk or wasted."

I continued, "Certainly the risks for MVA are very high when driving drunk or wasted. Hence, it is good for them to avoid drunk driving and have the person who did not drink to drive them. Due to the confusion and double vision that may result from being drunk, the tendency to drive recklessly and cause an accident with casualties or fatalities is very high. Sober drivers are more cautious and alert to their surroundings and road situations than wasted ones. When drunk, that alertness fades out and irrationality sets in making it easier for the drunk person to indulge in risky driving than when sober. These make it quite a challenging task to successfully operate a vehicle appropriately when wasted. Additional points to note include facts that when driving drunk and in the company of friends or people who are also drunk or tipsy, the risk of crashing increases. Most parties occur at night time. Well, more crashes involving teenage and young adult drivers happen at nighttime. Being drunk behind the wheels compounds the problem and increases the potential for fatalities in such accidents."

She wanted all her questions answered as she carried on, "So when a person is wasted, she sees things in double?"

I was certain. "Yeah, a wasted person may see things spinning or double, their eyes may roll, and their head may spin too." She wondered, "So why then do these girls go through this trouble? Why do these party girls put themselves through that? It sounds tiring and unfortunate. Oh dear! Mom, I can't even imagine what you are explaining—rolling eyes, seeing double, oh wait, double vision, right? And confusion? Ugh! Why go through all that pain and hassles for alcohol? I do not see any good reason, but you never know."

I wasn't sure there was a good reason either to drink excessively and become wasted or drunk, so I concurred with her, "I agree with you. There is not a plausible reason for drinking in excess." We both smiled. I insisted, "There are other consequences of alcohol. You may see in the news that people became aggressive in bars or nightclubs, began fighting, or even engaged in a gunfight or shooting battle. Sometimes alcohol is the culprit for such aggressive actions and/or reactions because drunkenness potentiates increase in negative reaction time."

While we were discussing the topic, in my opinion it was the best time to tell her a bit more of what I knew on the matter. "You see, the worse of it all is that long-term alcohol abuse or frequent consumption in excess has long-run repercussions, including health problems which may include not only significant confusion and memory loss but also health issues such as the Korsakoff syndrome and, worst of all, the alcoholic liver disease, also known as ALD."

She looked perplexed. "Okay, Mom, you just lost me, or maybe I lost you. Mom, translate those words in English." Then she laughed. "I am not a health-care professional, Mom. The ADL and Korsa-what-drome? What are these types of illnesses?" She asked apparently more interested in the conversation than I anticipated. I laughed and briefly explained Korsakoff syndrome, insisting, "Korsakoff syndrome is simply the deficiency in B vitamin thiamine. That is not the worse health-related consequence anyway. The ADL is the real issue. That occurs after years of heavy alcohol consumption. The thing is, our liver is one of our noble or vital organs. A healthy liver helps process vitamins, sugars, fats, and proteins. Are you with me now?" I inquired. She nodded in affirmation.

I pursued, "Now when diseased, the liver, like any other vital organ, loses its potential to function effectively. When it malfunctions, guess what happens?" She frowned. "The person dies?" I nodded. "Sometimes they do die. Very close but not there yet in this case. The person's life is at risk because liver disease is life threatening. Persistent long-term exaggerated alcohol use or abuse can severely damage the liver, therefore causing ADL. And ADL, at its worst, is what is known as liver cirrhosis. Yes, then it can easily kill the person. You get the picture?" I took a deep breath. "Yes, ma'am. So, the person dies!" she exclaimed. "Yes," I responded. "But maybe a car crash is what may take their lives before the liver is attacked," I intimated. "Either way, Mom, abusing alcohol is not worth doing. Whether you drive drunk or you go to bed often drunk, you are closer to a sad end, it seems, than your peers who are sober at all times." I concurred "You are darn right, child! You got it!" Engaged in the conversation, I added, "You see, babe, the dangers for young girls who drink alcohol indiscriminately and get wasted is that they may easily fall prey to predators who would easily abuse them sexually and even physically." She looked perplexed but smiled.

Know that the dangers of sexual and physical assault on college campuses often occur after the young lady is intoxicated with alcohol. We need for you to know that alcohol has a relaxant effect that may cause generalized body weakness and somnolence to a lesser degree, and hyper-somnolence and unconsciousness to a higher degree. Hence, if a girl drowns her belly with alcoholic drinks, she may pass out and sleep deeply, leaving herself vulnerable to a predator who may abuse her. It may not matter that the girl was drinking in the company of her good friends. It is often those close guy friends that may end up sexually utilizing and abusing their wasted and unconscious female friends on campus. You are learning and must be very vigilant, young lady, alright? "Drinking alcohol has absolutely no advantages to or for you. You know my stance on this subject matter. In your place, I would avoid drinking it until such time in your adulthood that you know you are mature enough to say yay or nay to social drinking and you can tell yourself when enough is enough of it."

She asserted, "I have no intention of tasting it now. And I am not sure what I will do after I turn twenty-one. It is several years from now. I have time to think about it. Alcohol appears rather difficult to handle. That is why these girls on the social media posts are wasted and behaving badly. They can't handle it. Why drink it if you can't handle it? Why hurt yourself? I hope that if I ever drink, it will be in moderation. The very idea that a girl could be easily raped on a college campus by her own guy friend just like that because she passed out from drinking alcohol is pretty scary. What in the world!" That sounded somewhat encouraging. I wanted to be sure she understood that aside from behavioral implications, other ramifications were associated with being wasted or drunk. I declared, "Unfortunately, babe, that is the kind of world we live in. Young ladies must know the truth to be better prepared when socializing. Furthermore, law enforcement agents are excellent at enforcing the law and impose legal sanctions on people who drive drunk. Legal consequences for DUI include either revoking or suspending the driver's license.

Also, the courts may decide to have the drunk person undergo alcoholism therapy in an alcohol rehabilitation center. These are traceable footsteps that stay in people's records. Not good at all for any one's reputation, especially not a lady's. She smiled. "Why is society's eyes more on women than men? When a guy does some weird stuff like passing out and being wasted, some people may easily forget he did. But when the same thing happens to the opposite gender, it becomes a real issue and concern. Why, Mom?" My response was not what I would have liked for it to be. I smiled back. "It will probably remain that way forever. Maybe people think a lady's reputation is more precious than a gentleman's, I suppose. I am not sure. Often, men get away with behaving badly. Women don't. And often, scrutiny on female actions, values, attitudes, and behaviors is higher than for the male counterparts."

Little Things Make the Difference— Lady

I hear from my parents and others that life in the societies of yesteryears was very different from contemporary society. Some of our friends have also shared that their parents often discuss the changes that are very evident between "their time" and now. My response to discussions that evoke some of the disparities is usually geared toward "generational differences, improvements in science and technology, and situational challenges." Currently, we live in a very fast-paced world, and our lives are filled with countless kid-related activities in addition to our career responsibilities. I often say we do not have sufficient number of hours in a day to accomplish what we need or must do in a twenty-four-hour period. The rush of life has easily taken its toll on some of us to the extent we often forget to do some of the little things that matter, and that may make the difference in a situation or someone's day, week, month, or life. There are certainly myriad little things that as ladies, we could do to make a difference daily. For our daughters, I initiated the principle of **being a lady** and explained with the following examples what that could mean.

I recently visited and spoke with JJ, a manager at an acute care hospital. We discussed various health-care organizations and our positions. We were having a serious but very good discussion. She asked me if in my position as a corporate employee I ever make my own copies at work. I described the organizational structure and explained to her the administrative makeup of the campus housing my office. I indicated to her that the campus had three administrative assistants with whom I work and who could and would assist me when I need help printing or copying documents for various purposes. Two of these employees are campus administrative assistants, and one is a corporate administrative assistant to the vice president of operations that I reported to.

JJ explained to me that at the organization where she worked, there were no assistants, and she does what she needs done by herself. I asked her what kinds of things she would need help with, and she replied, "Changing the ink in the copier, making fast copies, putting paper in the printer…" I grinned at her, but she did not look content at all. I transformed my grin into a broad smile and responded, "Yes, I have three very fine ladies who would readily assist me at work when needed. However, I rarely ask them for help of that nature. It must be very pressing and impossible for me to complete such tasks to request their assistance. They each have a lot to do and are administrative assistants, so you can imagine in how many different directions they get pulled. Aside from the corporate assistant, I work very closely with the other two. What I do is, instead of asking them for help, I go to them when I have a downtime, which is very rare, and ask them how I can be of service to them. Often, when preparing for hospital meetings such as the quality council meeting, medical executive committee, or governing board meetings, they each fulfill the requirements of their individual role in that realm, and the hospital director whom I oversee fulfills her role in preparing the meetings. However, I could ask for additional this or that if I determine we need more documentation to support data presented at the meetings. But I make sure to not add to their already full and overflowing plates. I intentionally make sure to ask what I can do to assist especially during such times. Not surprisingly, each time I offered to assist them, they had me help with one or two things to get their job done. When all is said, and done, I make sure to send them a token of appreciation and a note expressing my gratitude for their hard work and service.

JJ appeared amazed at what she was hearing, "You see, JJ, I try to act like a lady. This means that it is important for me to understand and know how to do the little things around the office that need to be done and not leave them for an assistant to do. What I try to do as a leader is serve others, especially those that often serve us. As a lady, I think of what I can do to ease their workload and therefore assist them accomplish part of their responsibility and not necessarily what they can do for me as the corporate person coming to attend their hospital's meetings. I add papers to the copier when needed. I assist with putting packets together, I change the printer's ink when necessary instead of asking someone to do it for me, I push the cart filled with credentialing files and take it to the medical executive committee meeting locale when need be, I do what it takes to make sure that our team's work is excellently done by helping them in such little ways."

JJ looked perplexed. Her eyes widened as I spoke, and her smile broadened with each of my sentences. She exclaimed, "How fantastic! And you said 'as a lady?' You are truly a lady. Those are some of the little things that make a difference in a person's day at work." Our encounter reminded me to share with our daughters the little things that may make the difference and set them apart as "true lady," according to JJ's words.

I was reminded by her that ladies have a way about them whether at school, in the office, on the roads, in their vehicle, at the gym, or in the grocery store. There is something about ladies that is distinguishing. Ladies certainly get frustrated at work like every normal person, but they can keep their cool in challenging circumstances and remember to do the little things that make the difference in other people's lives whether it is for administrative assistants or others.

On the highway, for example, I got screamed at years ago when a woman exited her vehicle, leaving her kids in the car to walk up to my vehicle to scream at me for making a poor entrance onto the road. A lady is one whom when confronted with such a situation would maintain her calm and remain as cool as a cucumber.

A lady on the highway understands that public arenas are for communal use, so she exhibits no aggression on the road but maintains a calm composure and a zipped lip when a hasty, reckless, or uncompromising driver swings ahead of her, is almost pushing her off the road, or even gives her the finger or tongue on the highway.

Dr. Krauss, an outstanding lecturer at the university where I did my MBA once asked us this questions in class: "How would you react on the highway if an aggressive driver is behind you, is honking his horn for you to let him or her pass, or wants to pass you hastily without any warning or is even pushing you off the road so he can pass?"

Several of us shared our views and responses. He continued, "Why would you react that way?" There were several responses. For some, it was being a lady. For others, it was "doing the little thing that may make the difference in that person's life, not knowing why they were in such a rush, what their crisis was, and the idea that the road is for all of us to use, so we must remember to be civil and kind as we share it communally."

In such a circumstance, a lady would calmly create space for that driver to enter in front of her without hesitation. And prior to changing lanes, the lady would indicate using her lights to notify other users of the road of her intent to change lanes. Although we would all agree that some delirious drivers push other users of the roads to the tips of their nerves, a lady is an understanding, considerate, and courteous user of the roads who remembers to make way for a struggling road user, who uses her indicators to appropriately communicate on the roads because such little acts may make the difference, especially on our roads where the potential for an accident almost always lingers.

Dr. Krauss, whose classes I thoroughly enjoyed at the University, asked many other questions that made us think and share our viewpoints. He challenged us as students and was very transformational. There were excellent reasons to every question he asked us. On a different day in class, he asked us to each share what our pet peeves were and to explain the reasons for the pet peeves.

One that I shared with our class was tardiness. A lady does her utmost to make it to appointments, rendezvous, class, church, meetings, and other appointments on time the best she can. Professionally, I am known to arrive very early at work, usually the first or one of the first people to arrive, and last to leave.

Recently, often tired and oblivious to time zones as a result of traveling to different states for my work, I failed the practice and arrived last or late for some social gatherings. Additionally, tiredness began making it difficult for me to be timely at places where Manny had made reservations for us.

Kay, Court, and Manny did a tag team one Valentine's Day and decided to set the clocks at our house, on my phone, and in my car thirty minutes ahead of time. The clocks are normally set ten minutes ahead of time to help us out with timing. I went to bed for a nap and as usual was too fatigued to wake up when my alarm rang. I requested another ten-minute nap. Kay woke me up on time.

When I ultimately got ready to leave the house, I felt bad that we were running behind schedule per Manny's reservation. I profusely apologized. He calmly said, "We did what we needed to do to make sure we remained on schedule and arrive on time for the occasion." I did not understand and asked "We will never make it there for our reserved time. What do you mean?" Smiling, our daughters explained that they assisted their dad in planning a surprise event for me. "You guys are not late. Mom, you will be on time. Stop apologizing." Not knowing that the times on the clocks around our home were incorrect, I responded, "Well, looking at that time, we are running late." They all smiled mischievously, looking at each other. Kay finally explained, "You will be on time. We changed the time on all the clocks you see around here, on your phone, in your car, everywhere. The clocks are all thirty minutes ahead. The time right now is this minus thirty minutes. You are ahead of schedule, but with your drive time, you should be on time, like a lady. Those are the words we have heard for as long as we have been Ursula's daughters—like a lady. And, ladies, do not go late to planned or scheduled appointments, reservations, and so on. Ha! But tired ladies also need some good rest. Haha!" Laughing and nodding, I exclaimed, "No way! You all played time mischief to allow me catch a bit more rest? Thanks, brood! You all are the best! So, what's the real time now?"

Court chuckled. "Time for you and dad to dash out of here for your date so you are not tardy."

When all was said, and done, we agreed again that a lady would keep to time and do what it takes to avert tardiness. We had discussed the importance of being on time. It was comforting to see that our daughters helped me keep time when they realized tiredness could interfere with my respect for a principle that I dearly propound. A lady should leave home well ahead of time for any occasion not just for respect of the people awaiting her timely arrival but also to prevent her from hurrying on the roads, driving aggressively, cursing like a sailor as she drives due to her being in a haste, and running red lights. Respecting time to avoid the consequences of rushing on the highway is a great way to be or remain a lady by doing this little thing that may make a difference in varied ways.

Some of the little things done that could make the difference include what my dad said to me as a kid. My dad always said to us, "You dress your best on Sundays because you are going into the house of God and you want to visit Him respectfully, so look great for Him." This stuck with me because that was it. Growing up, my parents were principled about dressing per the occasion's dress code, and there was no compromise on the subject.

As an adult lady, I realized that dressing appropriately for the occasion was a true little thing with immense significance. Dad was right. And to me, he is indisputably always right! We have heard in certain situations or occasions someone curiously ask, albeit under their breath, "What is she wearing? What in the world is she wearing? This is not the place to come dressed like that! What was she thinking?" or "Boy, why is she dressed like she is in her backyard, working on her plants and flowers?" These are comments that have made heads turn at social gatherings, including private and public dinners, luncheons, parties, school functions, charity events, etc.

Simply put, being a lady could entail doing a little thing such as dressing appropriately for the occasion. Take the time to take care of yourself as a lady in this little way. Reserve wearing sports shorts at the appropriate time and for the right event and place. As lady should not wear gym-like and workout clothing to church because those are reserved for going to the gym, and there is a good reason those are called gym or workout clothes.

The understanding is that jeans are very popular in certain cultures, and so they may work well for a dress-up or a dress-down day/occasion, which may work almost everywhere. It is cool, and I like it. However, as a lady, reserve the jeans for occasions where jeans may be appropriate because of the absence of a dress code for that occasion. As a lady, respect for your host and the occasion should prompt you to do this little thing that may make the difference in very many ways. In sum, this translates to "attire appropriateness for place and time."

Keep the Peace—Family Matters

As humans and members of a large community of people, friends are an important part of each of our lives. Katie A., a sweet friend, gave me a small stone frame on which is engraved the words "Friends are the families we chose for ourselves." My family has been blessed with amazing family friends that we cherish so much. Indeed, in times of crisis and in our absence, our daughters would run to some of our best friends before they try to make it to our families. That notwithstanding, we raised our girls to understand our principle that **family is very important, matters and comes first.** As blood relations, my family should be the first place my daughters go to in case of an emergency.

I love my family dearly. My best sister recently visited us from England, and we had the time of our lives, reminiscing, singing, dancing, praying, laughing, and crying together. Our daughters witnessed the abundant love that we shared. My family visited my sister last summer and shared an equally fabulous time with she and her family. During her recent visit, in conversation relating to our family, I told my sister, "I am related to my family but I had no control over that. I love my family very much, and I do not take any one of them for granted, but, boy, sometimes the bickering is so much, it is tiring. We need to fix this. While we have amazing friends, families share a relationship sealed by blood. It should be thicker they say, right?" She looked at me, equally frustrated with our family shenanigans. She agreed, "We love each other, but our differences in opinion, values, and even communication styles are clear, and we dispute over almost everything. Come on and read this e-mail and tell me what you think about it and if there is a good reason to communicate in that manner. There are insults all over the message. And the tone is very condescending."

I truly wanted to enjoy my time with her and mom, and did not want to discuss our family. I thought to myself that she was visiting from England, and we had to make the most of our time together. She insisted on me seeing the mail and began reading it aloud. I joined her, and we both read the mail and several other similar messages on her phone. When we finished reading the exchanges and commenting on it, I noticed she appeared forlorn discussing this and immediately understood that although some of us get along greatly and have maintained our original strong bond with each other, the persistent collective disunity and frequent fracas between certain siblings have taken their toll on her.

She is, after all, the big sister to all of us. For me, she is the big sissy I always wanted to have—caring, loving, understanding, kindhearted, and forgiving. "We need to create time to work this out fairly and amicably among all of us. Our parents want us to live in peace and keep the peace between us. How can we bring everyone together in peace and to keep the peace?" I queried, looking straight into her eyes.

Experiences between my siblings and our daughters' multiple questions and my desire to ensure our girls remained each other's best friend prompted me to establish the principles of family is very important, matters and comes first, within my family with Manny and our girls.

During my childhood, adolescence, and young adult life, I would never have imagined that my family would ever argue or fight each other. We were inseparable, loving, understanding, caring, kind to each other, very united, and leading a great life.

There was not a sign that could have made me imagine that we would experience big, serious brawls with lasting negative impact on our relationships. But as we matured and our parents aged further, the donnybrook began full force, and divisiveness ensued as silos formed. Oddly, this has lasted a very long time, with brief periods of intermission before another heated argument and fight. I sometimes think to myself, as families, we love each other, but we also love to hate each other, and, yes, we sometimes hate to love each other. I am not sure why the former and latter happen. Apparently, when father has a lot of equity, children fight for/over it, some vying for the fattest share of everything, and being jealous at the smallest gains some make on this or that, while others remain insatiable and greedy no matter what, seeking control of everyone and everything. What a world! And reality is, the world is real, and in the real world, in our modern societies, several families bicker among themselves for varied reasons or without a plausible motive. Notwithstanding, it does not have to be bad if the involved family members are willing to avert a deep conflict through understanding of their differences.

The world is far from being a perfect place, and our earthly life is hardly a perfection. For this and other reasons such as our peculiarities, conflicts do exist as part of life and part of every relationship. Born of the same parents or not, our idiosyncrasies make for our uniqueness as individuals which is no different in a brotherly and sisterly relationship. We are all different from each other. And families are made up of unique individuals who each have different dreams, interests, values, aspirations, personalities, manners, and even approach to communication, as my older sister indicated recently.

Our uniqueness and differences as individuals predispose us to have interpersonal conflicts. My older sister asserted recently, "We have differences in values and opinions and argue over everything, but we need to make up after the arguments. We are a family. Begrudging each other will not help resolve the issue." Conflicts are natural and can be resolved quickly once and for all, especially in a family, if all parties involved are understanding and forgiving. However, I have learned from my own family that strategies and pathways used or not used to resolve serious conflicts can create deeper problems. And problems don't just become deeper in a day; it takes time, not an awful long time, but it does require time for small cuts caused by serious arguments to balloon into eschars difficult to debride and clean up. Nonetheless, my perspective is that no wound is impossible to heal and close with willful forgiveness, and when the love of and for family is firmly implanted within us, with an early understanding from family values and principles that family is very important, it matters, and it comes first in all appropriate situations.

Family should be the first place where reasonable individuals demonstrate goodwill, understanding, and tolerance. The absence of such basic principles from family experiences might create soured feelings. Such feelings may worsen, especially if some siblings are haughty and devoid of kind sisterly or brotherly considerations. **Keep the peace** is the principle that I shared with my daughters as critical in maintaining family unity. Keep the peace in this *Compass* means to make and maintain peace after a conflict. Keeping the peace is the responsibility of each family member because family matters. I've heard people say home is where the heart is. Well, I say family is where the soul is because it is where we grew up with the people that know and understand us best, have our best interest at heart, and love us unconditionally. As we guide our kids through life, it is imperative to be principled about how family greatly matters, and set the example for our daughters to always be there for each other, and have each other's back, and to keep the peace between them, even and especially when we are gone from their midst.

Cradling Love and Trust

Considering the aforementioned principles, I explained to our girls that excellent and lasting sibling love and friendship, when formed at a very tender age, could be very enduring. However, siblings who squabble a lot as kids and say things such as "I hate my sister" from a tender age may grow up loving each other more due to maturity, lessons learned, and better understanding of the other.

We raised our girls to believe that because family matters first and foremost, they should be best friends and inseparable. I consciously raised them to understand that "loving each other unconditionally is crucial in our family, respect of each other's body is critical, and therefore hitting, kicking, or biting the other and physical fights are prohibited in our family." Since having them, I continue to pray for enduring love, understanding, peace, and unity between them. Although they argue now and then for one reason or the other, their age difference made it easier for a tight bond to establish between them very early. Kay cared tenderly for Court as an older sibling. She helped to change her nappies, play with her, read to her, sing to her, and comfort her when she screamed for me. On her part, Court looked up to Kay as they grew up. I wanted them to have a relationship later in life that was built on a solid foundation of love, trust, and friendship. Believing that a powerful bond that could withstand and resist the boldest of tempestuous times should begin very early at home as they grew up, I included Kay in Court's care from the day she was born so she would learn to be there for her sister from her cradle with love and attentiveness. Their age difference was a factor that proved to be helpful in this endeavor, and Court learned to run to her big sister when she needed a sisterly cuddle or something to drink, wanted to play, and so on. The idea was to generate their love, trust, and care for the other from their infancy. My hope was that their confidence in the bond they share would be superb once they could trust each other. I had no idea what I was trying to do would work but as a matter of principle, I did what I believed in. As they grew up, I realized that their very different personalities also helped them get along easily and intensified their loving relationship. Kay will hardly start an argument and rarely gives a repartee when Court becomes argumentative. When both girls were teenagers as I was completing this manuscript, my plan appeared to have worked perfectly. They never raised a finger at each other and have never fought. They are tightly connected and fiercely protective of each other. However, I do not know what will happen as they mature, leave home, make new friends, marry, have their own families, and live apart from each other. The thought of living them here someday with an indelible reminder of how we raised them, how we would like for them to maintain their firm sisterly bond and tie their respective families together in love, respect, trust, and understanding, coupled with my personal family experiences and their questions about my family, helped me to initiate these principles to guide them into their adulthood as best friends who firmly and unconditionally love eachother.

Breaking Is Infeasible

Even though there are organizations that foster relationships and networking among women, it appears to me sometimes that it is harder for the female gender to maintain a solid relationship between them than it is for men. Seriously bothersome is seeing that women naturally bicker among themselves more than men do. In more general terms, viewed through personal lenses, these are my perspectives after so many years on earth. Whether you agree with these notes on inter-feminine rapport or dispute them, it does not have to be that way. We need to network more, form stronger bonds that are practically infeasible to break, and learn to better understand and trust each other more. Collaboration among women should begin right in the family circle. Considering the principles of family matters, for girls who have siblings, it is important to cultivate a special relationship among you all, especially with your sisters. The ties between you should be powerful and solid to the extent that breaking it becomes an infeasible consideration by whomever. Sisterly relationships should be one that friends, partners, spouses, and other close individuals understand it is impossible to tear or damage. Fundamentally, family is where the soul is as "home is where the heart is," so it is critical to build strong family ties to protect the soul. I shared with my girls that the foundation for family ties that are infeasible to break is love. I hold this belief as a sinful woman who tries to lead a good Christian life and mostly look to the prescriptions of the Word of God to answer some of the most daunting questions I encounter.

In 1 John 4:7 (NABRE), we are told, *"Beloved, let us love one another, because love is of God; everyone who loves is begotten by God and knows God."* Love as a foundation for a solid relationship is further expressed in 1 Peter 4:8 (NABRE), *"Above all, let your love for one another be intense."* When you hear your daughter say "I hate you" or "I hate my sister," dialogue with her to explain why she would say that. Then seriously dissuade her from saying those words and for harboring such a negative sentiment for her sister. Even if she says it without believing she does truly hate her sister, the hatred versus love might stick in her speech, mind and deeds. Further, strongly rebuke those words through prayers. In 1 Corinthians 13:13 (NABRE), we understand that, *"So faith, hope, love remain these three; but the greatest of these is love."* Love is highly rated by God who loved us first. As His followers, we reserve the responsibility to enlighten our daughters that love is also the bedrock of family ties.

Love is intangible, yet it is the biggest and most powerful ingredient for a soul's contentment. I guided our daughters by telling them that love is the indispensable spice for every good thing imaginable, and I encouraged them to have steadfast mutual love for each other and to express the love daily. I reminded them that God said love, sincere love, is a crucial seal for a lot of things. To support and uphold the principle, before going our separate ways daily, we say I love you to each other, and our girls are maintaining this as I write. As we are not guaranteed tomorrow, if that is the last time we see each other, we know that we expressed our love and best sentiment prior to parting. The reciprocity of this beautiful sentiment is explained in Romans 12:9–10 (NABRE), *"Let love be sincere…Love one another with mutual affection."*

Scanning my family dynamics helped me understand that our naturally marked differences as humans make it difficult for us to not fight. Considering that love is the most understanding of feelings, we must try to identify its presence or absence between our daughters and encourage its existence or birth as the underpinning for a long-lasting, enjoyable relationship between them, even while we are no longer here to mediate their differences and keep the peace. The difference that love can make in a relationship, which may be the missing link with some of my siblings, is further illustrated in 1 Corinthians 13:4–8 as the *"way of love."* The lines indicate how central love could be in the relationship and dealings between siblings.

> "*Love is patient, love is kind. It is not jealous, [love] is not pompous, it is not inflated, it is not rude, it does not seek its own interests, it is not quick-tempered, it does not brood over injury, it does not rejoice over wrongdoing but rejoices with the truth. It bears all things, believes all things, hopes all things, endures all things. Love never fails.*" (1 Corinthians 13:4– 8, NABRE).

I imagine this is what we call true love. Sincere love is very enduring and is like a fortress. It can withstand a tsunami without the fear of being destroyed. It never fails. And the thought of breaking it will remain infeasible even after we as parents leave them when our journey on earth ends. Using the principles of family is very important, comes first and keeping the peace to guide our teenage girls into adulthood can give us hope that this the kind of love would exist and endure between our children.

Staying Close

Fundamentally, sisters should share a continued friendship even after the older sister leaves home for college or moves temporarily to a foreign country for continued education. The foundation of their initial strong bond would support and hold true even when distance stands between them. Discussing with our daughters who say they would love to live close to each other, I shared with them that in some situations, living close to siblings does not necessarily mean that they are close to their fullest extent or capacity. But that siblings are individually and collectively responsible for the relationship that exists between them whether they live a few miles apart or dozens of kilometers away from each other. They are each accountable for their level of commitment and engagement in fostering the endurance of love in their sisterly relationship. I advised them that to ensure that they stay close to each other and not feel like they are far apart no matter the distance, they should believe, have faith and confidence in each other, respect and understand one another, and *Create* time for each other. I initiated the principle of *Create* for them to use in fostering their relationship in their adulthood. In *Create*, you will find that each letter is indicative of something special to consider in your relationships:

C – **Commit** to communicate with each other in an open and honest manner, share your feelings, and be comforting and supportive of one another.

R – **Respect** each other and their families no matter their family makeup or circumstance.

E – **Evaluate** your rapport, take inventory of where things are, and fix misunderstandings as they occur so minor issues do not degenerate to a large proportion.

A – **Admit** it when you are at fault and apologize for your shortfall. There is no perfection on earth, and we are all liable to make mistakes. Accept the other's apology, forgive and move on.

T – **Traditions**, have traditions that you honor as part of your family experiences together. Initiate traditions for Thanksgiving, Christmas, Easter, New Year's Day, and or birthdays etc. Traditions provide a solid basis for reinforcing unity, enduring family ties, and continuity.

E – **Express** your love for each other often and without reserve. Ensure your love is infectious and shared between your families.

Peaceful Gatekeepers

Some of the gentlemen that court our sisters end up becoming their spouses. During courtship, it is crucial to discuss family values, highlight their significance in your lives, unequivocally underscore the importance of your relationship with your siblings, and identify them as an invaluable part of your life, as the case may be. The men we ultimately marry and share our lives with "till death do us part" do become one of the most important men and people in our lives. We begin and create another family with them. Our heartthrobs and our children's dad or the father figure in our children's lives, they also become quite an integral part of us. Thus, it is important to court and then marry men who are peace-loving, God-fearing and family-oriented. Such men are more likely than not to be peaceful gatekeepers of their wife's family interests, including but not limited to their relationship with their siblings.

During courtship, discuss family relationships when/as appropriate. Your boyfriend should understand the level of trust and friendship existing between you and your sister long before talks of matrimony. In our imperfect world, unfortunately some women are married to men who knowingly or inadvertently cause their spouse to fight with and begrudge some of their family members rather than enable unity between siblings. Peaceful gatekeepers are essential to foster loving family, sisterly rapports.

Should your spouse ever tell you something disheartening about your sibling, something that raises questions, concerns, doubts, or worries in your mind, remember to *Create* time and dialogue about it. My hope is that girls would allow the love they share and exemplify as siblings to transfer to their children, grandchildren and further pass it on to the generations after them through *Create* while ensuring that they marry men who are peaceful gatekeepers.

Forgiveness

Like I said to my sweet sister whom I love so much, each of us just happens to have been born into a family because our Lord decided that way, not because we made a choice to be born into that family and have the siblings that we do have. My fervent belief is that divine and inexplicable circumstances determined we would belong to a family unit because we were born into that family. We must respect that, like it or not. We cannot change it. God blessed our parents with children—that is us, siblings, and we are sealed in the relationship as siblings. As loving siblings argue and fight sometimes, it was important to have a principle **forgiveness** to guide our girls to adulthood.

"What is the worst thing a sibling can do to me?" I sometimes wonder. "Nothing," my response follows. A very long time ago, we learned in the Bible (Genesis) that Joseph was sold into slavery by his brothers, causing their father excruciating feelings of pain and loss. What could be worse for me or you? Nothing, truly. Nothing compared to what Joseph and his father endured due to the brothers' evil deed. Joseph and his brothers were bound by blood and destined to meet again, though under different circumstances. Wondering why this comparison? The lesson is, I want you to see how Joseph treated his brothers when he recognized them. Consider how much he gave them to take back home—his tears, his big, golden, forgiving heart for the ones who maliciously and skillfully sold him into slavery.

I share this story to teach our daughters about the principle of **forgiveness**, and to steep them in thoughts and lessons of pardon, understanding that sibling issues have been present from the time of our forefathers and will always be there, and that forgiveness is very important for peace to reign. During my faith journey, some very big personalities demonstrated what forgiveness means, whether for family, friends, acquaintances, or those who are unknown to us. Pope John Paul II—the pope I grew up learning about, watching the news about, whom my parents met—is the one great Catholic I have engraved in my memories as a hero of my faith, the one with an incomparable magnanimous heart who had forgiven from his hospital bed a man who attempted to take his life away by shooting him four times in different parts of his body. Pope Jon Paul II did not think of his attempted assassin as any other but one deserving mercy, pardon; and he would quietly sit close to him, listen to him, and personally extend him mercy and forgive him just two years after a painful and long recovery following the assassination attempt. The pope's message to the world on forgiveness was simple. He said, "The only way to peace is forgiveness." My hero growing up, I looked up to him for example and tried to listen to anything that he said or did or messages that came from him as our church, parents, or news had it. Following the papal messages of family, forgiveness, love, and Christianity, growing up, and even today, some of my daily prayers to God are as simple as "please Father, lead me, guide me, take control of my being and my actions, that I may love and forgive today as You lead me. I have faith in You, my Lord. Thank You, Jesus. Amen."

Despite our human imperfections, siblings can try to be like Joseph and be forgiving instead of going crazy after a fight with a sibling. Further, I could simply do what my childhood Catholic hero advised we do in order for peace to reign—forgive. Pope John Paul II set the tone for all humankind. He did not just forgive a very dangerous individual, he consistently preached about forgiveness till the end of his life, and with love, we all saw how he met the man who was declared his enemy by the entire world, teaching us all the importance of forgiveness. Similarly, Pope Francis has shared with us his message of mercy, insisting it is the Lord's most powerful message. He has also invited all of us to pray the "mercy chaplet," which entails divine assistance that is essential for our hearts and souls to help us disseminate forgiveness and love. Forgiveness is a critical principle for parents to guide the teenage daughters to adulthood because one thing is certain: they will be at peace after forgiving each other.

Worth remembering is what Pope John Paul II said of families: "The history of mankind, the history of salvation, passes by way of the family…The family is placed at the center of the great struggle between good and evil, between life and death, between love and all that is opposed to love." Understanding that even the pope acknowledged that family issues do exist, it is therefore worth remembering his statement above regarding potential family issues and remember to approach them with grace and love, and to forgive.

Discussing the principle with our daughters, I shared that acknowledging that family is very important, after a fight they should avoid going over the issues in your head but rather remember to *Create*. They should forgive quickly, allowing the forgiveness to come from their heart because holding a grudge is one of the darkest things that a soul can harbor, in my opinion. By begrudging a sibling, one hurts self by holding their spirit hostage. You do yourself harm when you refuse to forgive someone, not to mention your family member. Conversely, it is very liberating to forgive and let go, no matter what a sibling did. Therefore, growing the seed of forgiveness in our daughters as we guide them into adulthood is critical because there is no perfect being on earth. The worst of us are endowed with something good and worthy while the best of us certainly have our flaws. Each of child will make a mistake and will need the other's forgiveness, and accepting this as the truth and believing that you are neither worse nor better than your sibling who hurt you will help with your process of forgiveness.

The many important principles that are the pivot of this section include (1) Diversity and inclusion, (2) Absolute no underage drinking, (3) Being a lady and all that it entails, (4) Family is very important, it matters, and comes first, (5) Keep the peace, and (6) Forgiveness.

SECTION 7

MY OPEN LETTER TO OUR DAUGHTERS - PRINCIPLES

My darlings Kay & Court!

Preparing to have each of you was very special. I had prayed to the Lord for you to come into our lives as parents. I believed then that He was answering my prayers. It was a terrific first experience to have Kay. I was blown away by this littlest person who had lodged in me and was now here with us. Waiting to have Court was challenging. We thought we would be left with Kay as our lone child but our good Lord delivered and honored us with her. We bless the days you both came into our lives.

We have journeyed together amazingly. Raising you two was quite a daunting task. I felt somewhat terrified by the idea of being responsible for two little people who relied and depended on me for everything, from their meals, protection, to education, and their successes and failures in life. I was unsure of what I was doing as a mom, but I tried to rely on what I gleaned from your sweet grandma, Martina, magazines about child–upbringing, my education in health sciences, my personal believes, and of course my Father in heaven.

My gut told me to do what I could the best I could without fuss, worries, stress or pressure of any kind. So, I decided we would journey together as we have done through it, the way we did. As you now young adults, I hope that the principles shared here which we used in guiding you to adulthood would stay with you forever!! Besides, I'd like to share with you open secrets about some things that I hope you remember as you make your way through the beautiful but crazy world.

Remember God in your daily lives in your words and deeds. Commit to Him, have faith in Him and follow His pathway. Seek to please Him by doing His will instead of trying to satisfy humans. Be cognizant of your environment, and even if or when the decision you make is not a popular one with that environment, make sure it is the right thing to do by the Lord and move on.

Do not seek perfection. Like I say to the both of you often, perfection does not exist on earth. You do not have to be perfect or try to find perfection in people, objects or situations. Strive for excellence and do your best always, and in all your endeavors. There is no perfect human. We all have imperfections, and shortfalls. I have very many of them as you know, but I try to make the most of who I am and what I have, and do my best which is excellent but not perfect. And be happy with that.

Be purposeful with your words. Remember as you proceed in life that there is great power in the words you speak. You have heard me say this over and over. Some say, "Do not jinx yourself." The truth is like I told your dad when I first met him, be a purposeful speaker because I learned in the bible that "there is life and death in the words we speak" or something like that. So, speak blessings, not cursing because that may be the jinx. Speak positively, with hope.

Be honest. Remain honest with yourself, your feelings, your perspectives, your surroundings and relations. Be you, and those who love you will accept and love you for being an honest and sincere person rather than a caricature of what societal prescriptions may be.

Love yourself. We each are unique with idiosyncrasies bestowed upon us as gifts from our loving Father. Love the gift that you are in our world, and give others what you can but do not try to change you for others. Remember to keep yourself safe and healthy. Do the things you like such as blogging, writing, dancing, reading, running, playing the piano, arguing cases in court, leading a team…, according to your individual gifts. Don't beat yourself for any reason whatsoever. You are a gift. Love you as a gift.

Laugh as often as you can, smile, and enjoy the good things of life. Lead your daily life in happiness and to the fullest like I have often suggested at home. Life is a special gift so enjoy it reasonably. Be funny and make fun of yourself like we often do at home. Laughs and smiles are contagious. Consequently, they may positively impact the people in your surroundings, speak to your warmth and add some light to someone's challenging day, situation or circumstance. None of us is certain of tomorrow's availability for us, so enjoy today as a happy person and let tomorrow take care of itself.

Love with all your heart and give love where it is due. Love is something that I hope you are not unnecessarily selfish with. Love comes very naturally to us. It is essential to be loving beings to our family, friends and communities. However, I hope you do not live in someone's shadow out of love. Love yourself enough to not do that. And be you even in love.

Be kind. I hear some people talk about current social and moral decadence, that we are experiencing a culture of consumerism, narcissism, individualism, self-aggrandizement, and their abrasive ramifications on our children and their generation. Remember that the world does not revolve around you nor one individual no matter how much "stuff" they amass. Be kind in all the forms of kindness imaginable but do not disregard yourself and or your needs in the process. Be nice, courteous, civil, understanding, and benevolent as appropriate. I read many years ago that "One good turn deserves another." May-be. However, I know from personal experience that our good deeds live and follow us everywhere whether we think about them or not. Be kind because it is the right thing to do.

My former beloved boss, SVP Chris Bergh once said to me in a meeting with over nine formidable hospital executives, "Ursula you are too nice." The team immediately responded: "We love her. You get more done with honey than with vinegar." I never thought of niceness as being kind but my peers told me a lot about myself after that meeting that made me understand how easy but worth it, it is to be kind even in highly demanding professional environments. Be kind.

When necessary, let go. Remembering all the lessons learned during Kay's last year of high school and Court's eighth grade, prompted me to write this. Proud of the amazing young ladies you have become, I want to support your words that "When a door shuts, it is because another will open" or "one phase ends so another may begin." It is truly unnecessary to be dependent or hold onto things, people, sad memories or situations when common sense dictates that we shouldn't. As you let go of the worthless, create room for the things that are worth it, and welcome them with open arms. Never look back with regrets, move on with grace, and full of hope. Each thing in life happens for a great reason, even though sometimes we can hardly make sense of it while questions flood our heads. Remember our all-time favorite from the Sound of Music: "When the Lord closes a door, somewhere he opens a window." Everything happens for a reason.

When you are wrong, acknowledge your error and ask for forgiveness. We are not perfect beings and are bound to make mistakes. It is humbling to say, "I am sorry I hurt or wronged you", but it is very liberating to do or say that. Do it with class, grace, mean it, and have peace of mind once done. It was great to have this discussion with the both of you and I am thrilled you understand the selflessness involved in doing this.

Life may treat you unfairly. We have been down this road before and discussed this thoroughly. Remember what you told me on a card that you wrote for me: "God gives serious challenges to those He has equipped with the capabilities to deal with them." Life is beautiful but our world may sometimes be brutal with unfair practices especially towards minorities. When you feel like life is unfair, you know who to call on and where to go for solutions. Remember that God often says no to one thing because He has a yes for another. Go to Him with all your needs, fears, worries. Pray to Him and He will be there for you. Be strong ladies, be very resilient and hold onto your faith in our God the Father, the Son and the Holy Spirit.

At no time in your life, and in no circumstance should you be stifled. If a community or an organization consistently does not appreciate you, undervalues you or tries to diminish your worth, do not stay there. Have the courage to move on, change any circle of negative influence, and seek an environment that appreciates your worth. Remember to surround yourself with people who provide you positive energy, appreciate you for you, and at your rightful value.

Like we wrote in the UA acres book, I will always love you. My love for you both has always been unconditional. No matter who you become, what you become, what you do or do not do, what you accomplish or fail at, whether you miss your target or hit it, I will always love you from the bottom of my heart. Therefore, for as long as I live, I will always be there for you with open arms and LOVE. And when I am no longer here on earth, I will watch over you from heaven with a smile and the same abundant LOVE.

Mommy☺

Appendix

Karen Michelle Bell's Persuasive Speech: "Stop Bullying Now"

The purpose of my speech is to raise awareness of bullying and convince my audience to start taking action.

I. Intro
  A. As of 2012, 282,000 students are physically bullied in secondary school every month. Close to 1,692,000 children have been attacked so far this year. At the end of this year, 3,384,000 bullies will have attacked secondary students. (L)
  B. Imagine you are walking down the halls of a school and see a child being bullied. How many of you will actually intervene, stand up for the victim, or do something? Reverse the roles. Would you want someone to come to your aid?
  C. Having witness bullying firsthand, and knowing friends who have been victims of bullying, this is a topic I'm deeply concerned about. My research has deepened my knowledge and understanding of the topic, and I hope to do the same for you. (E)

Using my research with incidents I have witnessed, I've put together a presentation in which I hope to convince you to take a stand against bullying. The main branches of bullying—its causes, effects, potential solutions and outcomes—must be reviewed before determining what final steps to take to end this issue.

II. Body
A. Bullying in schools
1. What causes kids to release such aggression towards their peers? What has caused bullying to evolve into such a monstrous epidemic?
   a. Practice starts at home
      i. Parents may be abusive, or they may hold and display characteristics of a bully. When kids see or endure this, they begin to believe that it's ok.
      ii. Their siblings may bully them at home.
   b. Kids may be insecure
      i. Usually bullies have personal problems.
      ii. To feel more powerful, they take out their anger or frustration on their peers.
      iii. Bullies may have also been victims themselves.
   c. Bystanders
      i. Too Many of us are too scared to take a stand
      ii. Adult intervention–4%
      iii. Peer intervention–11%
      iv. No intervention–85%
      v. We are too worried about being judged for doing the "un-cool" thing.
2. What does this all eventually result to?
   a. Insecure kids decide to retaliate
      i. Kids torment others, and display unwanted, aggressive behavior to feel better and more powerful.
   b. The bullying damages the victims' state of mind (P)
      i. Low self-esteem
      ii. They become more sad

    iii. Endure more fear and helplessness
    iv. Increases harmful and suicidal thoughts
  3. Extent—Bullying is on the rise in our country
     a. In 2010, 1 in 7 kids were bullied (L)
     b. In 2012, 1 in 4 kids are bullied (L)
     c. A whopping 160,000 kids stay home every day in fear of being bullied at school (L)
     d. Every seven minutes, a child is bullied (L)
  4. Personal Experience—In my elementary school, there was a girl in my class with Diabetes type 1. A group of girls, with issues at home, taunted her in the locker rooms because of her appearance. As a result, she cried in the bathroom stalls. (E)
B. Solutions
  1. Solutions to stop bullying include the following.
     a. Speak up
        i. If you witness or endure bullying, tell someone. Particularly an adult.
        ii. Also, whether you are a witness or victim, try telling the bully to stop.
     b. Do not be aggressive, violence is never the answer. Remain calm. Yet firm. Avoid the exchange of any negative energy between you and anyone else. If you do this, you are less like to escalate the problem, and further the bullying.
     c. Do not bully back
        i. Don't encourage the bully to continue the behavior by stooping to their level.
     d. Don't stay alone with the bully
        i. Avoid negative confrontation.
        ii. Don't encourage aggression
        iii. Don't agree to meet them alone
  2. Expectations

a. Once you have notified an adult, expect them to take appropriate action to seize the behavior. If It's your parent, they may meet with the principal. If it's your school admin., then expect disciplinary action.
b. If telling the bully to stop, he/she may not stop initially
   i. Repeatedly standing up for yourself or others may cause bully to stop.
   ii. OR, the bully may only seize once an adult reinforces rules and disciplinary action.
3. Personal experience
   a. Recently, a group of 7 girls bullied my friend by sending her verbal death threats because of a friendship she held. When she finally reported it to the principal, the girls were punished. (E) This is just one example that shows that telling an adult has a positive effect.
C. Outcome expected—It's important to stand up for the bullied.
   1. Advantages of supporting the victim
      a. The victim becoming aware of the support he/she has (P)
      b. Victim acquires a higher self-confidence (P)
      c. Victim regains a voice, knowing that people are willing to help. (P)
      d. By helping someone who is being bullied, you gain internal self-satisfaction from effectively lending a helping hand to a bullied individual. (P)
      e. You also gain respect from your peers for standing up to a known evil and fighting for a good cause.
   2. Eliminating the problem—How do we eliminate this problem?

- a. Ask your school to start a bully awareness/ anti-bullying club.
- b. Encourage bully awareness meetings.
- c. Do NOT be afraid to report bullying and speak up. You can trigger a chain reaction in which everyone will defend bully victims.

III. Conclusion

- A. Bullying has always been an issue, but more so recently. Our schools are a common setting for it. So, we should say something when we see opportunity to.
- B. Kids' behavior all depends on how parents bring them up, and their inner feelings. Bullies emerge from unstable homes and it continues because people rarely speak up. There are steps we all can take, hoping for positive outcomes.
- C. Bullying is more than a joke; it's taking lives of children everywhere, too often. Kids are living in fear, while many others are causing fear.
- D. Think back to the question I asked earlier. Now, would you help a kid you saw getting bullied? Go out there and speak up for the kids who can't anymore. Use your voice for those who have lost theirs.

Glossary

"AEE" – Alliance for Excellent Education
"ALD" – Alcohol liver disease
AP – Advanced Placement
BAL – Blood alcohol level
BAC – Blood alcohol content
BFF – Best friends forever
CDC – Centers for Disease Control and Prevention
CEO – Chief Executive Officer
CFM – Christian Family Movement
CNO – Chief Nursing Officer
COR. – Corinthians
CREATE – Commit, respect, evaluate, admit, traditions, express
DFW – Dallas/Fort Worth
DHPPR – Determination, hard work, patience, persistence, and resilience
GPA – Grade point average
DUI – Driving under the influence
LEDD – *Listening, engagement, dedication, devising*
LOL – Laugh out loud
MCAT – Medical College Admissions Test
MED – Medical Executive Committee
MVA – Motor vehicle accident
NIAAA – National Institute on Alcohol Abuse and Alcoholism
NIH – National Institute of Health
OS – Overbrook School
PCP – Primary care physician
PETD – Patience-, energy-, and tolerance-demanding children
PSAT – Preliminary Scholastic Aptitude Test

Glossary

RESPECTFUL – Rapport, explicate, support, protect, encourage, communicate, trust, forgive, unbiased, listen
RN – Registered Nurse
TBI – Traumatic brain injury
TN – Tennessee
TV – Television
TX – Texas
UA – Ursuline Academy of Dallas
USA – United States of America
US – United States
WBI – Workplace Bullying Institute

INDEX

A

abuse, 21, 26, 36, 37, 42, 43, 44, 50, 51, 53, 59, 132, 185, 217, 218, 318, 326, 327
abusing, 25, 44, 54, 309, 327
abusive spouse, 51
academic, 63, 65, 71, 72, 74, 75, 81, 82, 83, 84, 89, 93, 95, 98, 103, 118, 120, 122, 132, 139, 144, 145, 146, 148, 149, 151, 153, 154, 170, 171, 194, 202, 289, 309
academics, 24, 148, 232
accept, 30, 102, 155, 176, 245, 299, 303, 352
accident, 47, 221, 313, 317, 320, 321, 322, 325, 333, 363
action, 36, 37, 54, 64, 83, 90, 103, 131, 166, 204, 222, 236, 260, 307, 357, 360
actions, 29, 40, 49, 71, 90, 134, 175, 205, 214, 221, 250, 251, 258, 260, 326, 329, 348
admiration, 34, 127, 305
admonish, 19
adolescent, 19, 35, 39, 40, 75, 80, 81, 101, 106, 107, 122, 123, 125, 129, 132, 134, 217, 262, 285, 286, 309, 310, 323
advocate, 50
affirmed, 25, 31, 33, 47, 117, 128, 142, 149, 153, 166, 173, 275
affirming, 32, 297

afraid, 43, 57, 83, 190, 213, 215, 237, 238, 254, 256, 312, 361
aggression, 45, 177, 332, 358, 359
aggressive, 19, 23, 37, 44, 46, 161, 190, 192, 195, 322, 326, 332, 358, 359
airport, 22, 23, 24, 113
alcohol, 12, 46, 49, 51, 130, 133, 134, 136, 271, 306, 307, 308, 309, 310, 311, 312, 313, 314, 315, 316, 317, 318, 319, 320, 321, 322, 323, 324, 325, 326, 327, 328, 363
altercation, 55
American Medical Association, 161, 201, 375, 376, 377
angel, 15, 18, 49
anger, 17, 45, 46, 48, 51, 215, 245, 307, 358
antidepressants, 48
anxiety, 46, 199, 253, 270
apologize, 22, 166, 171, 206, 209, 345
appreciate, 34, 40, 125, 177, 185, 212, 214, 216, 270, 300, 305, 355
argue, 16, 31, 32, 44, 337, 338, 340
arguments, 16, 29, 105, 134, 339
ashamed, 25, 43, 48, 237
assault, 36, 42, 43, 44, 177, 311, 327
assistance, 28, 90, 144, 208, 330, 348
assumption, 50, 66, 104, 105

Index

astonishment, 32
attitudes, 19, 40, 46, 104, 129, 132, 180, 189, 190, 198, 199, 212, 216, 217, 218, 222, 280, 286, 300, 329

B

Barbara Walter's, 34
bashing, 54, 55
beaten, 18, 25, 27, 29, 30, 31, 33, 34, 37, 38, 39, 46, 50
beating, 19, 21, 24, 25, 27, 31, 33, 34, 36, 37, 38, 39, 42, 43, 45, 46, 49, 51, 57, 59, 161, 222
beats, 25, 27
behaviors, 17, 18, 19, 33, 39, 40, 45, 50, 57, 58, 65, 129, 132, 134, 136, 169, 190, 191, 194, 198, 217, 222, 286, 306, 323, 329
believing, 31, 244, 254, 286, 342, 349
belittle, 35, 190, 215
belt, 29, 36, 38
BFFs, 28
biting, 45, 104, 340
blame, 47, 170, 192, 315
bless, 21, 243, 244, 275, 351
bond, 59, 132, 134, 207, 281, 337, 340, 344
break up, 51
bruises, 48, 180
bullied, 50, 169, 171, 173, 176, 183, 185, 188, 192, 196, 200, 202, 209, 210, 212, 357, 359, 360, 361
bullies, 176, 177, 179, 180, 188, 192, 193, 195, 196, 197, 201, 202, 210, 211, 212, 215, 286, 357, 358
bullying, 12, 44, 104, 161, 163, 166, 167, 168, 170, 171, 172, 173, 175, 176, 177, 179, 180, 181, 183, 184, 185, 186, 187, 188, 189, 190, 191, 192, 193, 194, 195, 196, 197, 198, 199, 200, 201, 204, 205, 206, 207, 209, 210, 211, 212, 214, 215, 282, 357, 358, 359, 361
Bullying, 161, 170, 171, 177, 191, 192, 193, 199, 357, 358, 359, 361, 364, 375, 377, 378

C

callousness, 44
caring, 16, 30, 46, 79, 88, 135, 228, 256, 276, 283, 314, 337
Catholic, 5, 15, 24, 35, 75, 103, 105, 117, 118, 120, 125, 137, 138, 144, 151, 205, 217, 225, 226, 228, 231, 232, 233, 236, 238, 241, 242, 250, 254, 347, 348, 378
celebrate, 28, 262, 305, 316
celebrity, 262
challenges, 30, 39, 40, 42, 45, 57, 70, 76, 77, 78, 79, 85, 93, 94, 95, 96, 101, 116, 119, 121, 142, 145, 148, 202, 204, 211, 213, 249, 260, 312, 329, 355
challenging, 5, 17, 31, 40, 41, 42, 51, 57, 58, 59, 65, 78, 92, 95, 101, 118, 122, 143, 145, 149, 151, 198, 246, 268, 325, 331, 351, 353
charity, 335
chemist, 97
chemistry, 61, 97
Child Protective Services, 27
Christian life, 226, 227, 233, 342
church, 52, 67, 98, 123, 126, 205, 208, 217, 225, 226, 227, 231, 232, 233, 234, 236, 238, 251, 267, 333, 335, 348

CNN, 36
cognitive skills, 34, 62, 68
college, 48, 49, 64, 67, 74, 75, 77, 80, 81, 83, 97, 100, 107, 108, 109, 110, 112, 127, 128, 134, 136, 137, 138, 139, 141, 142, 143, 144, 145, 146, 147, 148, 149, 150, 151, 152, 153, 154, 155, 156, 157, 186, 230, 231, 232, 233, 238, 250, 254, 276, 307, 308, 310, 311, 312, 316, 318, 319, 320, 327, 328, 344
colleges, 83, 110, 137, 138, 144, 146, 150, 153, 156, 289
comfort, 21, 22, 48, 58, 313, 340
communication, 28, 34, 45, 86, 136, 170, 177, 209, 270, 336, 338
competition, 30
confess, 16, 200
confession, 16, 225, 228, 233
confide, 47
confidence, 25, 46, 58, 98, 109, 238, 254, 264, 281, 341, 344, 360
confident, 19, 45, 54, 55, 58, 63, 97, 100, 202, 289, 306
conflict, 44
consequence, 30, 32, 80, 151, 199, 326
contempt, 54
conversation, 26, 28, 32, 33, 37, 50, 53, 72, 79, 84, 96, 99, 102, 107, 108, 115, 116, 121, 122, 131, 147, 148, 156, 157, 175, 208, 210, 211, 214, 217, 241, 247, 260, 262, 265, 270, 306, 324, 326, 327, 336
conversations, 16, 18, 30, 80, 81, 85, 86, 94, 105, 122, 138, 142, 155, 156, 217, 222, 248, 260, 267, 270, 273, 274, 296, 300, 304

cooperate, 45
correct, 17, 34, 42, 43, 57, 95, 168, 193, 216
counterproductive, 32
critical thinkers, 38
crying, 20, 22, 40, 94, 163, 165, 174, 219, 239, 245, 246, 255, 256, 314, 315, 336
cuddle, 21, 341
cuddled, 22, 239
cursed, 48, 219
cursing, 45, 219, 222, 334, 352
cyberbully, 206
cyberbullying, 177
cycle, 37, 38, 185

D

depression, 46, 51, 136, 250
destroy, 17, 51, 175, 228
destroying, 23, 26, 171, 279
destruction, 37
destructive, 50, 198, 199, 311
devastation, 51, 79
dialogue, 28, 34, 129, 132, 267, 346
disagreements, 44
discipline, 37, 44, 46, 51, 59, 244
disconnected, 48
discontent, 20, 172
discussions, 6, 16, 18, 19, 32, 45, 78, 85, 137, 186, 198, 207, 218, 267, 272, 283, 312, 318, 329
disputes, 44
disrespectful, 35, 101, 174, 183, 214
diversity, 12, 88, 282, 290, 291, 293, 296, 299, 300, 301, 302, 303, 304, 305
divorced, 25
drink, 49, 50, 85, 132, 133, 307, 310, 315, 316, 317, 319, 320,

Index

322, 323, 324, 325, 326, 327, 328, 341
Drinking, 50, 327
drug, 46, 132, 134, 136, 308, 309, 311, 318, 321, 322
drunk, 130, 189, 306, 307, 308, 314, 315, 317, 318, 320, 321, 322, 324, 325, 326, 327, 328
dynamics, 59, 198, 260, 274, 343

E

economic, 43, 67, 82, 109, 112
educational, 12, 59, 60, 61, 63, 74, 76, 79, 81, 82, 83, 86, 92, 94, 97, 99, 100, 101, 102, 104, 106, 107, 109, 110, 120, 135, 141, 146, 147, 149, 156, 157, 170, 200, 246, 256, 293, 300, 304
elementary, 35, 50, 70, 72, 73, 74, 83, 104, 105, 225, 231, 232, 254, 260, 272, 274, 275, 285, 359
embarrassed, 47, 53, 181, 202, 209, 210, 237
emergency, 27, 131, 236, 313, 317, 320, 336
emotional, 16, 26, 39, 44, 46, 51, 59, 155, 163, 166, 169, 222, 260, 266
emotions, 29, 45, 58, 169, 313
empower, 19, 106, 209
empty, 48
encourage, 5, 16, 44, 64, 65, 95, 102, 126, 152, 193, 196, 208, 209, 214, 274, 279, 282, 284, 293, 343, 359, 364
encouraging, 5, 38, 58, 82, 92, 109, 116, 137, 162, 190, 195, 201, 206, 242, 247, 280, 293, 300, 304, 328
enduring, 33, 42, 202, 240, 257, 263, 273, 340, 344, 345

energy, 39, 40, 81, 94, 111, 114, 268, 269, 270, 355, 359, 363
engineer, 97
enlighten, 22, 61, 200, 205, 300, 343
envied, 48
equal, 29, 55, 104, 226
errors, 38, 97, 151
expectations, 32, 45, 59, 135, 146, 271

F

fair, 45, 46, 90, 213, 286
Farmers Branch, 92
fatigued, 22, 252, 333
feeling, 38, 41, 56, 86, 102, 104, 133, 156, 163, 167, 169, 197, 201, 247, 262, 266, 298, 313, 344
fight, 28, 31, 49, 94, 95, 155, 176, 184, 193, 195, 196, 200, 202, 205, 210, 211, 213, 214, 276, 279, 337, 343, 346, 349
fights, 30, 208, 340
financial, 83, 109, 110, 113, 169, 170, 182, 184
forbearance, 48
forgive, 18, 48, 49, 210, 240, 251, 274, 282, 348, 349, 364
forgiveness, 18, 50, 200, 206, 209, 258, 281, 282, 347, 348, 349
forgiving, 282, 337, 339, 347, 348
fortitude, 48
foundational, 50, 59, 62, 74, 81, 82, 266
French, 92, 93, 319
friend, 5, 24, 25, 26, 28, 29, 30, 32, 35, 43, 50, 64, 72, 74, 76, 79, 117, 127, 129, 130, 132, 143, 144, 172, 175, 176, 178, 186, 187, 202, 203, 205, 208, 213, 231, 234, 241, 242, 248, 249,

257, 261, 262, 263, 266, 267,
268, 269, 271, 274, 276, 277,
279, 280, 281, 282, 284, 286,
294, 295, 296, 297, 298, 307,
313, 314, 316, 317, 320, 328,
336, 360
friends, 6, 12, 18, 26, 28, 29, 44,
47, 50, 53, 54, 61, 75, 76, 85,
90, 99, 100, 112, 117, 119, 121,
123, 124, 125, 126, 127, 128,
129, 130, 132, 133, 134, 135,
136, 137, 138, 139, 141, 144,
166, 170, 172, 173, 178, 179,
200, 201, 205, 207, 210, 215,
217, 222, 226, 231, 234, 236,
241, 242, 250, 253, 258, 259,
260, 261, 262, 263, 264, 265,
266, 267, 268, 269, 270, 271,
272, 273, 274, 275, 276, 278,
279, 282, 284, 285, 286, 294,
295, 296, 297, 298, 300, 301,
302, 311, 312, 313, 314, 315,
316, 318, 319, 320, 321, 324,
325, 327, 329, 336, 340, 341,
342, 347, 353, 357, 363
frustrated, 41, 45, 52, 164, 168,
187, 189, 331, 336
frustrating, 21, 41, 244
frustration, 40, 45, 358
frustrations, 48
fun, 5, 28, 29, 54, 68, 69, 70, 71,
76, 88, 90, 103, 108, 119, 126,
133, 178, 197, 204, 214, 241,
267, 268, 270, 271, 272, 274,
295, 296, 317, 353
furious, 20, 42, 126

G

gatekeepers, 337, 346
generation, 38, 105, 269, 302, 353
good behavior, 32, 46, 58

grace, 5, 26, 32, 40, 127, 226, 228,
240, 247, 249, 250, 299, 354
grateful, 5, 6, 19, 21, 27, 42, 73,
256, 258
great leaders, 38
grounded, 16, 41
grumbling, 19, 20
guidance, 49, 62, 144, 146, 150,
157, 209, 244, 281

H

Halloween, 204
harassment, 161, 180, 192
harmony, 30
harshness, 38
hate, 53, 197, 211, 338, 340, 342
health sciences, 97, 106, 351
high school, 47, 50, 64, 65, 66, 67,
70, 73, 74, 76, 77, 78, 79, 81,
83, 92, 93, 96, 105, 107, 108,
109, 110, 117, 118, 122, 124,
125, 127, 128, 132, 136, 137,
138, 139, 141, 142, 144, 145,
146, 147, 148, 149, 151, 152,
153, 154, 156, 157, 176, 178,
194, 200, 214, 217, 231, 232,
259, 260, 263, 264, 265, 272,
275, 277, 284, 293, 298, 304,
306, 307, 308, 309, 311, 312,
323, 354
hit, 15, 19, 22, 23, 24, 25, 27, 30,
31, 32, 34, 43, 44, 46, 47, 50,
52, 164, 165, 187, 221, 229,
310, 355
hitting, 21, 22, 23, 27, 31, 32, 33,
43, 44, 45, 46, 51, 52, 59, 340
homework, 24, 35, 70, 71, 85, 89,
91, 93, 94, 126
hope, 23, 25, 27, 37, 102, 105,
111, 137, 165, 184, 190, 240,
241, 246, 247, 248, 253, 254,
255, 257, 258, 261, 263, 273,

Index

274, 286, 328, 341, 343, 352, 353, 354, 357
hostile, 48
humiliate, 35
humiliating, 35, 44, 180, 181, 184, 194, 203
humiliation, 51, 55, 59, 179, 185, 209
hurting, 25, 31, 49, 51, 167, 169, 348

I

immature, 46, 189
inclusion, 12, 290, 293, 294, 296, 300, 301, 302, 303, 304
infancy, 39, 68, 268, 341
infectious, 40, 135, 162, 163, 345
insidious, 43
Instagram, 206, 306
insults, 54, 55, 337
interactions, 46, 54, 145, 193, 260, 284, 290, 293
intimidated, 18, 35, 103
intimidating, 18, 74
intimidation, 205, 207, 282, 285

J

jealous, 48, 195, 272, 338, 344
Jo Frost, 39, 57, 59
judge, 36, 37, 42, 43, 50, 51, 59

K

kicking, 105, 161, 340
kindhearted, 312, 337
kindness, 5, 15, 16, 17, 18, 197, 264, 353

L

laughing, 27, 53, 130, 145, 179, 253, 256, 280, 336
lawyer, 76, 97
listen, 29, 33, 50, 65, 68, 69, 84, 85, 94, 121, 129, 134, 137, 149, 166, 186, 196, 205, 281, 282, 283, 348, 364
listening, 29, 41, 68, 84, 87, 95, 117, 123, 136, 151, 182, 197, 200, 226, 228, 299, 322
little lady, 26, 27, 207
London Heathrow, 19
love, 5, 15, 16, 17, 18, 23, 30, 31, 32, 33, 34, 39, 47, 52, 72, 96, 97, 152, 185, 196, 198, 212, 215, 227, 229, 231, 233, 239, 240, 243, 245, 247, 248, 250, 251, 252, 253, 255, 257, 258, 264, 268, 272, 278, 301, 322, 336, 338, 339, 340, 342, 343, 344, 345, 346, 348, 349, 352, 353, 354, 355
loving, 13, 15, 16, 17, 30, 51, 58, 62, 71, 135, 215, 228, 230, 231, 240, 255, 257, 264, 273, 282, 285, 286, 314, 315, 337, 340, 341, 346, 352, 353

M

manifestation, 33
mass, 85, 98, 99, 208, 225, 228, 230, 232, 237, 279
math, 77, 83, 92, 93, 96, 97, 98, 104, 121, 122, 149
mean, 27, 29, 31, 35, 38, 39, 41, 44, 48, 53, 79, 95, 96, 99, 100, 101, 157, 165, 166, 167, 169, 171, 175, 176, 178, 201, 202, 203, 206, 210, 218, 274, 276, 285, 322, 333, 354

memory skills, 34
mental illness, 46
mentality, 39
Michelle Obama, 34
middle school, 35, 47, 55, 74, 76, 83, 103, 104, 202, 260, 263, 268, 272, 274, 275, 276, 301

N

naughty, 32, 34, 38, 39, 42, 57, 58
negative, 17, 18, 19, 31, 40, 42, 44, 54, 94, 101, 131, 132, 135, 192, 197, 280, 300, 311, 313, 322, 326, 338, 342, 355, 359
nice, 22, 25, 47, 48, 55, 58, 126, 164, 201, 208, 214, 219, 261, 264, 274, 276, 286, 320, 353, 354
nightmares, 19, 49
noise, 20, 22, 28, 143
nun, 16, 76, 97, 100, 225, 227, 274
nurturing, 16, 17, 46

O

Oprah, 63
Overbrook School, 6, 83, 88, 93, 99, 170, 250, 363

P

pain, 20, 21, 22, 31, 38, 39, 40, 42, 44, 50, 162, 168, 177, 250, 309, 325, 347
partners, 35, 91, 186, 342
patience, 5, 18, 26, 34, 39, 58, 72, 111, 112, 208, 247, 264, 363
peace, 93, 124, 134, 169, 170, 206, 209, 215, 226, 232, 240, 247, 286, 337, 339, 340, 343, 346, 348, 354

peer pressure, 123, 125, 127, 131, 136, 282
peers, 5, 26, 35, 60, 61, 79, 80, 85, 90, 103, 104, 112, 121, 122, 123, 125, 126, 127, 130, 132, 133, 135, 136, 156, 166, 169, 171, 172, 173, 174, 176, 185, 186, 188, 191, 195, 197, 198, 200, 207, 210, 211, 212, 213, 214, 215, 217, 235, 236, 261, 262, 267, 272, 274, 276, 293, 297, 300, 303, 305, 307, 324, 327, 354, 358, 360
perspectives, 6, 30, 32, 61, 66, 78, 85, 100, 106, 138, 143, 149, 196, 199, 218, 260, 278, 283, 298, 342, 352
persuade, 49, 176, 196
PETD, 39, 41, 43, 44, 58, 59, 363
physician, 97, 131, 363
physics, 55, 73, 97, 104, 122
pills, 49, 284
playbook, 40
playdates, 26, 57, 259, 296
policies, 85, 95, 195, 200
poor, 32, 36, 66, 81, 82, 101, 103, 107, 108, 111, 170, 174, 186, 212, 262, 279, 308, 332
pornography, 279, 282
positive, 39, 40, 58, 111, 135, 136, 143, 149, 280, 355, 360, 361
posture, 18
potential, 17, 34, 37, 51, 60, 78, 88, 95, 103, 105, 111, 118, 119, 136, 142, 144, 155, 171, 194, 201, 202, 211, 270, 274, 279, 280, 284, 300, 307, 310, 312, 325, 326, 333, 349, 357
power, 36, 48, 54, 172, 173, 180, 189, 192, 197, 201, 210, 231, 233, 239, 254, 255, 256, 257, 302, 352

Index

prayer, 23, 215, 233, 236, 237, 239, 241, 243, 244, 249, 251, 253, 254
praying, 21, 190, 226, 227, 230, 231, 232, 236, 238, 240, 244, 250, 251, 256, 280, 336
pregnant, 19, 68, 74, 136
prescriptions, 95, 342, 352
President Barack Obama, 289, 302
privilege, 32, 253
probability, 40, 51, 107, 138, 201
problems, 32, 42, 45, 79, 94, 98, 279, 310, 312, 326, 339, 358
protect, 23, 39, 79, 130, 196, 213, 243, 244, 279, 282, 342, 364
protective, 341
PSAT, 92, 153, 363
psychiatric disorders, 52
psychological issues, 51
puberty, 40
punched, 22
punishment, 12, 22, 31, 32, 33, 34, 37, 38, 42, 43, 46, 51, 57, 59, 175

R

racial, 43, 289, 302
rape, 311
raped, 328
rapport, 264, 266, 268, 277, 278, 281, 284, 342, 345
rationale, 39, 71
rebuilding, 49
reciprocity, 264, 343
recovering, 51
relationship, 15, 16, 46, 48, 50, 59, 98, 129, 136, 146, 155, 181, 192, 233, 251, 253, 254, 255, 259, 264, 265, 268, 269, 270, 272, 273, 279, 280, 281, 284, 285, 300, 320, 336, 338, 340, 341, 342, 343, 344, 345, 347
relationships, 51, 54, 77, 80, 126, 128, 132, 135, 139, 141, 195, 198, 226, 259, 260, 263, 265, 267, 269, 270, 277, 279, 282, 300, 301, 338, 341, 346
remorse, 38
repercussions, 19, 37, 38, 43, 59, 311, 326
Repression, 45
resilient, 51, 207, 284, 285, 286, 355
resolution, 44, 50, 79, 84, 118, 206, 310
respect, 28, 31, 42, 45, 90, 118, 127, 130, 135, 154, 189, 196, 198, 212, 262, 264, 266, 268, 278, 281, 290, 300, 303, 304, 305, 334, 335, 340, 345, 347, 360, 363
respectful, 29, 72, 215, 265, 269, 270, 273, 274, 277, 280, 284, 285
rudeness, 30, 54
rules, 18, 45, 59, 95, 154, 182, 196, 198, 212, 281, 360

S

safe, 22, 23, 89, 91, 111, 130, 165, 173, 192, 211, 274, 317, 352
scare, 29, 215
scared, 18, 130, 221, 234, 236, 358
scars, 26, 51
science, 18, 92, 118, 177, 252, 267, 329
scientific, 97
screamed, 20, 314, 316, 332, 340
secret, 24, 43, 213, 238, 309
segregated, 99
self-control, 45
self-discipline, 51

self-esteem, 46, 51, 54, 58, 109, 122, 180, 184, 191, 193, 195, 213, 358
self-respect, 26, 45, 212, 271
serious, 16, 19, 33, 73, 80, 94, 102, 135, 136, 140, 148, 165, 173, 182, 191, 192, 204, 207, 210, 214, 236, 244, 262, 267, 271, 273, 285, 317, 329, 338, 339, 355
sexual behaviors, 132
shame, 38, 48, 56
shameful, 21
shield, 39, 250
shortcomings, 46
shy, 18, 47, 172, 209, 273, 293
sibling rivalry, 30
siblings, 15, 16, 44, 94, 317, 337, 339, 340, 342, 343, 344, 345, 346, 347, 349, 358
signal, 34
silence, 43, 154, 182, 190, 266, 268, 315
silent, 31, 33, 130, 190, 246
slapped, 20
sleeping pills, 49
sleepover, 28, 57
smack, 15, 19, 21, 22, 23, 25, 28, 34, 41, 52
smacking, 19, 20, 24, 32, 43, 51, 57
smoke, 129, 132, 133
smoking, 129, 130, 279
social gatherings, 333, 335
solutions, 91, 95, 195, 208, 211, 256, 312, 355, 357
soothing, 21
squabbles, 30
stability, 16
status, 67, 100, 111, 116
stranger danger, 41
strength, 5, 45, 48, 123, 127, 227, 247, 248, 250, 286, 305

stubborn, 39, 40, 148, 174
studying, 18, 74, 86, 92, 93, 104
succeed, 17, 67, 73, 81, 82, 83, 84, 92, 93, 105, 109, 114, 115, 116, 121, 138, 152, 201
success, 17, 39, 73, 76, 83, 85, 91, 92, 93, 95, 98, 109, 110, 111, 112, 113, 116, 120, 121, 122, 127, 145, 146, 147, 148, 151, 199, 264, 313, 316
Supernanny, 39, 42, 59
support, 5, 16, 40, 60, 77, 81, 91, 93, 98, 125, 141, 146, 148, 157, 168, 173, 175, 193, 236, 254, 264, 266, 275, 276, 279, 282, 330, 344, 354, 360, 364

T

teach, 19, 29, 39, 43, 45, 51, 57, 69, 90, 136, 137, 198, 199, 207, 249
team, 85, 92, 119, 121, 172, 176, 178, 183, 186, 187, 191, 197, 198, 199, 201, 205, 210, 216, 264, 274, 297, 298, 299, 304, 331, 333, 354
tears, 25, 30, 48, 163, 166, 169, 178, 239, 240, 242, 245, 246, 248, 252, 286, 347
teen pregnancy, 106, 136
testimonies, 37, 236
the intruder, 47, 170
therapy, 50, 168, 202, 216, 321, 328
tick-tock, 50
timid, 18
tolerance, 39, 40, 41, 81, 125, 191, 196, 339, 363
tolerate, 30, 41, 125, 171
torture, 38, 51
tough love, 33
transgenerational, 37

Index

truancy, 40, 65, 81, 91, 106, 282
trust, 48, 51, 59, 126, 129, 154, 206, 211, 212, 213, 227, 229, 231, 246, 250, 253, 254, 255, 257, 264, 266, 273, 278, 281, 340, 342, 346, 364

U

underage drinking, 279, 282, 306, 310
understanding, ii, 13, 16, 19, 34, 38, 40, 43, 46, 53, 57, 62, 68, 69, 71, 82, 85, 88, 90, 93, 95, 103, 104, 106, 114, 118, 142, 146, 148, 149, 153, 168, 189, 207, 218, 226, 233, 247, 254, 264, 265, 266, 273, 277, 283, 286, 290, 291, 296, 299, 303, 304, 332, 335, 337, 339, 340, 343, 347, 353, 357
upbringing, 30, 31, 57, 351

V

vaping, 12, 279, 282
victimization, 205, 207, 210, 285, 378
violence, 43, 44, 45, 46, 51, 359
violent, 37, 43, 50
virtue, 40, 216
vision, 82, 91, 93, 109, 112, 115, 116, 303, 325
vulnerable, 43, 327

W

whooping, 34
witnessed, 24, 33, 42, 54, 127, 185, 188, 189, 190, 196, 199, 216, 230, 254, 320, 336, 357
Word of God, 238, 342
worship, 244, 249, 258

Y

yelling, 16
YouTube, 36, 193

References

Alliance For Excellent Education. Retrieved from http://all4ed.org/.

Alliance For Excellent Education: Caught in the Crisis Fact Sheet: Achievement Gap. Retrieved from http://all4ed.org/?s=&category=achievement-gap&show_only=reportsfactsheets.

Alliance For Excellent Education: Caught in the Crisis Fact Sheet: High School Graduation Rate. Retrieved from all4ed.org/State-data/nation/.

American Psychological Association. www.apa.org.

"Bullying." 2001. Journal of American Medical Association. http://jamanetwork.com/journals/jama/fullarticle/193777.

Bullying Statistics. www.bullyingstatistics.org.

Bursch, B. 2010. "Preventing and Treating Bullying and Victimization." Journal of American Medical Association. http://jamanetwork.com/searchresults?q=Bullying&allJournals=1&SearchSourceType=1&exPrm_qqq={!payloadDisMaxQParser%20pf=Tags%20qf=Tags^0.0000001%20payloadFields=Tags%20bf=}%22Bullying%22.

Canadian Red Cross. www.redcross.ca.

Cardichon, J., and P. Lovell. 2015. "Below the Surface: Solving the Hidden Graduation Rate Crisis." Alliance for Excellent Education. http://all4ed.org/reports-factsheets/belowthesurface/.

References

Centers for Disease Control and Prevention. Retrieved from https://www.cdc.gov/.

Centers for Disease Control and Prevention: Youth Risk Behavior Surveillance System (YRBSS). Retrieved from http://www.cdc.gov/healthyyouth/data/yrbs/index.htm.

Centers for Disease Control and Prevention. "Youth Risk Behavior Surveillance, United States, 2011." http://www.cdc.gov/MMWR/PDF/SS/SS6104.PDF.

Education Resource Information Center (ERIC). Retrieved from http://eric.ed.gov/.

Espelage, D. L., and G. Gianluca. 2014. "Peer Victimization, Cyberbullying, and Suicide Risk in Children and Adolescents." Journal of American Medical Association. doi:10.1001/jama.2014.3212.

Healthy People. 2020. Retrieved from https://www.healthypeople.gov/.

Henniger, M. L. 2005. Teaching Young Children: An Introduction. 3rd ed. Upper Saddle River, NJ: Pearson Education, Inc.

Jain, S. 2013. "Experiential Training for Enhancing Intercultural Sensitivity." Journal of Cultural Diversity, 20(1), 15–20.

McAfee, O., and D. J. Leong. 2002. Assessing and Guiding Young Children's Development and Learning. 3rd ed.). Boston: Allyn& Bacon, Prentice Hall Inc. A Pearson Education Company.

Merriam-Webster Dictionary since 1828. Retrieved online from http://www.merriam-webster.com/.

Moreno, M. A., M. F. Furtner, and F. P. Rivara. "School Bullying." Journal of the American Medical Association. doi:10.1001/archpediatrics.2011.166.

Morrison, G. S. 2004. Early Childhood Education Today. 9th ed. Upper Saddle River, NJ: Prentice Hall Inc. A Pearson Education Company.

Nansel, T. R., and M. D. Overpeck. 2003. "Operationally Defining 'Bullying'—Reply." Journal of American Medical Association. doi:10.1001/archpedi.157.11.1134-a.

National Center for Education Statistics. Retrieved from https://nces.ed.gov/annuals/

National Center for Education Statistics. Retrieved from http://nces.ed.gov/.

National Institute of Health. Retrieved from https://www.nih.gov/.

National Institute on Alcohol Abuse and Alcoholism (NIAAA). Retrieved from https://www.niaaa.nih.gov/.

National Institute of Child Health and Human Development (NICHD). Retrieved from https://www.nichd.nih.gov/Pagesindex.aspx.

Sanner, S., Baldwin, D., Cannella, Kathleen, A.S., Charles, J., & Parker, L., (2010). "The Impact of Cultural Diversity Forum on Students' Openness to Diversity." Journal of Cultural Diversity, 17(2), 56–61. Retrieved from http://search.proquest.com/docview/365966874?accountid=35812.

School Crime Supplement (SCS). 2009. Retrieved from

References

https://safesupportivelearning.ed.gov/survey/school-crimesupplement-scs-national-crime-victimization-survey-ncvs

Senior, D., J. J. Collins, and M. A. Getty. 2011. The Catholic Study Bible. 2nd ed. Madison Avenue, NY: Oxford University Press Inc.

Shwartz, W. "New Information on Youth Who Dropout: Why they Leave and What Happens to Them. For Parents/about Parents." Education Resources Information Center (ERIC). http://eric.ed.gov/.

Strong American Schools. Retrieved from strongamericanschools.org.

United States Census Bureau. Retrieved from https://www.census.gov/.

US Department of Education. Retrieved from http://www.ed.gov/.

World Health Day 2012. Retrieved from www.who.int/mediacentre/news/release/2012/whd_20120403

Workplace Bullying Institute. Retrieved from: http://www.workplacebullying.org/.

Workplace Bullying Institute. Retrieved from http://www.workplacebullying.org/individuals/problem/definition/